The Development of British Naval Thinking

In this book, Britain's leading naval historians and analysts have come together to produce an investigation of the development of British naval thinking over the last three centuries, from the sailing ship era to the current day. It will describe the beginnings of formalised thought about the conduct of naval operations in the eighteenth century, its transformation through the impact of industrialisation in the nineteenth century and its application in the two world wars of the twentieth. The book concludes with a review of modern British naval thinking and the appearance of naval doctrine against the uncertainties of the loss of empire, the Cold War, nuclear weapons and the huge changes facing us as we move into the new millennium. How perceptive and distinctive was British naval thinking? Where did British ideas come from? Did they determine or merely follow British experience? Do they explain British naval success? The contributors to this volume will try to answer all such questions in a book that should be of considerable interest to the maritime community around the English-speaking world.

Geoffrey Till is the Dean of Academic Studies at the UK's Command and Staff College. He has written widely on maritime matters. His most recent book is *Seapower: A Guide for the 21st Century* (Routledge 2004).

CASS Series: Naval policy and history
Series Editor: Geoffrey Till

This series consists primarily of original manuscripts by research scholars in the general area of naval policy and history, without national or chronological limitations. It will from time to time also include collections of important articles as well as reprints of classic works.

1 *Austro-Hungarian Naval Policy, 1904–1914*
   Milan N. Vego

2 *Far-Flung Lines: Studies in Imperial Defence in Honour of Donald Mackenzie Schurman*
   Edited by Keith Neilson and Greg Kennedy

3 *Maritime Strategy and Continental Wars*
   Rear Admiral Raja Menon

4 *The Royal Navy and German Naval Disarmament, 1942–1947*
   Chris Madsen

5 *Naval Strategy and Operations in Narrow Seas*
   Milan N. Vego

6 *The Pen and Ink Sailor: Charles Middleton and the King's Navy, 1778–1813*
   John E. Talbott

7 *The Italian Navy and Fascist Expansionism, 1935–1940*
   Robert Mallett

8 *The Merchant Marine and International Affairs, 1850–1950*
   Edited by Greg Kennedy

9 *Naval Strategy in Northeast Asia: Geo-strategic Goals, Policies and Prospects*
   Duk-Ki Kim

10 *Naval Policy and Strategy in the Mediterranean Sea: Past, Present and Future*
   Edited by John B. Hattendorf

11 *Stalin's Ocean-going Fleet: Soviet Naval Strategy and Shipbuilding Programmes, 1935–1953*
Jürgen Rohwer and Mikhail S. Monakov

12 *Imperial Defence, 1868–1887*
Donald Mackenzie Schurman; edited by John Beeler

13 *Technology and Naval Combat in the Twentieth Century and Beyond*
Edited by Phillips Payson O'Brien

14 *The Royal Navy and Nuclear Weapons*
Richard Moore

15 *The Royal Navy and the Capital Ship in the Interwar Period: An Operational Perspective*
Joseph Moretz

16 *Chinese Grand Strategy and Maritime Power*
Thomas M. Kane

17 *Britain's Anti-submarine Capability, 1919–1939*
George Franklin

18 *Britain, France and the Naval Arms Trade in the Baltic, 1919–1939: Grand Strategy and Failure*
Donald Stoker

19 *Naval Mutinies of the Twentieth Century: An International Perspective*
Edited by Christopher Bell and Bruce Elleman

20 *The Road to Oran: Anglo-French Naval Relations, September 1939–July 1940*
David Brown

21 *The Secret War against Sweden: US and British Submarine Deception and Political Control in the 1980s*
Ola Tunander

22 *Royal Navy Strategy in the Far East, 1919–1939: Planning for a War against Japan*
Andrew Field

23 *Seapower: A Guide for the Twenty-first Century*
Geoffrey Till

24 *Britain's Economic Blockade of Germany, 1914–1919*
Eric W. Osborne

25 *A Life of Admiral of the Fleet Andrew Cunningham: A Twentieth-century Naval Leader*
Michael Simpson

iv *CASS Series: Naval policy and history*

26 *Navies in Northern Waters, 1721–2000*
   Edited by Rolf Hobson and Tom Kristiansen

27 *German Naval Strategy, 1856–1888: Forerunners to Tirpitz*
   David Olivier

28 *British Naval Strategy East of Suez, 1900–2000: Influences and Actions*
   Edited by Greg Kennedy

29 *The Rise and Fall of the Soviet Navy in the Baltic, 1921–1940*
   Gunnar Aselius

30 *The Royal Navy, 1930–1990: Innovation and Defence*
   Edited by Richard Harding

31 *The Royal Navy and Maritime Power in the Twentieth Century*
   Edited by Ian Speller

32 *Dreadnought Gunnery and the Battle of Jutland: The Question of Fire Control*
   John Brooks

33 *Greek Naval Strategy and Policy, 1910–1919*
   Zisis Fotakis

34 *Naval Blockades and Seapower: Strategies and Counter-Strategies, 1805–2005*
   Edited by Bruce A. Elleman and Sarah C.M. Paine

35 *The US Pacific Campaign in World War II: From Pearl Harbor to Guadalcanal*
   William Bruce Johnson

36 *Anti-submarine Warfare in World War I: British Naval Aviation and the Defeat of the U-Boats*
   John J. Abbatiello

37 *The Royal Navy and Anti-Submarine Warfare, 1944–49*
   Malcolm Llewellyn-Jones

38 *The Development of British Naval Thinking: Essays in Memory of Bryan Ranft*
   Edited by Geoffrey Till

The Development of British Naval Thinking

Essays in memory of
Bryan McLaren Ranft

Edited by Geoffrey Till

LONDON AND NEW YORK

First published 2006 by Routledge
2 Park Square, Milton Park, Abingdon, OX14 4RN

Simultaneously published in the USA and Canada by Routledge
270 Madison Ave, New York, NY 10016

Routledge is an imprint of the Taylor & Francis Group, an informa business

© Geoffrey Till for editorial; individual chapters, the contributors.

Typeset in 10/12pt Times NR by Graphicraft Limited, Hong Kong
Printed and bound in Great Britain by Antony Rowe Ltd, Chippenham, Wiltshire

All rights reserved. No part of this book may be reprinted or reproduced or utilised in any form or by any electronic, mechanical, or other means, now known or hereafter invented, including photocopying and recording, or in any information storage or retrieval system, without permission in writing from the publishers.

British Library Cataloguing in Publication Data
A catalogue record for this book is available from the British Library

Library of Congress Cataloging in Publication Data
The development of British naval thinking : essays in memory of Bryan Ranft / edited by Geoffrey Till.
  p. cm. — (Cass series—naval policy and history, ISSN 1366–9478)
  Includes bibliographical references and index.
  1. Great Britain. Royal Navy—History. 2. Great Britain—Military policy. 3. Naval strategy. 4. Naval education—Great Britain—History. I. Till, Geoffrey. II. Ranft, Bryan. III. Title. IV. Series.
VA454.D459 2006
359′.030941—dc22
                                                                 2005025819

ISBN10: 0–714–65320–9 (hbk)
ISBN10: 0–714–68276–4 (pbk)
ISBN10: 0–203–48562–9 (ebook)

ISBN13: 978–0–714–65320–4 (hbk)
ISBN13: 978–0–714–68276–1 (pbk)
ISBN13: 978–0–203–48562–0 (ebook)

This book is dedicated to the memory of Professor Bryan McLaren Ranft

Contents

	List of Contributors	xi
	Foreword	xiii
	ADMIRAL OF THE FLEET SIR JULIAN OSWALD, GCB	
	Acknowledgements	xvi
1	Introduction: British naval thinking: a contradiction in terms? GEOFFREY TILL	1
2	The idea of naval strategy in Britain in the eighteenth and nineteenth centuries N.A.M. RODGER	19
3	The development of education in the Royal Navy: 1854–1914 ANDREW LAMBERT	34
4	Corbett and the emergence of a British school? GEOFFREY TILL	60
5	1914–18: the proof of the pudding ANDREW GORDON	89
6	Richmond and the faith reaffirmed: British naval thinking between the wars GEOFFREY TILL	103
7	All sorts of wars: British naval thinking and technology in the Second World War JOCK GARDNER	134
8	British naval thinking in the nuclear age RICHARD HILL	160

| 9 | **The discovery of doctrine: British naval thinking at the close of the twentieth century** | 182 |
| | ERIC GROVE | |

| | **Epilogue: Professor Bryan McLaren Ranft** | 192 |
| | GEOFFREY TILL | |

| *Bibliography* | 195 |
| *Index* | 208 |

Contributors

Jock Gardner is now a civil servant in the Naval Historical Branch, Portsmouth, having previously served in the Royal Navy for nearly 30 years, where he was a specialist in anti-submarine warfare. In the last decade he has made contributions to many historical conferences, presenting papers on twentieth-century naval historical topics internationally. He has also contributed to several books and has had many articles published. His previous works include *Antisubmarine Warfare* (1996) and *Decoding History: The Battle of the Atlantic and ULTRA* (1999). He is now working on a biography of Admiral Sir Bertram Ramsay.

Andrew Gordon is a reader in the Defence Studies Department at JSCSC. He has a Ph.D. in War Studies from King's College London, and is the author of two books: *British Seapower and Procurement Between the Wars* (1988) and *The Rules of the Game: Jutland and British Naval Command* (1996). He is currently working on a book on Admiral Fisher. He is a former Lt Cdr in the Royal Naval Reserve.

Eric Grove is Senior Lecturer in the department of politics at the University of Salford. He is also a Fellow of the Royal Historical Society, a Vice President of the Society for Nautical Research and Member of Council of the Navy Records Society. Earlier publications include *Vanguard to Trident* (1987) (the standard work on post-1945 British naval policy) and *The Future of Sea Power* (1990). His latest book is *The Royal Navy Since 1815: A New Short History* (2005).

Richard Hill served for 40 years in the Royal Navy, including four tours in the Ministry of Defence, retiring in 1983 in the rank of rear admiral. He was then Chief Executive of the Middle Temple until 1994. He wrote and lectured extensively on naval and maritime subjects from 1970 onwards. His ten books include *Maritime Strategy for Medium Powers* (1986) and the *Oxford Illustrated History of the Royal Navy* (1995), of which he is General Editor. He was Editor of *The Naval Review* from 1983 to 2002.

Andrew Lambert is Laughton Professor of Naval History in the Department of War Studies, King's College, London. A Fellow of the Royal Historical

Society, his books include *The Crimean War: British Grand Strategy against Russia 1853–1856* (1990), *The Last Sailing Battlefleet: Maintaining Naval Mastery 1815–1850* (1991), *The Foundations of Naval History: John Knox Laughton, the Royal Navy and the Historical Profession* (1998) and *War at Sea in the Age of Sail 1650–1850* (2000). His latest book, *Nelson: Britannia's God of War* was published in October 2004. Professor Lambert has also taken naval history to the broadest audience with a number of television appearances. In 2001 he took part in the BBC series *The Ship*, a reconstruction of Captain Cook's first Pacific voyage, as a crew member and historical consultant. He wrote and presented the three-part series *War at Sea* for BBC2, broadcast in February 2004.

Admiral of the Fleet Sir Julian Oswald, GCB At the end of a long and successful career in the Royal Navy, Admiral of the Fleet Sir Julian Oswald served as C-in-C Fleet, Allied C-in-C Channel and C-in-C Eastern Atlantic from 1987 to 1989. From then to 1993, he was First Sea Lord and Chief of the Naval Staff and First and Principal Naval ADC to the Queen. Since then, he has maintained his maritime interests, which include publications of aspects of maritime strategy and British defence policy.

N.A.M. Rodger is Professor of Naval History at the University of Exeter and a Fellow of the British Academy. Author of innumerable books, his *The Command of the Ocean, 1649–1815*, the second volume of his *Naval History of Britain*, was published in 2004, winning the the Duke of Westminster Medal for Military Literature in 2005.

Geoffrey Till is Dean of Academic Studies at the Joint Services Command and Staff College and a member of the Defence Studies Department of King's College, London. In addition to many articles and chapters on various aspects of defence, he is the author of *Seapower: A Guide for the 21st Century* for Frank Cass, published in 2004. Next in the pipeline is a study on naval transformation. With Bryan Ranft, he co-authored *The Sea in Soviet Strategy* (2nd edition 1989). His works have been translated into nine languages, and he regularly lectures at staff colleges and conferences around the world.

Foreword

Admiral of the Fleet Sir Julian Oswald, GCB

To write this preface to a book in honour and memory of Bryan Ranft enables me, in a very small way, to repay part of the debt I owe him, for it was he who first opened my eyes, and those of many of my contemporaries – young Acting Sub-Lieutenants at the Royal Naval College, Greenwich at the time – to the value and importance of reading about, discussing and learning from the deeds of our naval and other military and political predecessors and understanding the context in which their campaigns and battles had been won and lost.

Bryan was no ordinary Professor of History (I hope such a description is neither impertinent nor paradoxical!). His style was quite different from that of the history masters at Dartmouth, who taught those of us who spent four years there. He wanted us to make the mental adjustment from schoolboys who learnt to undergraduates who studied. His style was challenging and he didn't like his time wasted, but if you were genuinely interested he would go far out of his way to help and encourage you. Many years later, while serving as a captain, I asked him if he would look at some work of mine with which I was less than satisfied. Shortly thereafter, over an excellent lunch, he carefully, kindly and helpfully suggested how I could improve it and remove inconsistencies. Throughout his life he remained the man to whom I found it easiest and most rewarding to turn in such circumstances. He always had some good ideas and quite unselfishly shared them.

It is of course totally appropriate that this volume, dedicated to his memory and carrying contributions from his colleagues, friends and protégés (I am proud to count myself in all three categories), should examine the development of British naval thinking in the last 50-odd years. This the contributors do admirably. But how are we to balance our judgement of and assess the relative merits of chapters written by academics, by naval officers and by those who can justifiably be categorised as both?

Consider first the contribution potential to British naval thinking of the straight professional naval officer (I hope there are no crooked ones!). Even those most interested by and concerned with the development of contemporary naval strategy will only devote disjointed segments of their careers to actually working in and having responsibility for this field. At other times their priorities, rightly, will be with commanding a happy and efficient ship or commando, the intricacies and challenges of equipment procurement or support, or their personal development as officers in their chosen of many specialist disciplines. At such times they will probably retain a watching brief on developments, perhaps through the pages of *The Naval Review*, or other more official publications, but for large periods of their careers this cannot be their top priority.

Much reduced regular services leave a smaller pool in which to find the necessary talent and the willingness to engage in these types of study, which may well appeal only to a minority anyway. There are some helpful interventions. The military M.Phil programme (godfather – Denis Healey), a growing number of productive links between the armed services and the universities, the Joint Services Command and Staff College, the improvements to the Royal College of Defence Studies syllabus and more. However it is neither difficult nor ill-advised to come to the view that naval and marine officers on their own will have a strictly limited ability to advance naval thought. But in combination with others? Let us see.

Undoubtedly the star of the pure academic (are there any impure ones?) is in the ascendant. Much more work is now done openly, for example the review panel for George Robertson's Strategic Defence Review on which academics were well represented, with less or no security constraints and with the realisation that many non-military areas of interest and concern (oceanography, climatology, the exploitation of the sea's resources, seaborne trade, piracy and the whole law of the sea canvas) play an increasingly important part in the evolution of naval strategy. (This subject is explored most interestingly in Richard Hill's chapter). Are academics' views accepted, welcomed, agreed in dark blue/lovat circles? I think so, definitely. From (Sir) Michael Howard and his invocation of the profession of arms, which restored a measure of public acknowledgement, and perhaps even more important, acceptability of defence, when its ethos was at a low point, the intervention of academics has been broadly beneficial, widely accepted by the naval community and increasingly influential with politicians. Their contribution to public and political debate, their growing recognition exemplified, for instance, by the appointment of Lawry Freedman as the first Defence Professor, and the inauguration of the Defence Lecturer Programme, were all significant milestones. The academics' place in the defence firmament seems to me assured, understood and welcomed both by the professionals and by ministers.

But what of the small but highly significant corps of those who are, or were, both academics and naval officers: Sir Herbert Richmond, Professor Jeffrey Switzer and Captain Stephen Roskill in the past, Richard Hill and Jock Gardner today? Are they valued as they should be? Do they carry weight in both campuses?

Let us consider Captain Stephen Roskill as an example, and a fine one – a professional, dedicated and brave naval officer to his fingertips. Invalided from the service he loved, he turned initially to recording its history in the Second World War and later to a widening interest in naval strategy. His Senior Research Fellowship, later Pensioner Fellowship, at Churchill College Cambridge, evidences his acceptance by the academic community. But after taking off his uniform were his views still sought and accepted by senior naval officers? The evidence is strongly in the affirmative. His son Nicholas recalls a stream of admirals visiting their home at Blounce. Some may well have wished to engage him in discussion about how Stephen perceived, and intended to record, their performance in the Second World War, but many others clearly saw, in this professional sailor turned academic, a penetrating mind which was still very much turning on the issues and challenges of the day and the future.

Stephen Roskill is particularly interesting because he had strong and well recorded disagreements with politicians (Sir Winston Churchill), scientists (Professor Lindemann), naval officers (Admiral Dreyer) and academics (Arthur Marder) – and I have to say that he seems to have come out on top almost every time! By any measure his contribution as an academic/naval officer seems to me to rank among the very best.

Perhaps in summary one could say that both the naval officer in the role of strategic thinker and the academic engaged in British naval thought have played enormously useful parts in the challenging and difficult task of developing naval policy. A special place, however, should be accorded to those who have combined these two roles. Both academic and naval communities are likely to listen just a touch more attentively to those who have a foot in both camps. Bryan Ranft would clearly have understood this, he was totally pragmatic, and I think this goes a long way to explaining why he took so much trouble to try and instil just a little academic virtue into us young professional naval officers. I doubt he saw a future Richmond or Corbett in our ranks, but he did see that we could be a lot more use if we approached our careers with an analytical and questioning attitude to our history and some understanding of the enduring verities of seapower.

Reverting to my own relationship with Bryan, with which I began, and looking back on the way he challenged us, one might accuse him of pessimism. Actually I think it was nearer realism. He was perfectly aware that the Royal Navy we served could never regain the pre-eminence it enjoyed in the time of our grandfathers – and he no doubt felt that it was only sensible to disabuse us of any untoward notions of grandeur. In a long and highly observant life this wartime soldier turned eminent naval historian saw enormous change in the United Kingdom's standing in the world. Realistically I think he wanted to prepare us for further, not always welcome, changes.

Thank you, Bryan, for making me think.

Acknowledgements

I would like to thank Admiral Sir Julian Oswald for writing the foreword to this volume, and all the other contributors for their help and patience in this project. The contributors, of course, are only responsible for their own sections of the book. I would like to thank some of Bryan Ranft's former colleagues for their help, particularly Mr Stuart Thomson, Mr Jonathan Farley, Mr Wilf Taylor and Captain Duncan Ellin. Chris Hobson and his excellent staff in the splendid library of the Joint Services Command and Staff College, Shrivenham, have been extraordinarily helpful as usual. My academic colleagues at Shrivenham have been supportive, especially Jon Robb-Webb. My secretary, Mairi McLean, has helped me in innumerable ways, particularly in compiling the bibliography. My wife, Cherry, has again put up with some very late nights, long delays in bookshops and provided faultless underway replenishment. Finally, Andrew Humphrys and his team at T&F have been forgiving for a project that was astern of station for far too long.

1 Introduction
British naval thinking: a contradiction in terms?

Geoffrey Till

> My strategy lectures are very uphill work. I had no idea when I undertook ... [the task] ..., how difficult it was to present theory to the unused organs of naval officers.[1]

This celebrated quotation from the correspondence of Sir Julian Corbett, the foremost British naval strategist whose work will be considered later, nicely encapsulates the notion that the British, and in particular the Royal Navy, do not 'do' strategy and, more insultingly still that 'naval thinking' is essentially a contradiction in terms. This fits in with a preference for practical, down-to-earth empiricism, rather than the theoretical philosophising which many think distinguishes the British from many of the other Europeans.

Reflecting on the problems of the Royal Navy of the eighteenth century in pinning down their habitual enemy, the French, into as many decisive engagements as it would have liked, John Clerk of Eldin pointed to the French, '... having acquired a superior knowledge, have adopted some new system of managing great fleets, not known, or not sufficiently attended to by us'. This all went to show, he thought, that

> Though a superior degree of knowledge in naval affairs be evidently of the utmost consequence to the inhabitants of this island, yet the subject of naval tactics has long remained among us in a very rude and uncultivated state.[2]

Mahan likewise lamented the fact that not only were British naval officers not 'instruit' in the French sense, they did not want to be: 'To meet difficulties as they arise, instead of by foresight, to learn by hard experience rather than by reflection or premeditation, are national traits'.[3] The problem, many complained, was particularly acute in the late nineteenth century. According to one observer who went by the soubriquet T124, 'it has to be confessed that in abstract thought concerning the problems of naval warfare' the Navy's 'achievements had not been outstanding'.[4]

Such claimed deficiencies in British naval thinking might be thought especially surprising given the evident centrality of naval and maritime concerns to Britain's security, prosperity, and even its identity and sense of itself. The Navy was well regarded by people and government. While the Army was perhaps a necessary evil, so far as Pitt was concerned the Navy was: 'That great foundation of our strength, of our glory and of our characteristic superiority over the rest of the nations of Europe'.[5]

The Navy provided Britain's fundamental security, it was associated with beneficial trade, economic, social and political liberalism and the restraint of arbitrary power at home and abroad. Thus the ringing tones of Robert, Earl Nugent, in a debate in the Lords, in September 1745:

> Let us remember that we are superior to other nations, principally by our riches; that those riches are the gifts of commerce, and that commerce can subsist only while we maintain a naval force superior to that of other princes. A naval power, and an extended trade reciprocally produce each other; without trade we shall want sailors for our ships of war, and without ships of war we shall soon discover that the oppressive ambition of our neighbours will not suffer us to trade.... [If] our trade be lost, who can inform us how long we shall be suffered to enjoy our laws or our liberties, or our religion? Without trade, what wealth shall we possess? And without wealth, what alliances can be formed?[6]

A whole variety of assumptions underlay Earl Nugent's position. Some of them had to do with the cultural and social dimensions of maritime power. Perhaps, ultimately, the most important of Nugent's claims was a strong sense that a maritime priority chimed in well with what Britain's leaders and opinion-formers thought were 'British values' and their sense of the kind of country they wished Britain to be. As Mackinder remarked: '... liberty is the natural privilege of an island people'.[7] The historic association of seapower with open trade on the one hand and with conceptions of freedom and liberal democracy on the other has been much discussed recently.[8]

There is a geophysical strand to this as well – namely the sense that the British are 'an island race', insulated from the sordid affairs of the continent of Europe by the English Channel. This common perception has in fact been challenged by those who point out that national identity is based on interaction with others and that Britishness is partly a consequence of cross-channel links and partly of the '... extended network of communication, diaspora and culture created by the eighteenth century British Empire'. But whether the emphasis is put on the islander aspect of the British, or on the fact that they were at the heart of a major sea-based empire, both would help justify the assertion that 'salt water runs in the veins of every true-born Englishman'.[9]

Secondly, every now and again, the international context moved in directions that were less benign than usual. The year 1745, when Nugent made

Introduction: British naval thinking 3

his speech was, after all, the year of the very dangerous Jacobite rebellion, a real reminder of how vulnerable Britain could be. As one speaker remarked in a particularly interesting debate in 1743, such dangers required a standing Army to guard against invasions and raids, which the Navy would not always be able to prevent:

> Yet considering the great Number of disaffected persons we still have amongst us, even the landing of a small Number of foreign Troops might very well disturb our domestic Tranquillity, if we had not a sufficient Number of regular Troops to send against them at their first landing.[10]

Such threats also caused much concern in the nineteenth and twentieth centuries. Maritime power could indeed be a great source of national strength, but it was a source of vulnerability too, especially given Britain's dependence on the security of its merchant shipping. In 1929, the then prime minister, Ramsay MacDonald, put it like this:

> In our case, our navy is the very life of our nation. We are a small island. For good or for ill, the lines of our Empire have been thrown all over the face of the earth. We have to import our food. A month's blockade, effectively carried out, would starve us all in the event of any conflict. Britain's navy is Britain itself and the sea is our security and our safety.[11]

Thirdly, in this period 'Britain' was actually not just a collection of mist-shrouded islands off the European mainland, it was a worldwide empire, held together by a network of shipping routes. The British Empire may have begun in a 'maelstrom of seaborne violence and theft' but it was transformed into the world's most powerful polity through a process of 'globalization with gunboats'.[12] As Jeremy Black has recently reminded us, its maritime character was and is still not always fully appreciated.

Partly this was because the nature of the empire itself underwent significant change. At first this 'empire of the sea' was limited to trading outposts, maritime colonies and old-fashioned mercantilism, but increasingly it spread inland and became 'territorialised', the province of soldiers and colonial administrators:

> Nineteenth century empire is generally seen in terms of power and expansion on land. The dominant image is of a line or square of redcoats confronting charging natives. The geographical focus is on India and, towards the close of the century, Africa. Ideas associated with David Livingstone or Rudyard Kipling are those of the interior: the dark forests of Africa for the former, distant hill-stations and mountain valleys for the latter. All of these were indeed important, but they draw

attention from the naval power on which the British position rested, and that provided a consistent existent goal throughout the period, linking the years immediately after Waterloo to the late Victorian era. Expansion on land relied on Pax Britannica at sea, naval hegemony providing the secure background to force projection. This hegemony combined with industrial growth and a liberal entrepreneurial ethos to encourage and sustain the commitment to free trade and a liberal international order that was to be a defining feature of nineteenth-century British imperialism. This commitment to free trade was also to be of great importance for economic growth across the world, although the 'globalisation', or, at least, openness to markets, it fostered also caused major problems of adjustment, and the benefits it brought were spread very unequally. Trade, rather than costly expansion on land was the source of Britain's status as the world's wealthiest nation, and thus of her power, more particularly the resources that were to underwrite government revenues, while maritime strength was also crucial to the image of British power.[13]

All these assumptions were exemplified in the maritime agenda of Tory opposition to the Walpole administration in the mid-eighteenth century. Its defiant Britishness was illustrated by constant references to the danger that the '... whole strength of the British Empire was to be steer'd by the Hannoverian rudder'.[14] Patriotic Britons should not permit the '... sacrifice of the wealth and interest of Great Britain to the narrow views and petty concerns of a German Electorate ... We ought as far as possible to enjoy the Advantage Nature has bestowed on us of being an island, and consequently to keep as free as we can from all quarrels of the continent'.

The British should defend their interests not other peoples'. It was '[u]n pardonable to neglect a necessary maritime war for the security of our Trade and Navigation for an unnecessary land war' since this would leave '... our commerce a prey to a piratical enemy, our losses unrecompensed, our injuries unavenged and our Honour unretrieved'. It made sense to concentrate resources on the Navy and the Marines, rather than on an Army operating on the mainland of Europe:

> We ought to disband a great part of the troops we have now on foot, in order to be able to increase our naval Force, because it is upon that alone, after the balance of Power upon the Continent is destroyed, that we must depend for the continuance of our future Independency.

Naval forces, moreover, would be much cheaper for the mercantile sea-trading British to provide because Britain had twice as many hulls, ports and seamen as anyone else. The Navy would also offer sufficient and cost-effective defence against the risk of invasion: 'You can be in no danger from any Invasion that can be made upon you, as long as you have a superior

Force at Sea'. Moreover, a standing Army was a permanent, unnecessary and unnatural threat to civil liberties.

It was all summed up by one speaker in the debate like this:

> If they should attack before their having such a Fleet ready, and we should confine ourselves to our own Element, without wasting our Strength in romantic Expeditions upon the Continent and maintaining numerous land Armies, we should be gainers by the War, by destroying their plantations and putting an entire Stop to their Trade, and thereby ridding ourselves of our greatest Rival in Manufactures and Commerce; so that I do not know, but it would be one of the greatest Favours the French could do us to provoke us to a Sea War, and one of the greatest Injuries we can do ourselves, is to engage without Necessity in an expensive land one . . .

Clearly, in these debates, the opposition's vision of Britain was of a country that was strong, that should be invulnerable to external attack and proof against insurrection at home, free from the threat of tyranny and aloof from the petty quarrels of Europe. Above all, it was prosperous, mercantile and profoundly maritime.

Of course, there was more than a dash of political hyperbole in all this. The Walpole administration and its successors were equally aware of Britain's maritime imperatives, but were apt to make the point that things were not as simple as the opposition claimed, especially when there was no power balance on the continent of Europe for Britain to manipulate to its benefit as cost effectively as the opposition claimed it could. Instead the British would need physically and substantially to intervene on the mainland in order to avert the grisly prospect of a malign *imbalance* of power the other side of the water, which might have maritime implications which even the Royal Navy would not be able to handle. In Queen Anne's time, it was claimed the British had forced the French to maintain substantial land forces thereby preventing them from building ships and converting troops into marines:

> By land we beat them out of the Sea. We obtained so great and so many Victories at land that they were forced to neglect their Sea Affairs, in order to apply their whole strength both in Money and men to defend their country . . . at land.

In fact, there was a degree of exaggeration to both sides of this argument, for these were essentially politicians rather than professional strategists after all. In fact, the argument that intervening ashore forced Britain's eighteenth-century adversaries to switch effort from the sea back towards the land has been exaggerated.[15]

More significantly perhaps, the notion that Britain could, because of its maritime strength, dominate the scene with a kind of Olympian ease is also something of a romantic myth. Usually it was not a question of Britain's adopting either the 'bluewater' or the 'continental' school but of a mixture between the two that reflected the strategic circumstances of the time.

Part of the process of striking the right balance was for the claimants on both sides to state their case with maximum effect. Enunciating the maritime myth itself was a necessary part of the process, and this explains why at times of strategic upheaval – such as the end of the nineteenth and the beginning of the twentieth centuries – it reoccurred with major effect, and was closely associated with an explosion of naval and strategic thinking. At such times, the association of the Navy with beneficial trade, economic, social and political liberalism and the restraint of arbitrary power at home and abroad was rediscovered and re-emphasised. This regenerated the 'English naval myth' stretching back to the half-remembered glories of the first Elizabeth, and was celebrated in the late Victorian and Edwardian imperial age by the ballad poetry of the likes of Rudyard Kipling and Henry Newbolt:[16]

> Effingham, Grenville, Raleigh, Drake,
>   Here's to the bold and free!
> Benbow, Collingwood, Byron, Blake,
>   Hail to the Kings of the sea!
> Admirals all, for England's sake,
>   Honour be yours and fame!
> And honour, as long as waves shall break,
>   To Nelson's peerless name![17]

This was a re-affirmation of a symbiotic relationship between the Navy and Britain so close that ignoring it would be like trying to write the history of Switzerland without mentioning its mountains.[18] Seapower could be not merely an instrument of British policy, but its objective. 'What really determines the policy of this country' said Sir Edward Grey in 1911, 'is the question of Sea Power. It is the naval question which underlies the whole of our European policy'.[19]

'The British peoples,' thought the journalist Archibald Hurd, 'are incurably maritime – by geographical distribution, by instinct, and by political bias, because sea power has always suggested freedom'.[20] No other people, added Commander G.S. Bowles, inhabited such 'a small densely crowded island approachable by outside trade solely across the sea'. The consequent maritime element of 'Britishness' was described and explained at the time by the historian G.M. Trevelyan like this:

> The universality of the Englishman's experience and outlook – quite as marked a characteristic as his insularity – is due to his command of the ocean which has for more than three centuries carried him as explorer, trader, and colonist to every shore in two hemispheres.[21]

Not surprising then that so many Britons should apparently consider that, 'The ends o' the earth were our portion, The ocean at large was our share'.[22]

It also seemed to follow that the country had to have a Navy worthy of its maritime character and it was a fundamental point that these interests made Britain both strong and, at the same time, vulnerable. Thus Clowes,

> No one can foretell exactly what a naval war between powers of the first importance will be like, or what surprises it may bring forth; yet we all know that, if Great Britain be a party to that war, the issue must be decisive of her fate. Either she must maintain, and indeed increase, the glories of her naval past by coming triumphantly out of the contest, or she must lose everything that now gives her a unique position in the world.[23]

A Navy second to none, singly or in combination had to be aspired to and nurtured. It is no coincidence that in the early 1890s, the Nelson tradition was so thoroughly rediscovered because that seemed to encapsulate everything that Britain represented. It was astonishing thought Laughton that both in Britain and around the world, 'Nelson is almost a synonym for England's greatness. Aboukir and Trafalgar the true epitome of England's glory'.[24] Lord Esher described a visit to the naval college at Osborne in 1906:

> We went to the college this afternoon. Four hundred boys looking splendid. The gym is much improved. There is a portrait of Nelson hung in the gallery – with a motto under it in enormous letters: 'There is nothing the Navy cannot do'.[25]

The Navy was accepted as exemplifying 'the best of British'; indeed, the Navy, and everything it stood for, epitomised the essential characteristics of 'the island race' whose interests it defended. The Navy, in many ways, *was* Britain. Or, as one reviewer of Nicholas Rodger's majestic *Command of the Ocean: A Naval History of Britain, 1649–1815* put it, '... if you do not understand the importance of British maritime history, you can never fully understand Britain'.[26]

But, as Jeremy Black and others have warned, this basic understanding could easily be lost. He laments what he sees as the contemporary decline of this aspect of 'Britishness' although with the current emphasis on sea-based expeditionary operations and the joint approach in current British defence policy at one level and the continuing popularity of maritime history and documentary programmes on the television at another, one might well conclude that such pessimism at the moment is overdone.[27] On the other hand, the controversy over the BBC's meagre coverage of the Trafalgar 200 Fleet Review and the International Festival of the Sea rather supports this depressing case.[28]

But the real point is that awareness of the 'Britishness of seapower' has risen and fallen like the tides themselves in the changing context of Britain's fortunes, and that it could certainly not be taken for granted.

A need for naval thinking?

> There is no smartness about sailors. They waddle like ducks, and can only fight stupid battles that no one can form any idea of. There is no science nor strategem in sea-fights – nothing more than what you see when two rams run their heads together in a field to knock each other down. But in military battles there is such art, and such splendour, and the men are so smart, particularly the horse-soldiers.[29]

These reflections by Anne, Thomas Hardy's heroine in *The Trumpet Major*, nicely encapsulate the notion that naval thinking is indeed an oxymoron. But why, given the manifest importance of the sea to Britain, has naval thinking been comparatively neglected in Britain? There were, and perhaps are, some trivial reasons for the alleged reluctance of British naval officers to reflect on the wider aspects of their profession. It has to be admitted that the process can sometimes strike them as being quite boring. In some cases, those responsible for the education of officers at the naval colleges of Dartmouth, Greenwich and Manadon felt that abstract concepts might damage young or tender minds, not least because, as Winston Churchill once remarked:

> The seafaring and scientific technique of the naval profession makes such severe demands upon the training of naval men, that they have very rarely the time or opportunity to study military history and the art of war in general.[30]

T124 attributed the problem to two other things. 'No doubt', he said, the Navy's 'dazzling success at the turn of the previous century were partly responsible, by inducing a spirit of intellectual complacency'. But he also thought the absence of good history was to blame as well:

> There were plenty of naval histories, but they were mainly narratives. They told of the glorious exploits of the Royal Navy and of how they happened. What they did not tell was why they happened, and whether the policy that brought them about was well or ill conceived.[31]

Less obviously, there was and indeed is concern that the consequences of such thinking might prove too prescriptive and deadening for free-ranging operations on the open ocean. Corbett reproduced a seventeenth-century report which pointed out the essential difference between operations at sea and on land:

> ... it intended to enjoin our fleet to advance and fight at sea much after the manner of an army at land, assigning every ship to a particular division, rank, file and station, which order and regularity was not only improbable but almost impossible to be observed by so great a fleet in so uncertain a place as the sea.[32]

Compared to navies, armies in action disaggregate into much smaller units (down to platoons and very possibly individual soldiers). A strong sense of common purpose and prescriptive doctrine is the only thing that may bind them together in the confusion of battle. Fleets at sea need it too, of course, but to a much lesser degree, the argument goes. Hence the traditional British naval wariness about excessive conceptualisation and prescriptive doctrine; better to rely on an offensive instinct schooled by experience. The pantheon of naval heroes celebrated in paint at those self-same naval colleges is indeed dominated by people like Nelson who are held constructively to have broken 'the rules', whereas 'regulators' like Admiral Jellicoe observed and even invented them. Battles of lost opportunity such as Jutland and the inconclusive line engagements of the British and French in the eighteenth century on the other hand show, it is said, the ultimate futility of simply 'going by the book'.[33]

But the counter-view that the book has at least to be written has slowly gained ground through the twentieth and into the twenty-first century, such that the observations of Thomas Hardy's heroine appear increasingly wide of the mark. Instead, there has been a growing acceptance, even in the Navy, that maritime strategy does exist, does matter and should be thought about. This has, moreover, been reinforced by a keener sense of what the term actually means. Here a problem is that, like other words in the military vocabulary, 'strategy' has been adopted in common parlance, but adulterated in the process and has come not to mean much more than 'the way to get things done'. Accordingly, we talk of 'a strategy' for getting a mortgage, cutting a hedge or even 'body strategy'.[34] Perhaps because resuscitating the original meaning of the word could easily become a real chore, and one incidental to its immediate purpose, the otherwise excellent *BR 1806: British Maritime Doctrine* of 2004 ducks the issue and has no reference in its glossary to 'strategy' or even 'maritime strategy.'

The easiest thing to do in this situation is to seek to define the term as it will generally be used in this and other books. For a good start in that process we could go back to the definition offered by Sir Julian Corbett:

> By maritime strategy, we mean the principles which govern a war in which the sea is a substantial factor. Naval strategy is but that part of it which determines the movements of the fleet when maritime strategy has determined what part the fleet must play in relation to the action of the land forces; for it scarcely needs saying that it is almost impossible that a war can be decided by naval action alone.[35]

A number of themes emerge from this quotation, all of which will be addressed in this book. The first is the very obvious one that there is much more to naval operations and naval history than the guns of battle. Corbett wrote at a time when the concept of the 'operational level of war' was implicitly rather than explicitly considered. The nearest he comes to addressing this is in, not the battle, but *The Campaign of Trafalgar* with its emphasis on Nelson's efforts to link the strategic and tactical levels of war and to serve his country's aims by assuring the best conditions for the conduct of the battle. Naval thinking therefore covers *all* the levels of war, and not just the tactical matters of battle.

It also covers the relationship between the Navy and the other services. One of the most striking aspects of this familiar quotation from Corbett is the emphasis on what is now known as 'the joint approach'. To play their part as effectively as they might, navies need to be coordinated with land and indeed air forces.

The discussion is also clearly set at the highest level of war in which the focus is on the achievement of the broad aims of national policy. Remembering his Clausewitz, Corbett emphasises the point that strategy is about the use of the military as a means of achieving a political objective. Liddell Hart put it concisely when he defined strategy as 'The art of distributing and applying military means to fulfil the ends of policy'.[36] The following, equally familiar, but much broader quotation by Robert Osgood emphasises that naval operations need to be set in their overall domestic and international context:

> Military strategy must now be understood as nothing less than the overall plan for utilising the capacity for armed coercion – in conjunction with the economic, diplomatic and psychological instruments of power – to support foreign policy most effectively by overt, covert and tacit means.[37]

This comprehensive conception of strategy-making incorporates the other forms of power which also have their part to play in the achievement of political ends. Economic, diplomatic and psychological means may serve the same purposes and, indeed, the armed forces can be used to influence other people's behaviour in very many non-lethal ways. Osgood's definition also implies that 'strategy' is by no means limited to periods of war but applies in peacetime as well. There is, it would seem, much more to strategy than simply killing people efficiently, at sea or anywhere else. Strategy is not restricted to the conduct of war, but extends into peacetime. Osgood widens the agenda by emphasising differing types of strategy to include using your armed forces to win friends, or to influence their behaviour as much as coercing or deterring possible adversaries. The use of naval power, in short, needs to be considered not just as a distinct type of military operation but also as part of a comprehensive approach to strategy.

Accordingly, 'naval thinking' as discussed in this book involves reflecting on the nature, conduct and consequences of naval power in general, and setting these against their strategic setting. It may be intended to help sailors to understand and perhaps perform their roles rather better; it may be intended to help others understand the role of naval power, past, present and future.

One particular variant of naval thinking, which is also to be discussed later in the book, is the notion of doctrine – which is in effect the application of maritime theory in a particular time and place. If maritime strategic theory is likened to the art of cookery, doctrine is concerned with today's menus. It helps hard-pressed commanders concentrate the mind and it encourages general intellectual professionalism and coherence of thought and action among the military. It may often seem quite transient; with so much constantly changing (not least the terminology used) most would accept that there is an increased, rather than decreased, need for more generalised strategic thinking to help the bewildered sort important matters of the moment from those of permanent value.

Doctrine is these days applied to all levels of war, the strategic, the operational and the tactical. It tends to be more prescriptive than general maritime strategic theory, and narrower in focus. It tends to be least prescriptive at the higher levels, and most prescriptive when it takes the form of 'fighting instructions' and 'tactical procedures' and where the emphasis is much more on how to think and do things rather than on what to do and what to think about. Usually though, doctrinal formulations contain warnings against its being allowed to degenerate into 'dogma'. Its authority is therefore caveated by the reader's need to exercise his or her judgement in its interpretation and application.

Both maritime theory and doctrine are, however, largely based on the processing of historical experience and discovering what the Russians call the 'norms' of naval operations – or what is usually found to work. Several of the contributions to this book look in more detail at the role of naval history in the development of British naval thought, and it is clear that any examination of the evolution of British naval thinking should comprise not just the analysis of rigorous essays in maritime naval theory and formulations of doctrine, but also illustrative or influential works of naval history, statements of naval policy and their practical applications as well. Sometimes, after all, theoretical conceptions (about the protection of shipping for example) only become clear when they are 'realised' or put into practice in training, procurement or the conduct of operations. Naval theory and naval practice, past and present, can have a relationship that is truly symbiotic.

The difficulty, as Churchill pointed out earlier, is that these practical activities themselves may become so all-absorbing that they more or less exclude busy naval officers from metaphysical speculation about the nature of their profession. But merely developing or having experience is not enough. Sailors need to think about their business – otherwise, as Frederick the

Great famously observed, quite a few of his pack mules would deserve to be field marshals. Accordingly it was important that naval officers be educated to think about their profession.

This raises a last theme of this book – the business of naval education. Encouraging naval officers to take time out in order to reflect on their profession was and remains the aim of naval education and staff training at the Royal Navy's various educational establishments in Portsmouth, Plymouth, Dartmouth and Greenwich and now the Joint Services Command and Staff College at Shrivenham. The study of this aspect of naval thinking has tended to be rather neglected in the past although it is, at long last, now being addressed.[38]

Professor Bryan Ranft was closely associated with one important manifestation of this, namely the Department of History and International Affairs at the Royal Naval College, Greenwich, in which he spent most of his academic career. The Royal Naval College Greenwich, based in the beautiful late seventeenth- and early eighteenth-century buildings of the Greenwich Royal Naval Hospital was only established in 1873, in response to an Admiralty circular of 30 January of the same year, which talked about the need '... to provide the most efficient means of higher education of naval officers adequate to the constantly increasing requirements of the Service ... [and] ... and the highest possible instruction in all branches of theoretical and scientific study bearing upon their profession'. It was expected that the College would become a '... nucleus of mathematical and mechanical science, especially devoted to those branches of scientific investigation of most interest to the Navy'.[39]

Vice-Admiral Sir Astley Cooper Key, paradoxically an opponent of the establishment of the College, became its first Admiral President, with a Captain of the College acting in effect as Chief of Staff and a civilian Director of Studies to run an Academic Board of professors to supervise the four departments of Mathematics, Physical Science, Chemistry and Applied Mechanics and Fortification.

From the start, RNC Greenwich became a leading centre for scientific study, but as is discussed more fully by Andrew Lambert in Chapter 3, its role in the development of naval history and strategic thinking was much more hesitant and accidental. A lecturer in mathematics and meteorology, J.K. Laughton, more or less on his own initiative, developed a course of 6 down-to-earth and practical lectures on naval history (instead of the 30 originally recommended), but left in 1885 to become the country's first Professor of Naval History at King's College, London. Other luminaries of the period, including Rear Admiral Philip Colomb and Julian Corbett came and went.

Although as Lord Selborne told the House 'a naval strategy course, to include strategy, tactics, naval history and international law had been commenced at Greenwich for the benefit of the senior officers of the Royal Naval College',[40] the consensus at the time was against the practical value of the theoretical study of naval operations past and present, and these ventures did not prosper.[41]

The result was famously summarised by Churchill:

> When I went to the Admiralty I found that there was no moment in the career and training of a naval officer when he was obliged to read a single book about naval war, or even pass a rudimentary examination in naval history. The Royal Navy had made no important contributions to naval literature. The standard work on Sea power was written by an American Admiral. The best accounts of British sea fighting and naval strategy were compiled by an English civilian. The Silent Service was not mute because it was absorbed in thought or study, but because it was weighed down by daily routine and by its ever diversifying technique. We had competent administrators, brilliant experts of every description, unequalled navigators, good disciplinarians, fine sea officers, brave and devoted hearts but at the outset of the conflict, we had more Captains of ships than Captains of war. In this will be found the explanation of many untoward events.[42]

This depressing conclusion was echoed by some acerbic observers in the fleet:

> There were a number of shockingly bad admirals afloat in 1914. They were pleasant, bluff old sea-dogs, with no scientific training; endowed with a certain amount of common sense, they had no conception of the practice and theory of strategy or tactics. They had spent their lives floating around the world showing the flag and leaving behind them a most admirable impression of the nature of the British gentleman.[43]

Nor, for that matter, did the College itself have a much better conception. The Acting Sub-Lieutenants who formed the bulk of the students were given to '... disorderly and riotous conduct and excessive use of wine and spirits' as means of compensating for the tedium of a rigid and mathematics-dominated syllabus run by a set of professors who Admiral Fisher darkly suspected were more intent on feathering their own nests with outside consultancies than in advancing the cause of naval education.[44] 'There is a want of naval reality about Greenwich College', Fisher remarked, 'which reacts detrimentally on every officer who studies there'. The College survived Fisher's bitter opposition, however.

The experience of the First World War reinforced the perception that there was, after all, a clear need to study the profession of warfare at sea. Admiral Richmond, the College's Admiral President took a robust line on this:

> It is curious, though it is not really surprising, to see how unable most officers are to express themselves at all. They cannot analyse a situation,

they cannot define their objects in a given situation. The contrast between naval & military officers is remarkable. Of the soldiers ... all could write a clear appreciation & make a better plan than the Captains or Admirals. Many of the Captains cannot spell even passably.[45]

Such views became the justification for the establishment of the RN Staff College in 1919. Connectedly, a Department of History and English was at last set up in 1922. The first Professor of History and English at the Royal Navy College was Geoffrey A.R. Callender, MA, FSA, FR.Hist S. Appointed on 20 April 1922, he retired in September 1934, being succeeded by Michael Lewis CBE, MA, FR.Hist S. until January 1955, John G. Bullocke, MA until December 1962 and then Christopher C. Lloyd MA. FR.Hist S. until August 1966. All of these were naval historians but in the early days, and as will be discussed at greater length in Chapter 6, the history taught at Greenwich was of the inspirational rather than the analytical sort, and perhaps appropriately the greatest contribution to British naval thinking in this period was made not by a civilian academic but rather by Richmond himself.

By 1939, the Department was operating within what was in effect a naval university which ran some 21 varied courses every year. Much, but by no means all, of this activity was suspended during the Second World War although some 27,000 officers nonetheless passed through the College doors. Normal service was resumed in 1945 and the staff of the Department of History and English was increased from 2 to 12 in order to cope, particularly with the institution of the Junior Officers General Education and War Course (JOWC). Bryan Ranft was one of the new appointees, in 1946.

The JOWC was based on notions that had developed during the war, not least through the work of the Army Bureau of Current Affairs, that all members of the armed services should be encouraged to come to their own conclusions about *why* they were doing what they were doing.[46] It developed into a lively, undergraduate-level course for about 100 Sub-Lieutenants, and centred on study of the context in which naval operations were conducted – namely Britain and world affairs. It included such revolutionary concepts as private study periods and individual tutorials, reforms brought about sometimes in the teeth of the opposition of the likes of the Commander of the College in 1945, who thought his charges,

> ... would not work unless regimented and driven to it. They were incredibly 'low brow' and therefore evening societies would be a farce. Examinations were necessary to see who was working and as a sanction threat for the idle.[47]

The JOWC ended in 1958 when the entry age into the Royal Navy was raised to 18 and a third academic year was added to the course at the Britannia Royal Naval College at Dartmouth, which included significant study of history, both general and naval, as well as international affairs. A Special Duties Officers' Greenwich course (SDOGC) was introduced in 1958 and a Lieutenants' Greenwich course (LGC) in 1961. Bryan Ranft took over a department reduced in size and eventually retitled the Department of History and International Affairs (DHIA) in 1966. This came at a time of very considerable change at Greenwich. Many of the scientific and engineering departments were moved to the Royal Naval Engineering College at Manadon, and the Department of Naval Architecture to University College London. The only surviving academic departments were the large Department of Nuclear Science and Technology and the small DHIA directly responsible for teaching the SDOGC and the LGC. The DHIA also contributed to the WRNS Officer Training course, the main Staff course and the Senior Officer's War course as and when requested.

Greenwich was a federal institution, or in Callender's words '... a "Collegium" that is to say a group of departments, individually autonomous, but co-operating to direct the forces of nature for the use and convenience of the Service'.[48] The DHIA (just one professor and eight lecturers) was rather oddly regarded as entirely sovereign, theoretically equivalent to its much larger fellow units, and reporting directly to the Commander-in-Chief Naval Home Command at Portsmouth. This was important as successive heads of the Department considered that the independence of their academic advice depended on that autonomy and so were constantly wary of the danger of being swallowed up by the RN Staff College, with which, in the nature of things, they had to work closely. Geoffrey Callender had put the same point rather too strongly back in 1924:

> ... if you engage a Professor of History and then determine for him what he shall teach and what he shall not, you are modelling your conduct on the fool in the fable who bought a dog and then insisted on doing the barking himself.[49]

For professional educators operating within a military environment, the real issue was, and is, for the military customer and the academic service provider to find agreement, from their different perspectives, on what should be taught and how.

Bryan Ranft's aim, accordingly, was to tighten up the the Department and to ensure that the syllabus remained immediately and obviously relevant to the students and the Navy generally. The Department continued to focus on the international context of the time and the Royal Navy's role within it.

This tradition was taken further by his successor, Professor Peter Nailor (1977–88), the first Professor of History at the Royal Naval College appointed when already at the professorial rank in the university sector. Professor Nailor also brought with him a lifetime's expertise as a senior civil servant in the Admiralty and produced the definitive semi-official and publicly available study of the Royal Navy's Polaris programme.[50] He was succeeded in his appointment by the editor of this volume.

From 1966 to 1997, when the Royal Navy finally left Greenwich, the College, and the DHIA, were continually buffeted by several of the broader currents affecting the Royal Navy. The first was the relentless search for financial economies. Time and time again, Greenwich was faced with the prospect of the loss or shortening of its courses, or indeed with complete closure. It was an important part of the task of the College's two professors and heads of department to assist their naval colleagues in the continual battle to resist such calls, not least by the provision of continuity and useful links with former students who later became influential decision-makers.

The second battle, specifically for the DHIA, was to continue to demonstrate the need for a significant academic element to staff training. In the early days when staff training itself was regarded by a significant element of naval opinion as something of a rest cure and/or an 'appointing margin' for officers with awkward gaps in their careers that needed filling somehow, this was far from easy. Moreover the syllabus needed to be demonstrably 'relevant' to the Navy's preoccupations and, at the same time, professionally and cost-effectively conducted.

For this reason, the balance in the syllabi of courses between contemporary affairs and naval history shifted to the latter's disadvantage. In 1980, in the course of one of *The Naval Review*'s periodic laments about the decline of the study of naval history, Peter Nailor observed that history had become a victim of the Navy's preoccupation with electronics and guided missiles and its 'discovery of management'.[51] Staff courses were becoming more vocational, losing some of the civilising and mind-broadening aspirations that they used to have; they became, tauter, tighter, harder work, less fun – but more immediately and obviously useful and so less vulnerable to the budgeteers. The standing of staff training accordingly rose. Fewer senior officers came to Greenwich and prefaced their remarks to disheartened students with the observation that 'I didn't do any staff training and it never did me any harm'. The RN Staff College, one of the major units of the Greenwich campus, became much more cohesive, taking professional charge of its various courses in a more challenging way.

But, perhaps paradoxically, as staff training began to 'matter' more, the need to develop inter-service cooperation was increasingly recognised. The stress on 'jointery' was logically irrefutable and resulted in the final closure of the Royal Naval College and the opening of a brand-new purpose-built Joint Services Command and Staff College (JSCSC) first at Bracknell and then at Shrivenham in 2000. The ultimate reward for the work of Bryan Ranft and his colleagues, before and after, however, was that many of the achievements in service education of the 1966–97 period were, rather against the odds, wholly absorbed by the new JSCSC. Indirectly, the fact that British command and staff training is recognised as amongst the very best in the world is an important part of Bryan Ranft's legacy.

It is evident from all this that while both maritime theory and doctrinal formulations are the most conscious and rigorous aspects of the field of 'naval thinking', it is by no means restricted to them. There are other important dimensions to the subject as well, particularly the development and use of naval history and the analysis of the interrelationship between naval operations and their domestic and international context. This book will therefore seek to explore them all, and their interconnections.

In Chapter 2, Nicholas Rodger explores the extent to which the whole notion of strategy applies at all in the eighteenth century. In Chapter 3, Andrew Lambert analyses the contribution of naval history and naval historians to the evolution of British naval thinking in the nineteenth century. Chapter 4 describes the emergence of a self-conscious British school of maritime strategy in the years immediately before the First World War. In Chapter 5 Andrew Gordon considers the evolution of British thought during that conflict, while Chapter 6 takes that forward through the interwar period. Jock Gardner contrasts theory and practice as revealed by the experience of the Second World War in Chapter 7. Next, Richard Hill considers the evolution of British naval thinking in the nuclear age, a period when Britain found itself in a very different and difficult set of strategic circumstances. In Chapter 9, Eric Grove outlines the rediscovery of doctrine by the Royal Navy at the very end of the twentieth century, part of a conscious limbering up process for the challenges of the post Cold War world. The book concludes with an epilogue that lists the work and achievements of the late Professor Bryan McLaren Ranft to whose memory this volume is respectfully dedicated.

Notes

1 Cited in Schurman (1981) p. 44.
2 Clerk (1790) pp. 17–18, 147–8.
3 Mahan (1902) p. 77.
4 T124 (1940) p. 13.
5 W. Pitt, Speech of 27 Feb 1786. Reprinted in Pitt (1806) Vol. I, p. 281.
6 Speech, reported in *Gentleman's Magazine*, September 1745, pp. 465–6.
7 Mackinder (1969) p. 15.
8 For example, Padfield (1999) and (2003).
9 Wilson (2002) p. 204.
10 This and all subsequent quotations from speeches made by members of the opposition and of the Walpole administration may be found in the 'Journal of the Proceedings and Debates in the Political Club', *The London Magazine*, 1743. Esp. pp. 23, 58, 62, 134, 211, 212, 218, 221, 228–9, 279, 427, 437, 438, 541.
11 Ramsay Macdonald, 11 Oct 1929, cited in Air 9/108, Public Record Office, Kew, London (PRO).
12 Ferguson (2004) pp. 1, 17.
13 Black (2004) pp. 171–2.
14 See *The London Magazine*, 1743, op. cit.
15 Baugh (1988).
16 See for example Newbolt (1995).

18 *Geoffrey Till*

17 Henry Newbolt 'Admirals All' in ibid.
18 Rodger (2004) pp. lxiii, 48, 178, 235–6, 255.
19 Cited in Richmond (1939) p. 140.
20 Hurd (1918) p. 20.
21 These views are conveniently summarised in Aston (1927) pp. 82, 98.
22 Rudyard Kipling, 'The Lost Legion' in his collection *The Seven Seas* (1916) p. 77.
23 Clowes (1902) p. vii.
24 Cited in Hattendorf (2005) p. 174; see also MacKenzie (2005).
25 Letter 11 Feb 1906 in Brett (1934) p. 142.
26 'Putting the sea back in Britain', *The Economist* 20 Nov 2004.
27 Black (2004) pp. 361–2 et seq.
28 'History lost in a sea of uncertainty', *Daily Telegraph* 29 June 2005 and the Frank Johnson column, *Daily Telegraph* 2 July 2005.
29 Anne, in Thomas Hardy's *The Trumpet Major* (1925) p. 354.
30 Churchill cited in Lehman (1988) p. 25.
31 T124 (1940) pp.13–14.
32 Corbett (1904) p. 154.
33 For a wider exploration of this thesis see Gordon (1996).
34 *The Guardian Weekly* 23 April 2005.
35 Corbett (1911) pp. 15–16.
36 Liddell Hart (1967) p. 5.
37 Osgood (1962) p. 5.
38 See the forthcoming study by Dickinson referred to in the next footnote.
39 The definitive study of the establishment and development of the Royal Naval College, Greenwich, has still to be written. This material is derived from an early pioneering work by C.M. (Jerry) Dawson, a one time colleague of Bryan Ranft, namely *The Story of Greenwich* (Blackheath, London: privately published 1977), and the booklet *The Royal Naval College Greenwich Centenary 1873–1973*. See also Dickinson (1999). At the time of writing Dr Dickinson is working on a major study of the evolution of British naval education. See also Anon (1931), Callender (1939) and Lloyd (1966).
40 Clowes (1902) p. ix.
41 Lloyd (1966) p. 155.
42 Churchill (1927) Vol. I, p. 93.
43 King-Hall (1952) pp. 97–8.
44 Kemp (1964) Vol. II, pp. 107–9.
45 Marder (1952) p. 365.
46 Dawson, op. cit. p. 104.
47 Dean's Office file 1945.
48 Callender (1939) p. 22.
49 Letter to Richmond, 22 Dec 1924, in Goldrick and Hattendorf (1993) pp. 107–8.
50 Nailor (1988).
51 Peter Nailor, letter on 'Naval History' *The Naval Review*, 68 (Jan, 1980) pp. 66–7. This was written in response to (Captain) G.A. F(rench)'s 'Naval History' in the October 1979 edition, an article which prompted a deal of interest and the eventual reprinting of Richmond's 'The Importance of the Study of Naval History' in the April 1980 edition.

2 The idea of naval strategy in Britain in the eighteenth and nineteenth centuries[1]

N.A.M. Rodger

It is doubtful to what extent the idea of naval strategy existed in eighteenth-century Britain, nor for a good part of the nineteenth century. Though there are very many books and articles by modern historians professing to explain British naval strategy in this period, contemporaries did not, and could not, discuss it, for the simple reason that the English language did not have a word for strategy. That word itself first appeared in English about the year 1800, as a borrowing from French.[2] At that time, and for long afterwards, it was used in a sense close to the Greek original; it referred to the art of the general, rather than the admiral, and chiefly at what we would call the local or tactical level. Not until late in the nineteenth century can we say that the phrase 'naval strategy' was current in English in the accepted modern sense, and only then did it become the subject of public debate. To discuss 'British naval strategy' of the eighteenth and most of the nineteenth century is to impose an anachronistic modern category on the thinking of the time. The idea of British naval strategy must really mean the strategic element in British naval policy, as far as it can be isolated with the benefit of hindsight.[3]

Even this is misleading as far as the eighteenth century is concerned, for before 1815 it is scarcely possible to say that Britain *had* a distinct naval policy. Navies and fleets of course existed, and men had of necessity some ideas on how to use them, but those ideas tended to be pragmatic, often detailed, located within a general framework or attitude which was not spelled out with any exactness. In practice, British policy towards the outside world was a single subject, which had diplomatic, political, commercial, ideological, financial, military and naval expression according to the circumstances. Until 1782 the responsible ministers, the two Secretaries of State, shared between themselves (not quite equally) the responsibilities for home, foreign, military, naval and colonial affairs.[4] It was a strength of the system that it was capable of producing a unified foreign policy, and British policy-making in wartime was not altogether improved by the reorganisation of 1782, which divided the secretaryships into Foreign and Home (including military and colonial) Departments, and by the growing independence of the Admiralty (which by the 1790s was only nominally subordinate to the Secretaries of State). The creation in 1794 of the Secretary of State for War had a particularly unfortunate tendency to separate the formation of policy from its execution.[5]

The weakness of the system had always been that the ministers who made policy, in peace or war, had no detailed knowledge of military or naval affairs, and few expert advisers to provide it. Some ministers, and many if not most men active in politics, were not merely ignorant of administration and logistics, but explicitly denied the value of such knowledge, and derided those who relied on it.[6] In this situation, detailed planning was neither sought nor found, and naval policy even in wartime was apt to remain at a high level of generalisation. There was no naval staff in the Admiralty. Its tiny staff consisted almost entirely of civilian clerks engaged in routine administrative business.[7] The only sea officers present were the naval members of the Board of Admiralty. It was common, though not invariable, for the Board to include at least one senior officer of weight and experience, and this senior officer might or might not be the same person as the First Lord who presided over the Admiralty Board and represented the Navy in Cabinet. The junior members of the Board, who were essentially political placemen with no important functions, might include one or two officers, often elderly and long retired, but there was for long periods no more than one active sea officer on the Board. It was perfectly possible to have an Admiralty headed by a civilian, virtually without professional assistance. For much of the American War of Independence Lord Sandwich, the First Lord, had only one professional colleague, Lord Mulgrave, who was absent at sea and able to advise only by letter. The First Lord might and did settle grand strategy with his Cabinet colleagues, but it could only be worked out in detail by the Navy and Victualling Boards, on the administrative side, and the Commander-in-Chief, on the operational side.[8]

Commanders-in-Chief, however, were in no condition to supply the want of any specifically naval policy-making. The 'retinue' of an eighteenth-century British admiral consisted largely of domestics and young gentlemen hoping to rise on his patronage to become officers. His 'staff', in the modern sense, consisted of his secretary, who handled the administrative business of the squadron with the assistance of one or two clerks. In addition he might, but did not usually have, a First Captain (in addition to the Flag Captain) to assist him in handling his fleet, and he might entrust intelligence or diplomatic correspondence to the flagship's chaplain.[9] Otherwise he was on his own.

Nor was there any forum for the discussion of strategy, or indeed of any other aspect of the naval profession. There were no institutions of higher study for the profession of arms, and no idea of encouraging officers to study it. Intelligent Admirals hoped their officers would read books, but there was no professional literature they could suggest that dealt with strategy. There were manuals on navigation, gunnery, naval architecture and other technical subjects; and a growing interest in tactics and signalling;[10] but the literature on naval warfare in general consisted of a handful of works translated out of French, none of which dealt with strategy in any coherent fashion.[11]

Eighteenth-century Britain lacked any machinery for naval planning or policy-making because planning for war, or during war, was both less urgent and less useful to the Navy then than it is now. The fact that it took at least 18 months to mobilise the Navy as a whole, and many months to fit out individual squadrons, gave plenty of time to consider the circumstances of the moment.[12] Since intelligence, especially of distant theatres of war, was usually weak and sometimes non-existent, since the situation had often changed before a force could reach its destination, it was always difficult and often impossible to draw up detailed plans in advance. Everything at the tactical level, and a good deal at the strategic, had perforce to be entrusted to the initiative of the commander on the spot. All ministers could do was choose a good officer and fully brief him as to their intentions.[13] When all operations which became known outside the inner circle of ministers were invariably subject to the glare of publicity and a heavy fire of ignorant criticism, there were strong incentives to keep consultation to a minimum.[14] For all these reasons naval operations tended to be thought of as immediate and pragmatic concerns, and no articulated school of British naval strategy emerged.

When naval policy was debated, it was usually in an ideological rather than a practical context. Particularly in the first half of the eighteenth century, British policy towards the outside world tended to be seen through the distorting spectacles of popular politics. There was a wide discrepancy between Britain's actual position as a European state vitally interested in the balance of power on the Continent; and the popular perception of a naval strength so great that it could view events across the Channel with lofty indifference, and sweep up the commerce and colonies of the enemy with casual ease. Any failure to do so was attributed by the public to incompetence or treachery, while an officer like Vernon or Anson who had captured a Spanish town or galleon could be sure of public adulation and an instant political career.[15] The Act of Settlement of 1701, which regulated the Protestant succession to the throne, attempted to forbid any foreign monarch (meaning the Electors of Hanover) from allowing the interests of his Continental possessions to deflect his British policy. This made it easy for opponents of government to present any Continental involvement, especially (after 1714) an involvement with Hanover, as the poisoned fruit of illegal Continental entanglements. Naval campaigns and overseas expeditions, on the other hand, were the English way of warfare; patriotic and profitable. So what purported to be a strategic debate was in many cases a disguised form of ideological contest, where foreign policy acted as the surrogate of domestic politics.[16]

The real naval policy of eighteenth-century England is not to be discovered in the fevered stereotypes of parliamentary debates and popular journalism, and it is very often misunderstood by modern historians. For most of the eighteenth and nineteenth centuries, the Navy was not primarily concerned with imperial expansion or even overseas trade. It was above all a defensive force, the principal if not only safeguard of a country and a regime which felt itself to be permanently threatened by France or Spain, or both.[17] It is easy for the modern observer to underestimate the extent to which the English felt insecure with the greatest military power of the age a day's sail away across the Channel, and these fears were sharpened by the presence of a legitimate dynasty in exile, and by Protestant attitudes towards Catholicism. Foreigners likewise contrasted the febrile excitements of parliamentary democracy and the flimsy edifice of public debt with the solid permanence of absolute monarchy and the real wealth derived from land and population. Only the Navy safeguarded Britain, for which reason the bulk of the ships, especially the battleships, were always kept in home waters. In 1757, in the middle of the most succesful war of colonial conquest Britain ever fought, 71 per cent of the ships and 67 per cent of the men were serving in home waters, and another 12 per cent of the ships and 18 per cent of the men in the Mediterranean.[18] Between 1757 and 1762, 64 per cent of the 'ship days' of the Navy were served in home waters or the Mediterranean.[19] The ease with which the French could tie down a large proportion of the fleet simply by marching a body of troops to the Channel coast was a real strategic weakness for Britain, and helps to explain how often the French Navy held the initiative at sea in spite of having fewer ships.[20] This was especially true in the opening phases of eighteenth-century wars, when the French manning system tended to give the French navy a temporary advantage.[21]

In addition to its principal defensive role, the Navy could be used as a deterrent, but eighteenth-century British governments tended to overestimate the extent to which seapower was terrible, or even relevant, to the ambitions of their Continental rivals.[22] It worked in strictly colonial confrontations with France or Spain, on occasions, such as the Falkland Islands crisis of 1770 or the Nootka Sound incident in 1790, when those powers were not prepared to risk a general war.[23] It did not work against land powers with few or no overseas interests, as in the Ochakov Affair.[24] It did not work reliably in the Mediterranean, where the Royal Navy was far from home and facts of geography and the prevailing winds tended to work to the disadvantage of large squadrons.[25] Even in 1718–19, when France was a British ally and the Royal Navy could send its main fleet to the Western Mediterranean with a local base (Minorca), superior seapower proved to be a disappointment, though a Spanish army was ashore on the island of Sicily with only an inferior fleet to protect it. Not only did deterrence fail, forcing the British to fight an undeclared war at sea, but even the victory of Cape Passaro did not achieve its objective, and it was French armies ashore which eventually forced the Spaniards to withdraw. When the Spanish Navy again attempted to support expansion in Italy during the War of the Polish Succession (1733–5), the British did not feel strong enough to intervene.[26]

Compared to the main fleets, the Royal Navy's colonial squadrons were small and scattered, and their role likewise was defensive. Their task was to defend seaborne trade, in peacetime as much or more than in war. They were not meant primarily to defend British colonies, still less to attack enemy possessions, for both of which purposes the squadrons, and their bases, were too small and very badly placed.[27] On the occasions when the British mounted major colonial expeditions, large forces were always sent out for the purpose, and very often a temporary base had to be established.

Both at home and overseas, British naval policy in the eighteenth century followed patterns already established in the seventeenth century, and in some aspects long before that.[28] The most essential innovation was the rise of the Western Squadron. This development has been well studied by modern historians, and can be described with a good deal more clarity now than it ever was by those who were involved. The key years were between 1745 and 1747, and those chiefly responsible were the Duke of Bedford, First Lord of the Admiralty, his young assistant the Earl of Sandwich, their naval colleague Admiral Anson who commanded the Western Squadron during those years, and finally Admiral Vernon, as ever applying his powerful mind and violent temper to the issues of the day. Each of these perceived some elements of the strategy they were developing, but none of them ever set it out completely and clearly on paper.[29]

The essence of the strategy, as we can see it today, was the concentration of the most important British squadron in the Western Approaches of the English Channel. Here it lay to windward of the mouth of the Channel, and of the major Atlantic ports of England and France. From this position, the Western Squadron was able to meet most of the essential British strategic requirements. In case of invasion, the attack must necessarily be mounted from one or more of the Channel ports of France or Flanders. If the invasion came without heavy naval support, it could be dealt with by the local naval defences. If it were to be protected by a fleet, that fleet could only come from outside the Channel, and pass through the waters patrolled by the Western Squadron. In either case, the threatened coasts lay straight to leeward of the Western Squadron, which could run swiftly down upon any attacking force. When the British themselves undertook landings on the coast of France, the Western Squadron was able to support them, either by its direct presence (as at Rochefort in 1757), or by covering from a distance the work of a smaller squadron (as during the landings of 1758).[30]

It was equally well placed to protect British trade, covering the movements of convoys up and down the Channel, and likewise the shipping which used the Bristol Channel and the Irish Sea. By reaching southward across the Bay of Biscay, the squadron could intercept the commerce of St Malo, Nantes, Bordeaux and the ports of northern Spain. Most important of all, it was ideally stationed to watch Brest, and if necessary Lorient, Rochefort and even Ferrol. Modern historians often talk loosely of a 'traditional' British strategy of blockade, meaning the close observation of an enemy port to prevent ships getting in or out. Such a close blockade was extremely difficult to mount, and only for relatively short periods did the British find it both possible and desirable, but if it were to be attempted, above all on Brest, the Western Squadron was there to do it. For much of the eighteenth century, in practice, British practice was a loose or distant blockade, with the Squadron cruising in the offing, or sheltering in Torbay, and relying on cruisers and intelligence to give sufficient warning of enemy movements to permit interception. It helped that the westerly winds, which were most dangerous for the blockade of Brest, also made it most difficult to sail from (though not of course to enter) the port; while an easterly wind to bring a French squadron out through the Goulet would equally carry the English down Channel in pursuit.[31]

In all this a critical advantage for the English was the development of Plymouth Dockyard, founded in 1696 to support the cruiser squadron then operating in the Western Approaches, and rapidly expanded during the eighteenth century as it became the main base of the new Western Squadron. Though to leeward of Brest, and suffering from the same remoteness from the national centres of supply as the French base did, Plymouth maintained and reinforced in these waters the British superiority in maintenance and logistics on which their naval strength was built. Plymouth's docks, storehouses, gunwharf and victualling yard were the essential foundation which made possible the operations of the Western Squadron.[32]

The critical advantage of the Squadron was economy of force. By intelligently exploiting the facts of geography and prevailing winds, it allowed a single main fleet, from a single station, to discharge most of the essential strategic functions. That was the principle, as laid out by Sir Julian Corbett[33] and others long after after the event. Contemporaries were more concerned with the practice, and the practice presented endless difficulties. The 'single station' of the Western Squadron stretched from Cape Clear to Cape Finisterre: hundreds of thousands of square miles, in which it was impossible for a single fleet to be everywhere. For many purposes, especially the interception of enemy trade, the squadron was best broken up into small units, but of course it invited defeat in detail to break up the main fleet in the offing of the enemy's naval bases. If the Western Squadron concentrated on enemy warships in Brest or Rochefort, there was still no easy option. Close blockade gave the best chances of interception, but the risks and strains of keeping station on a dangerous lee shore throughout the year were very high. To lie at Plymouth, Torbay or even Spithead was easier and safer, but the enemy might easily come or go from their ports long before a British squadron could intercept them from so far away. Timely intelligence and numerous cruisers were essential in such a case, but they were far from guaranteeing success even when they were available, which often they were not.

Theory, which contemporaries did not have available, shows us how valuable the Western Squadron was. Practice, of which they had a great deal, showed them how difficult it was to exploit, still more to combine the advantages which in principle it offered. Nevertheless the experience of the 1740s, and still more the triumphs of the Seven Years' War, showed what was possible.[34] They showed that an essentially defensive arrangement also made it possible to isolate the colonies from European waters. The more the Western Squadron established a dominance of its area, the more difficult it became for French squadrons to sail from the ports of the Ponant, and the more easily British forces could operate in the West Indies and elsewhere, without fear of unpleasant interruptions. This process was always gradual, and never absolute. There never was a period when British control of European waters was so complete that expeditions could be despatched overseas without escort. What the Western Squadron made possible was a growing degree of security overseas, as its control of the Western Approaches became more assured. During the Seven Years' War, for example, British overseas expeditions increased steadily in size and number, but the forces which accompanied them did not increase proportionately, and by the closing months of the war it was possible for an improvised force with only a handful of warships to capture the great city of Manilla, completely isolated by successful naval campaigns on the other side of the world.[35] It had been the same story a few months before at Havana, though here a larger escort was needed to deal with the only substantial European squadron permanently based in the New World.[36] The Western Squadron made it possible to dominate the waters of the West Indies without the main fleet crossing the Atlantic. It was a naval strategy for winning America in Europe.

The strategy was based on the exploitation of geography, but geography left one serious flaw in it. The Western Squadron could do a great deal from its cruising ground in the Western Approaches, but it could not easily watch a port as far away as Cadiz, and it could not by any means cover Toulon. The fact that the bulk of the French fleet was divided between Levant and Ponant was a permanent strategic problem for France, but it was equally a problem for Britain. Though it was hard for France to concentrate her fleet, it was even harder for the British to control or counter the operations of squadrons from Toulon. To send a force to Gibraltar or into the Mediterranean divided the fleet, inviting the enemy to exploit their interior position to concentrate on either part. To ignore Toulon was to allow it to operate as a 'wild card' in naval strategy. The choice was an unpleasant one for the British, who never discovered a good answer to the problem. In the initial months of three successive wars, in 1744, 1756 and 1778, the Toulon squadron seriously embarrassed the British. Later in a successful naval war, the balance of forces might move far enough to allow Britain to station a powerful squadron at Gibraltar or Minorca, but in the opening stages of a war such a luxury was never available.

With hindsight we can identify the Western Squadron as the best solution possible to the strategic problems facing Britain in a naval war against France or Spain. Contemporaries, however, had neither hindsight nor strategic theory available, and they did not clearly appreciate how and why the

Western Squadron was so successful. In the middle years of the century, and especially after the Seven Years' War, Britain's outlook towards the wider world began to change fundamentally. The danger of French aggression seemed to many to have been decisively dispelled for the first time since the accession of Louis XIV. France's military reputation had been lost at the battle of Rossbach, her Navy crushed and humiliated, her overseas empire dismantled. Few Englishmen appreciated the threat posed by the growing naval power of Spain.[37] For the British the new fact was their growing overseas empire, increasingly the focus of policy. Hitherto the British had constructed an empire of trade, in which colonies were sought and desired only to the extent that they generated commerce and shipping. Now for the first time efforts were made to integrate the colonies with the mother country, to establish garrisons and levy taxes. For the first time men began to assert that Britain was an imperial rather than a European power, indifferent to the balance of power, unconcerned at her inability to construct an alliance of the traditional sort after the Seven Years' War. The Jacobite threat seemed to have finally faded away and the new monarch George III proclaimed himself indifferent to the fate of Hanover.[38]

Just when the landscape seemed to have changed forever, the American crisis of the 1770s put at risk what had only recently been identified as the core of British strength and prosperity. Past precedents hardly seemed of use in this situation; the government of Lord North committed a large part of Britain's small field army to the colonies, where British troops had never been before in such numbers, and tried to keep the peace in Europe by a policy of appeasement instead of the traditional pre-emptive mobilization. The result was that Britain found herself at war in 1778 in a worse situation than at any time since the sixteenth century, with the French Navy well ahead in the mobilisation race and equal in numbers of ships available, while Spain watched for a favourable moment to activate the Family Compact and provide an overwhelming superiority.[39] Not only was the situation worse, it was, or seemed to be, different. Of the British ministers, only Lord Sandwich, the First Lord of the Admiralty, appealed to the experience of former wars and urged that the main fleet be kept at home. His colleagues tended to follow Lord George Germain, the Colonial Secretary, in believing that in a war for America, America was the decisive theatre for which all others, including the Channel, should be stripped. Modern historians have tended to follow Germain too, and Sandwich never put his argument with convincing clarity. Though an intelligent man with longer experience of government than any of his colleagues, he had no concept of strategy, no tradition of analysis to fall back on. In this very dangerous situation it was doubly necessary to concentrate on the essential point, and the French decision to send the Toulon squadron across the Atlantic in the spring of 1778 gave the British an opportunity to make up for delayed mobilisation and achieve an early superiority. They threw it away by making an equivalent detachment from Keppel's fleet.[40]

Thus a war started in which the British repeatedly dispersed their strength in remote parts of the world. As Britain's peril from French and Spanish invasion fleets in the Channel grew greater, they took more and more of the ships and scattered them further and further away from the only waters where their presence might have won the war, and their absence nearly lost it. In doing so they negated most of their traditional advantages. Their well-equipped dockyards were left behind, and replaced by a handful of little careening yards ill situated and ill equipped to sustain large squadrons. Their victualling system, which had supported major operations with such success in the previous war, was demolished by the rebellion of New England and had to be painfully reconstructed from Irish ports. The existing sources of naval intelligence and the available cruisers (anyway far too few for a transatlantic war) were almost useless at such a distance from home. The worst of it was that by choosing, or allowing the enemy to choose, to fight in theatres of war 4000 miles away, the British gave up the possibility of effective strategic control. Eighteenth-century communications were too slow to allow fleets in the Caribbean to be controlled either from London or from New York. By conforming, for the first and last time, to the French practice of squadrons sent out 'en mission' to distant waters, the British effectively abandoned the direction of the war. Operations in the Western Approaches were near enough to be handled effectively, and experience had shown how success there could be developed to isolate and dominate the West Indies, and indeed the world. Success across the Atlantic could never have had such an effect, and in any case success was largely a lottery when it was impossible to know where or in what circumstances the fleets would meet. The battle of the Chesapeake in 1781, tactically ineffectual but strategically decisive, was fought almost by accident, between Admirals neither of whom had a clear idea of the situation. On the British side the Squadron was assembled more or less haphazardly only a few days before, and it was not even clear who was meant to be in command, let alone what the enemy was doing. Though many gross errors were committed, the essence of the problem was the insufficiency of long-distance communications, a problem to which the eighteenth century had no answer. Next year in the Caribbean the accidents of this sort of war fell out to the disadvantage of France, when Rodney defeated De Grasse at the Saintes in spite of what might very well have been a superior Franco-Spanish fleet. By then Sandwich and his naval advisers were seriously planning to disband the Western Squadron altogether and send the bulk of the fleet to the West Indies, which they would have done but for the fall of the North ministry.[41]

The British never made the same mistake again. The Battle of the Saintes in 1782 was the first and last major action ever fought by the principal British fleet outside European waters. Apart from the fortnight which Nelson's squadron spent in the Windward Islands in 1805, the principal British fleet did not leave European waters again until 1944. When war again broke out in 1793, the British had been cured of their obsession with colonies. Within Pitt's government the strategic debate would not have seemed unfamiliar to William III or Queen Anne. Lord Grenville, the Foreign Secretary, believed that the peace of Europe and the security of Britain could never be assured until the Jacobins were overthrown and France once more governed by a regime which could offer a stable peace. Henry Dundas, the Secretary for War, preferred to concentrate on purely British interests, building up the overseas commerce and financial strength on which her capacity to make war depended, while waiting for the French to overreach themselves and bring on their own downfall. Grenville therefore stood for the creation of Continental coalitions against France; Dundas preferred to avoid over-commitment to those who never delivered what they promised. But their disagreement was over means, not ends: Dundas entirely agreed that Britain's long-term security depended on a balance of power in Europe, he merely opposed wasting Britain's slender resources of manpower until there was a good prospect of obtaining it. The great West Indian expeditions of the 1790s, which he sponsored, were not designed to conquer territory for its own sake, but to deprive France of the commerce and financial strength the sugar islands produced – in short to gain the means of surviving a long war.[42]

Britain faced essentially the same strategic dilemma during the Napoleonic Wars. No lasting peace could be had until Bonaparte's limitless ambition had finally exhausted the resources of France and her empire, and aroused her enemies to unity. No opportunity was to be lost to advance that day, and in the meantime Britain could only safeguard and extend her trade and finances. Hence the war of commercial blockades between the Continental System and the Orders in Council, and hence too the defensive annexation of key overseas bases and points designed to protect British trade and open up foreign markets. Virtually all these, however, were achieved by the forces locally available. Neither fleets nor armies were spared from home, for it was in Europe that the essential decision was to be reached. There the British were most sensitive to any accession of naval strength to the French. They acted ruthlessly to prevent warships, enemy, allied or neutral, falling under French control. They dealt with the Dutch fleet in 1799, the Danes in 1800, 1801 and 1807, the Portuguese in 1807, and a Russian squadron in 1808; they attempted to reach Antwerp in 1809; they intended to take the Spanish fleet from Ferrol in 1800 and 1804, and contemplated a number of similar attacks on Flushing, Cadiz, the Texel, Vigo, Kronstadt, Cherbourg and Port Mahon.[43] When the final peace settlement was made, Britain happily surrendered most of her colonial conquests in the interests of a durable European peace. The key concern was that Antwerp, the dockyard port which threatened to destroy the basis of the Western Squadron, should never again fall into French hands. To that end the whole of the Dutch East Indies was handed back to strengthen the new kingdom of the Netherlands. The settlement of 1815 showed very clearly that the British had been cured of their obsession with colonial conquest. Bases were kept, and some colonies of settlement with particularly valuable export crops, but most of the conquered territories were restored. 'The undoubted Interest of England is Trade', declared a pamphleteer, 'since it is that alone which can make us either *Rich* or *Safe*, for without a powerful Navy, we should be a Prey to our Neighbours, and without Trade, we could have neither sea-men or Ships'.[44] Those words were written in 1672, but they might serve as a summary of the strategy of Henry Dundas, and the underlying rationale of the 1815 settlement.

Britain in the 1820s and 1830s followed a naval policy which much resembled that of a hundred years before. There was still nothing which could be called an idea of naval strategy; there was no professional study, no specialised literature, no public debate, no planning for war. Those who made policy still did so behind closed doors, and the policy they made was deeply traditional.[45] Virtually all the battlefleet was in reserve at home, while a small force of frigates and sloops was scattered about the world for peacetime purposes.[46] Professional attention was concentrated on the reconstruction of the fleet according to new and more powerful models; there seemed to be no need to give particular thought to how the ships might be used in wartime.

This began to change in the 1840s, when the coming of steamships and a more threatening international situation gave rise to the popular alarm that 'steam has bridged the Channel'. Unprovided with any body of naval doctrine and unskilled in the habits of logical thought, naval officers were vulnerable to the suggestion that new technology had rendered the lessons of the past obsolete. They found it difficult to present a coherent argument against the enthusiasts for fortification who in the 1850s and 1860s expended so much money and granite around the southern coasts of the British Isles. There occurred what has been called a 'militarisation', both of national policy, and specifically of naval habits of thought.[47] Nevertheless it is possible to exaggerate the extent to which a traditional strategy had been abandoned. The Navy's attention was firmly fixed on the reconstruction of the fleet, and the hugely expensive reconstruction of the dockyards which that entailed, but the fleet itself was clearly a traditional fleet for traditional purposes.[48] The costly 'harbours of refuge' which enjoyed a vogue in the 1840s and 1850s were intended to support squadrons of steamers at a time when their short range and poor seakeeping called for bases very close to their intended areas of operation.[49] The 'coast defence ships' built during and after the Crimean War, which have sometimes been derided as the negation of Britain's natural oceanic strategy,[50] were in fact an exact expression of the Navy's traditional function of commanding home waters. Their name, moreover, was a diplomatic gloss: they were actually coast *attack* ships, intended to operate off Cherbourg and Kronstadt, not Portsmouth and Plymouth.[51]

What was neglected during the hectic years of the 1860s and 1870s, when warship design changed continually, rapidly and unpredictably, was not the

Navy's traditional function of guarding the Narrow Seas. On the contrary, this remained in the centre of officers' thinking. In the high noon of empire, it was colonial defence and the protection of trade which tended to be pushed to the margins.[52] 'To the sailor, and probably the politician as well, the end of the three-decker meant the end of naval history';[53] modern-minded men like the naval officers of the 1880s, who had made their careers by their mastery of new technology, did not see much challenge in the peacetime work of an obsolescent cruiser fleet, and some of them regarded the protection of trade as inherently demeaning to an officer and a gentleman whose real work was to fight and win the great battle over the enemy which would settle the war in an afternoon and render all other naval operations irrelevant.[54] Indeed there was a substantial body of professional and lay opinion which regarded battleships alone as real warships, and everything else as essentially civilian craft maintained only for peacetime purposes.[55] There was a time when it was fashionable to deride the late Victorian naval officer, and the Admiralty of the day, as reactionary and obscurantist.[56] This is the exact opposite of the truth. In reality these men were deeply committed to modernity, they defined themselves by their mastery of new weapons and equipment, and they benefited from advanced technical training. Unfortunately they had received no education which tended to broaden the mind or develop the powers of informed judgement. They knew nothing of the history of their own Service. Highly trained but wholly uneducated, they were early victims of the modern fashion for scientific education. While their brothers went forth to rule the empire soundly grounded in philosophy and dead languages, naval officers were equipped only with 'the whole course of mechanics, the differential and integral calculus, hydrostatics, hydrodynamics and optics'.[57]

This mattered, because it was in the 1880s that for the first time a school of British naval strategy emerged. It was led largely by men who were connected with the Navy but not serving in it, and it concentrated on the problems of colonial defence and the protection of trade which had been for so long neglected. Many of these pioneer strategists founded their work on the study of naval history, which became an important instrument in a campaign for the intellectual reform of the Navy which led to the founding of the Naval Intelligence Department in 1882, and eventually (in 1911) to the Naval Staff. They used as their sounding board the Royal United Service Institution, and in 1893 established as their intellectual base the Navy Records Society. They may be said to have attained real public influence with the publication in 1890 of Alfred T. Mahan's famous book *The Influence of Sea Power upon History, 1660–1783*. Mahan himself was not a systematic thinker (nor of course British), but the immense success of his book made naval history and naval strategy fashionable, and made it impossible for naval policy to be made without reference to them.[58]

With the final acceptance of the twin sisters, naval strategy and naval history, this chapter comes full circle, for the historical understanding of British naval policy in the eighteenth century on which we still depend today is essentially the work of Sir Julian Corbett, Sir Herbert Richmond and their disciples, for whom the study of history and the formation of current policy were aspects of the same subject.[59] Not only did they bring the experience of the past to bear on the problems of their own day, they understood the past in terms of its relevance to their situation. Near the end of his life, in 1921, Corbett was asking 'What material advantage did Trafalgar give that Jutland did not give?'.[60] The result of this approach is that we still see large areas of British naval history through the spectacles of the 1890s. For this generation, imperial defence dominated their concerns. This was the aspect of naval warfare which had been so neglected, and in which Britain seemed to be so vulnerable. Moreover it was self-evidently the empire which made Britain great, and the Navy's claim to greatness was clearly that it had made the empire, and still preserved the empire. It was the Army and its partisans which now emphasised defence against invasion, which had once been the Navy's fundamental purpose. It was therefore natural for the naval historian-strategists to write history in which the Navy seemed to be the chosen instrument of imperial expansion. It then became, and for much of this century continued to be the case, that the size and composition of the Navy was usually justified (for example at the inter-war naval disarmament conferences) by reference to the needs of imperial defence and the protection of trade. It is not therefore surprising that the idea is still so widespread that the Navy was essentially an instrument of expansion, and that the bulk of its ships were usually abroad. In reality, as we have seen, this was true only of the brief and disastrous experiment of the American War. The British may not have had much idea of naval strategy as such during the eighteenth and nineteenth centuries, but they did have an almost consistent naval policy, and its first priority was always home defence.

Notes

1 This is a revised translation of 'Die Entwicklung der Vorstellung von Seekriegsstrategie in Grossbritannien im 18 und 19 Jahrhundert', in *Seemacht und Seestrategie im 19. und 20. Jahrhundert* ed. Jörg Duppler (*Vorträge zur Militärgeschichte* Band 18, Hamburg, 1999) pp. 83–103.
2 Middleton (1985) p. 22. The first citation in the *Oxford English Dictionary* (2nd edn) is 1810.
3 I have also discussed aspects of this theme in Rodger (1996a) pp. 38–60; and Rodger (1998) pp. 169–83.
4 Thomson (1932).
5 Mackesy (1984) pp. 14–15.
6 Woodfine (1988) pp. 71–90, at p. 74. Hall (1992) p. 131.
7 James (1938–9) pp. 24–7.
8 Rodger (1979) pp. 53–89.
9 Rodger (1986) pp. 17–18.
10 Adams and Waters (1995).

11 Hoste (1762). De Morogues (1767). De Villehuet (1788). Raymond (1788). On these writers see Granier (1993).
12 Rodger (1995).
13 Mackesy (1984) pp. 98–100. Hall (1992) pp. 47–9, 74–5.
14 Woodfine (1988) p. 77.
15 Wilson (1988). Jordan and Rogers (1989). Rodger (2000).
16 Hattendorf (1987a) p. 68. Pares (1936a). Roberts (1970). Black (1986). Rodger (1992) pp. 39–55.
17 Black (1992a) pp. 39–59, at pp. 39–43.
18 Hattendorf et al. (1993) pp. 381–82.
19 Rodger (1986) Appendix II.
20 Black (1988). Pares (1936a) pp. 456–7.
21 Meyer (1986). Le Goff (1990). Rodger (1995).
22 Tracy (1988).
23 Tracy (1974).
24 Webb (1980). Black (1992b) pp. 112–15.
25 Baudi di Vesme (1953) pp. 38–43.
26 Hattendorf (1987b). Black (1991) pp. 235–8.
27 Mather (1996). Pares (1936b). Baugh (1965) and Baugh (1994) pp. 194–6.
28 Davies (1992).
29 Duffy (1992b). Richmond (1920) Vol. III, pp. 6–8, 20–3, 82–4, 226–9. Ranft (1958) pp. 436–7, 441, 451–452, 459.
30 Corbett (1907) Vol. I, pp. 197–222, 260–302.
31 Ryan (1985). Middleton (1989).
32 Duffy (1992–4) Vol. I, pp. 182–91.
33 Corbett (1911) pp. 139–41, 195–6, 254–6.
34 Middleton (1989).
35 Tracy (1996). Cushner (1971).
36 Syrett (1970).
37 Merino Navarro (1981). Mühlmann (1975).
38 Mimler (1983). Niedhart (1979). Baugh (1994) pp. 203–13. Black (1989).
39 Baugh (1988b). Baugh (1992). Syrett (1998) pp. 1–16.
40 Rodger (1993) pp. 243–4, 275–9. Syrett (1991).
41 Rodger (1993) pp. 238–94. Syrett (1998) pp. 150–3, 167–8.
42 Mackesy (1974) and (1984). Duffy (1987), (1983) and (1998).
43 Mackesy (1984) pp. 122–5, 134–5. Hall (1992) pp. 81–2, 158–60, 168, 172, 175–9.
44 Quoted by Tracy (1991) p. 41.
45 Lambert (1996). Bartlett (1963). Beeler (1997) pp. 6–8.
46 Beeler (1997) pp. 26–35. I cannot agree with Partridge (1989) pp. 26–7 that the Navy had lost interest in home defence.
47 Hamilton (1993) pp. 118–31.
48 Lambert (1991).
49 Jamieson (1986) pp. 228–43.
50 The traditional view encapsulated by Parkes (1957) pp. 68–9.
51 Beeler (1997) pp. 19–22.
52 Ibid. pp. 210–36, mounts a strong defence of British naval planning in this era, arguing that as much was done as was possible or reasonable in the face of the threats then existing.
53 Schurman (1965) p. 3.
54 Semmel (1986) p. 85.
55 Rodger (1976) pp. 41–5.
56 Kemp (1977) pp. 16–31. Marder (1940) still indispensable for this period, is strongly marked by the same attitude.

57 Colomb (1898) p. 69. Gordon (1996). Rodger (1981).
58 Schurman (1965). Gat (1992). Ranft (1977b). Sumida (1997).
59 Schurman (1965) pp. 116–84. Goldrick and Hattendorf (1993).
60 Quoted from Corbett's Creighton Lecture in Hattendorf (1992) pp. 203–20, at p. 205.

3 The development of education in the Royal Navy: 1854–1914

Andrew Lambert

Education is a systematic form of instruction, designed to develop intellectual skills. While it would be valuable to consider all aspects of the Royal Navy's educational provision in this critical period, the key test of any armed force is its ability to meet the demands of war. Consequently this chapter will concentrate on educational provision to prepare officers for the higher direction of war.

The role of education in war planning can be divided into two sections. Both involve the development of intellectual skills. First it must equip the educated officer with the skills, rather than mere technical competencies, needed to master contemporary materiel issues, processes and information. Secondly it should prepare officers for the hardest tasks, tasks where there can be no clear guidance and they must make their own decisions, based on knowledge, doctrine and ultimately personal insight. An effective fighting service needs to master both elements, and harmonise them. For most of its long and highly successful history the Royal Navy has made adequate provision in the first area, but left the second to the free play of chance.

In the age of sail the transmission of understanding, and the formation of judgement, relied on personal contact, self-motivation and an apparently adequate supply of first-rate minds. In this sense the development of fighting doctrine, which used to be treated as the pinnacle of naval intellectual activity,[1] can be reduced to order by a little logic, and the simple tracing of a personal relationship. Indeed, as one of the brighter officers of the period under review recognised, tactical thought was of relatively little help when the problems became global and strategic.[2] Great victories were only secured when the enemy had been forced to take risks, by sound strategy.

Before considering the development of education it must be stressed that any successful armed force requires a nice balance between intellect and obedience. The Royal Navy did not, and does not, need an officer corps wholly composed of Admirals. Most officers are expected to follow their orders, and to exercise their judgement within fairly narrow limits. Consequently the educational provision of an armed force has to be carefully handled. Officers need to understand their professional duties before they can operate effectively in their current rank, and they need to prepare for promotion to the next rank. However, all officers are not equal, some will rise to the demands of independent authority, others will not. Education informs career development, and in most modern systems forms a significant element of the assessment process that determines progression.

The most important roles of any professional education system are to transmit understanding between generations, and to facilitate the exchange of ideas with professionals in closely related areas of activity. In the nineteenth century, the obvious connections were with the Army and the politicians. While the naval situation was essentially unaltered and unchallenged, it required no serious reconsideration. Naval officers did not need to study the role of naval power in national strategy because they did not have a case to present. It was hardly necessary to do so when the Army, led by experienced officers like Wellington and Burgoyne, understood the maritime strategic imperatives and the 'expeditionary' character of British strategy. However, there were important warning signs in 1847 when Burgoyne infamously leaked a letter from Wellington which appeared to denigrate the ability of the Navy to defend the British Isles.[3] That the Inspector General of Fortifications should seek to increase his budget by attacking the credibility of another service is unsurprising. This time his initiative misfired, but a decade later the same agenda would score a significant success. The Army was shocked out of its post-Waterloo complacency by problems in the Crimea, and then frightened into further educational reforms by the Franco-Prussian War of 1870–1. As the soldiers became better educated, and more self-confident, they began to question the hitherto unchallenged naval dominance of British strategy.

Normally politicians require guidance on strategic issues, but in the first half of the nineteenth century Britain was led by a generation remarkably well educated in war. There was no need to advise such masters as Canning, Wellington and Palmerston on the niceties of strategic/diplomatic policymaking. Only when that generation passed, with the death of Palmerston in 1865, was the Navy faced with the task of advising political leaders with little or no understanding of war.

Before we criticise our predecessors for their lack of modern systems we should assess the success of their methods. It could hardly be argued that when the Navy could produce such men as Nelson, St Vincent, Collingwood, Saumarez and Cornwallis it had any need of educational reform. Consequently the education of the Navy between 1815 and 1854 remained as it had been from time immemorial, reliant on the accidents of human transmission, and the relative frequency of conflict. The masters of war passed on their insights to their successors at first hand, on the quarterdeck, not in the schoolroom. The formal educational opportunities provided by the pre-Crimean Navy were limited to the primary and secondary level. Some officer cadets entered through the Royal Naval College at Portsmouth, where the curriculum imposed on 14- and 15-year-old boys provided an excellent basis for advanced mathematics and observational science, but offered little encouragement for analytical thought or reflection.[4] This was understandable – the Navy needed a steady supply of competent watch-keeping junior officers, from whom it expected the future leaders of the service to emerge, by the same haphazard processes as heretofore. The majority of cadets went straight to sea, where they soon became seamen. In 1837 the College was closed and all education was then provided by Naval Instructors, uniformed Warrant Officers or Chaplains. Within the limits of a shipboard existence they inculcated the basis for professional development: maths, science, French, drawing and some Latin.

Further education for commissioned officers was entirely voluntary, although there were professional advantages in completing approved courses of study. The gunnery training ship HMS *Excellent* in Portsmouth harbour offered specialist training and education, teaching the theoretical basis of gunnery at an advanced level. Those officers who took the opportunity tended to be among the most gifted technical minds of the age, and by the 1830s began to combine this study with steam engineering, which was also taught at Portsmouth. In addition they secured hands-on experience at one of the Navy's favoured engine suppliers. These opportunities prepared a select group of officers for an era of rapid and sustained technical change. Astley Cooper Key,[5] Arthur Hood and their contemporaries used this education to lead the Navy through a period of tremendous change.[6] Nor should the education at Portsmouth be seen as unduly narrow. This was an age that valued fundamental learning in a very limited range of subjects, and valued the formation of intellect above subject specific expertise. Not only was maths one of the very few university subjects, it was the only one relevant to a naval career.[7] The ambition was obvious, top marks at HMS *Excellent* 'being awarded only to those who attained proficiency in pure mathematics'.[8] However, college work did not guarantee success. One Captain who went back to college in the mid-1860s, with the hint of early employment for a successful volunteer, was disappointed. So was Key, then Captain of the *Excellent*, who wanted to encourage more officers to take this option.[9] Naval standards were high; Key's contemporary Montagu Burrows went from *Excellent* to Oxford, where he became Professor of History.[10]

Outside the College and *Excellent*, officers were left to their own devices. Some continued their education on board ship, or on shore; others attended university.[11] Here the relatively long periods of peacetime half pay provided ample opportunity for personal study, an opportunity that the best officers used. Nineteenth-century reforms tightened up the career structure, without providing a formal alternative. Junior officers, who spent the greater part of their time afloat, picked up their profession from those around them, as they always had. The professional character of the Captain was the most powerful influence.

While this might seem alarmingly inconsistent to modern eyes, lacking formal educational requirements and any higher level provision, the system in place in 1854 met the demands of the service. It produced a cadre of educated officers, provided a coherent strategic concept, sound operational orders and effective staff officers. To condemn it for not using modern, military-based labels to describe the department, officers and command systems would be anachronistic. There is a danger that historians are looking for a twentieth-century approach from a service still led by veterans of the Napoleonic wars. The assumption that large centralised staff and planning organisations were essential to the effective conduct of war was not accepted by any armed force in 1854 and serious educational provision was likewise uncommon. Tremendous changes would occur in the next two decades, but they were driven by the demand to create and to use mass conscript armies, based on reservists, and employing rail transport in theatres of war where hours could be decisive. The Royal Navy in 1854 faced none of these problems, and should not be criticised for failing to solve them.

In reality, the higher education of the Royal Navy had always relied on example; and the recent past provided all the examples the service required. Those who wished to master their profession needed to look no further than the two great masters of war who led the fleet at Trafalgar. Both recognised the vital role of history. Nelson read voraciously[12] while Collingwood enjoined his juniors to spend their time with 'books that treat of your profession, and of history'. Both men showed the benefits of sustained study in their clear and logical politico/strategic thinking, an area where mere naval learning and tactical finesse was not enough, and in the ability to express their ideas in simple, direct English. Both possessed an understanding of the higher direction of war essential to develop theatre strategies, defeat the enemy and work with soldiers, ministers, neutral governments and allies. Few of their precursors had shared these gifts – notoriously Lord Howe could not express himself effectively either verbally or on paper, while Lord Rodney did not bother to try. Nor did their successors in 1914 match this standard.[13] The heroes of Trafalgar were also fortunate that their words came down to posterity relatively unaltered. They left a rich legacy for thoughtful officers.

Although their assessment of the educational value of history would prove correct, mid-nineteenth-century Britain was barely at the dawn of modern historical method, and offered no formal historical education. The relative poverty of relevant historical work (leaving aside such isolated highlights as the *Naval History* of William James,[14] and Sir Harris Nicolas's *Dispatches and Letters of Lord Nelson*[15]), and the absence of a formal educational system for naval officers left intellectual development to the individual. If the subscription lists for some of the more important works published between 1815 and 1854 are any indication, the opportunity was not wasted. The two works cited sold in thousands, while Collingwood's *Correspondence*[16] ran through four editions, and all three were frequently referred to in contemporary correspondence. These texts offered an enquiring mind, insight and explanation; they attempted to comprehend the why as well as the when and where. While their value might have been improved by a well-delivered course of instruction, it would be incorrect to argue that officers were denied access to their professional past. The quality of reading matter was notably higher than that which had served Nelson. Between 1852 and 1857 Captain Geoffrey Hornby, ashore on half pay, spent his leisure time studying 'strategy (naval and military), mathematics, geography and Chemistry'. Consequently he found the Naval College course and examination easy.[17] Such preparation was essential for those who would lead the service, but was only possible because Hornby was unemployed for a long period.

In 1854 the Royal Navy went to war with a major power for the first time in 40 years, after a period of extensive activity and fundamental technical change. The Crimean War would not test the Navy's ability to fight fleet actions, protect trade or defend the home islands and extended empire, but it did make considerable demands on the Navy's intellectual capital.[18]

The fleets of sail-, paddle- and screw-propelled warships that fought in the Black Sea and the Baltic were commanded by experienced seamen, and staffed by engineers and officers with first rate technical training. Their guns were handled by trained officers and ratings, while the lower deck had just been transformed from a temporary job into a lifelong career. However, there was no system of education designed to prepare naval officers for the higher direction of war. Such preparation remained the province of the self-motivated and self-educated. Nor had there been any systematic attempt to collect and process the rich legacy of past conflicts.

The development of British strategy for the war with Russia combined technical expertise, local intelligence, historical comprehension and individual recollection. The main sources for Baltic war plans, strategic and operational, were the popular life of Nelson, written by Robert Southey, a detailed report on the state of the Russian coast defences and fleet prepared by the Deputy Hydrographer of the Navy, Captain John Washington, after a tour in mid 1853 and, in the absence of systematic and thorough historical analysis of the subject, the recollections and memoranda of Admiral Sir Thomas Byam Martin, the last surviving flag officer of the previous Baltic campaigns. For details of the 1808 to 1812 campaigns the Commander-in-Chief was issued with the journals of Admiral Lord Saumarez.[19] For the Black Sea theatre a similar combination of resources was deployed. Although the Royal Navy had never fought in that area, one ship had cruised those waters in 1829,[20] and several of its officers were sent back there. In addition the Admiralty could call on the Surveyor, Captain Sir Baldwin Walker, for more recent intelligence. He had been the effective commander of the Turkish fleet between 1840 and 1845.

In the absence of a modern educational provision the learning that shaped the conduct of war in 1854 was the experience of war, small scale and limited conflicts with lesser powers, under the command of veterans from the last great war. So long as the instruments and instrumentalities of war did not change too radically, and the intervals between wars did not grow too long, this system worked. The challenge for the Royal Navy, as for all major armed forces, lay in the next generation, when the stable world of pre-industrialised warfare was blown apart by technologies first used in 1854–6.

The Crimean War demonstrated that the Royal Navy had mastered the demands of contemporary strategy. This would be a war of coasts, as the Royal Navy had long anticipated. After Trafalgar the great war with France had also been a war of coasts, of power projection, bombardment and cutting out, occasionally illuminated by large scale amphibious operations. Copenhagen, Walcheren and Washington were the precursors of the Sevastopol campaign. While it could still rely on the old method of recovering and processing past experience to guide future application the Royal Navy would remain well educated.

There had been significant developments in the way the Navy thought about war, and these reflected a combination of war experience and new technology. The new focus was inshore, where effective operations depended on accurate navigational information. In addition the Crimea was the first steam war, increasing opportunities for power projection. This was no surprise, for the Royal Navy had been planning for such operations for more than a decade. Between 1840 and 1850 the Royal Navy developed the doctrine and equipment for offensive operations against major fortified harbours. The destruction of an enemy fleet in harbour would pre-empt any invasion attempt by France, and ensure an unrivalled command of the sea. While the focus of these developments was Cherbourg, the nearest and most obvious threat, the 'Cherbourg Strategy' was universally applicable. The combination of improved charts, intelligence reports and technical preparation meant the Royal Navy went to war with a fully formed strategy, which could be refined for application to other coastal fortresses.[21]

The Navy's only educational facility helped to develop this strategy. Captain Henry Chads of HMS *Excellent* observed: 'the real question of the day was how to destroy ships and arsenals with shells, and render such forts as Cherbourg useless to their possessors'. He experimented with very long range fire, using rifled weapons and larger charges.[22] The results exceeded his hopes. By 1853 he was confident that he could bombard Cherbourg with impunity. The dockyard would be badly damaged and the anchorage quite untenable. He recommended that this information be kept strictly confidential.[23]

The application of this important new capability, and the related theatre strategy, depended on accurate charts. In the mid-nineenth century British naval war planning was largely conducted by the Hydrographer's Department. From its inception in 1795 the Department had been a strategic resource for the Admiralty and, significantly, it was the only 'technical' branch located in the Admiralty building. Because naval operational and strategic planning were dominated by accurate navigational and related information, the Admiralty Board used the Hydrographer's Department as a war staff. The Department produced the operational plans issued the Commander-in-Chief of the Baltic Fleet in 1854.

The fact that the Hydrographer had a narrowly defined technical function may explain why his central role in the development and implementation of strategy has been missed. In 1853–4 the Hydrographer's Office gathered and processed intelligence on the potential theatres of war, developed and wrote the war plans, both strategic and operational, and sent officers to both theatres for surveying duties. These 'staff' officers quickly became central to operational planning, providing strategic advice for their Admirals. Captains Bartholomew Sulivan and Thomas Spratt planned every significant operation of war in the two main theatres. While college educated Sulivan handled all the details, from navigation to methods of attack,[24] the more narrowly scientific Spratt left the 'military' aspects to his senior colleagues and shared much of the planning with the Flag Captain, William Mends. However, these differences should not obscure the key role of the Fleet Surveying Officers, a role given ample credit at the Spithead Fleet Review of 23 April 1856, when the fleet was led by the two Baltic fleet survey ships.[25]

However, the Crimean War also witnessed a step change in the pace of naval technological advance and the passing of the last of Nelson's Captains. These developments called into question age old assumptions about the naval role in national strategy, devaluing past experience just as the Navy lost the principal sources of that understanding. This was not a particular problem in relation to the war fighting activity of the Royal Navy between 1856 and 1914, which was generally similar to that of the Crimea: coastal power projection and inshore operations against weaker, technologically backward states.

The real problem for the Navy came when it had to prepare war against a major opponent, since the primary tasks of fleet action, trade protection and home defence had not been tested in war since 1814. After 1856 there were no serving officers with any relevant experience in these tasks. Furthermore the wider politico-strategic context was blurred. The Navy had a pressing need to address the impact of technological, political and strategic changes on national strategy, and to prepare its senior officers to present their case to the political leadership. The invasion debate of 1858–61 demonstrated that the Army would no longer allow naval assumptions to pass unquestioned, and scored an early success when its better prepared officers outmanoeuvred the naval members of the invasion enquiry. To avoid future problems of this sort the Royal Navy needed a modern professional educational system, one that would equip its officers to explain their strategic concepts to politicians and the military.

The role of the Hydrographer's Office as the planning centre began to change as the surveying service became more narrowly professional. The tragic death of hydrographer John Washington in 1863 marked the end of an era. His overwork and legendary office habits stand as a metaphor for the schizophrenia of the post. Furthermore the Hydrographer's Office had no role in the primary tasks; the profile of the hydrographer between 1815 and 1865 reflected the secondary nature of planned and actual operations. For the next two decades war planning was largely untouched.

Attempts to form a naval staff, inspired by the Prussian example in 1870–1, failed.[26] However, we should not assume, as most modern commentators have done, that this is evidence of woeful neglect. Blockade, commerce protection and coast assault needed little further elaboration, and there is ample evidence that these basic strategies would have been used, had the need arisen. The responsible senior officers knew what was required. Between 1863 and 1884 there was no significant naval challenge, and no need to plan for improbable eventualities and battles with phantom fleets. Instead the Royal Navy was primarily used as the right arm of a long-term deterrent strategy. The key problem was, as Sir Julian Corbett later observed, to understand 'what the fleet makes it possible for your army to do'.[27] All the naval leaders of the era were familiar with the projection of power, at varying levels, and their combat experience was more likely to have been obtained on shore than afloat.

The lack of a staff and formal plans should not obscure the success of the late nineteenth-century Navy's preparation for war. The key problems of the period 1860–90 lay in harnessing new technology to existing strategies or, occasionally, adjusting strategy to meet a real improvement in capability. For such tasks the 'scientific' education of the *Excellent* system provided the foundation. However, once a rival fleet emerged, the primary strategic tasks would have to be re-examined and new doctrines prepared. If this was going to be done systematically, there was a need to master the experience of the past in a form that could be developed and transmitted as the core professional knowledge that defined the higher levels of the service.[28] The basic requirement was to develop an education system to replace the old personal transmission of understanding. While the need reflected the rapid development of new technology, the concept was widely accepted by contemporary professions.

With the introduction of a common cadet entry into HMS *Britannia* in 1858, in a three-year course, all officers could be expected to meet known standards. The curriculum remained essentially mathematical, and was too advanced for most boys to understand, let alone benefit from, and the error would be compounded by cramming the same material back into them later. This obsession with maths reflected the fundamental importance of the subject to all branches of the profession, the lack of an alternative intellectual focus and the high value accorded to it in all contemporary educational systems.

At the higher level it was widely assumed that the universal introduction of steam power had rendered the lessons of the sailing era irrelevant. This idea gained considerable currency in the coastal and riverine operations of the American Civil War, where armour, mines and heavy guns condemned old sailing ships to auxiliary roles. The dramatic success of the ram at the Battle of Lissa in 1866 appeared to complete the process. The only past worth studying was that of ancient galley warfare, a subject taken up by American, French, Russian and British officers.

The tactical emphasis in contemporary thinking reflected the need to solve the technical issues that would determine how ships would be used, before moving on to consider how such changes might affect the use of naval forces in national strategy. It was assumed that national strategy remained unaffected. This assumption was incorrect, although contemporary strategists, notably Mahan, argued that changing technology did not affect strategy. Unless they were exposed to a sophisticated historical investigation such assumptions were easily made, easily supported with selected evidence and easily accepted because they were convenient. In reality technical change between 1840 and 1880 fundamentally altered the strategic balance between land- and seapower. Steam ships greatly increased the range, scale and sustainability of naval and maritime power projection, and took naval power deep inland on navigable rivers. Armour and more powerful artillery enabled warships to overcome hitherto invulnerable fixed defences. The steam powered ship also simplified trade defence. Without coal and dry docks, hostile cruisers could not operate, severely limiting their impact. With Britain dominating coal supplies, dry-docking and telegraph cables, the trade defence problem was reduced to a minor issue. Curiously enough, John Colomb's pioneering studies of the problem in the mid-1860s missed this development because they focused on the growth of trade, not the changing nature of the threat.

It is also important to stress that the nineteenth-century Royal Navy lacked the most powerful stimulus to intellectual reform: catastrophic defeat. Consequently the process of change took longer, and appeared less dramatic. The initial British responses to technical change, focused on the politico-naval challenge of imperial France, were dominated by old ideas. By contrast the French challenge shifted to new strategies and alternative tactical systems. While this has been attributed to the superior education provided to French officers[29] the British were only waiting for the French to show their hand before overwhelming them in an arms race.[30]

However, the Navy did not have to wait long for a modern approach to education. After 12 years service afloat John Knox Laughton, a successful Cambridge educated naval instructor, came ashore to teach at the Royal Naval College, Portsmouth in 1866.[31] Already rated an outstanding teacher, he combined a first class mathematical mind with experience of war and impressive attainments in the observational sciences. His new students were the future leaders of the service, and Laughton realised that they needed a real education, not mere rote learning, if they were to master the theoretical basis of their subjects. This approach was evident in his first book, *Physical Geography in its Relation to the Prevailing Winds and Currents* of 1870, a powerfully argued attempt to comprehend oceanic and atmospheric circulation. It also offered an early insight into his educational methods. Having defined his subject he assembled a wealth of recorded data, from which he developed a theory that could explain the evidence: 'I have adopted a method which, though it differs essentially from that which has of late years been generally followed, is, I would submit, both more exact and more scientific. I have endeavoured to explain the phenomena which are observed, rather that to observe phenomena in illustration of theoretical views'.[32] Despite its scientific origins this educational method was universally applicable. Laughton used it for his 1872 textbook on surveying,[33] and recognised that it could also be used to analyse war. His data would be provided by naval history, while his generalisations would support the educational process and build a coherent doctrine to replace the old personal transmission of understanding.

These ideas were not unique. Laughton was influenced by the intellectual climate of his day and, like any serious educator, the needs of his students. In 1872 the staff and students of the gunnery training ship HMS *Excellent* formed the Junior Naval Professional Association (JNPA), a discussion forum for professional and scientific subjects, and opened an essay competition to consider the impact of modern guns, torpedoes, rams and mines on tactics. Laughton's 'Essay on Naval Tactics' skilfully combined the technical and mathematical knowledge required to formulate the precise manoeuvres so beloved of pioneer steam tacticians, with a wide understanding of past experience, both British and French, from which he derived the enduring principle of tactics, achieving a concentration of force against a portion of the enemy's formation.[34] For all its apparent simplicity this was the basis of Nelson's tactical approach, and the key to his success. Mathematical training had equipped Laughton to analyse evidence with logic and rigour, and to formulate general rules from his analysis.

The Royal Naval College was moved to Greenwich in 1873, largely to placate the local electorate.[35] In public the transfer was presented as an opportunity to expand naval education and improve links with the universities. Yet, while the move witnessed a marked increase of staff, from 2 to 15, and a slight broadening of the curriculum, the courses for anyone above the rank of Sub-Lieutenant remained voluntary, and entirely technical. As a result, the much heralded opportunity to improve naval education was wasted. The Navy had not wanted to leave Portsmouth, while the politicians did not care what they did, as long as they did it at Greenwich. The courses of study proposed, and largely carried into effect were essentially practical, upgraded training, and all directly relevant to junior careers:

1   Pure mathematics, including geometry and calculus.
2   Applied mathematics, including mechanics, optics and the theories of heat, light, electricity and magnetism.
3   Applied mechanics, theories of structures and machines.
4   Nautical astronomy, surveying, meteorology and chart-drawing.
5   Experimental science, physics, chemistry, metallurgy.
6   Marine engineering.
7   Naval architecture.

8   Fortification, military drawing and naval artillery.
9   International law, law of evidence and naval courts martial.
10 Naval history and tactics, including naval signals and steam evolutions.
11 Modern languages.
12 Drawing.
13 Hygiene, naval and climatic.

There were no courses dealing with strategy, planning, diplomacy or politics. The syllabus awarded a maximum of 1500 marks for all subjects. Of these 500 were for algebra, geometry and trigonometry, and 400 for navigation and nautical astronomy.[36] This syllabus, with the exception of naval artillery, law of evidence and courts martial was being taught by the end of the decade to a large but amorphous body of officers, many of whom were volunteers. The overwhelming importance of mathematics and scientific subjects reflected the mood of the age, and the needs of the service, up to a point. The course did nothing to prepare officers to exercise command, develop judgement, strategic insight or political wisdom. It completed their 'training', but it did not start their education.

Yet even this was too much. By 1880 college attendance had dropped from 237 to 180, revealing a fundamental flaw. As the senior Greenwich course was not compulsory it was not part of an overcrowded officer career structure.[37] The Navy needed to study the higher direction of war, a need that could not be met by a compulsory six-month Sub-Lieutenants course, which was little more that a repetition of the *Britannia* syllabus.[38]

While teaching at Portsmouth, Laughton recognised that the Navy was losing touch with history, which he thought was the key to effective education. When faced by an accelerating, technical revolution men who had grown up with the centuries-old certainties of the wooden sailing ship were convinced that the past had become 'a useless branch of knowledge'. Laughton stressed that a 'scientific' study of history, in contrast to the haphazard, romantic stuff that then passed for naval history, would produce 'lessons of the gravest meaning' for the study of strategy, administration, tactics, discipline and all other aspects of naval service. It was the *only* basis for a coherent educational system, and a modern written doctrine.

Initially Laughton devoted his efforts to the pressing issue of the day – tactical doctrine. He linked a scientific analysis of the capabilities of ships and weapons with principles derived from past experience. As the committees that set out the college curriculum had expressly mentioned history, Laughton was disappointed when the President, Admiral Sir Astley Cooper Key, only provided time and funds for half a dozen lectures a year on a course that was optional.

Laughton was looking to the future. His approach would have borne fruit when the current Sub-Lieutenants reached the highest ranks. The wisdom of his proposal is evident when one considers that a Sub-Lieutenant on the 1873 course, Prince Louis of Battenberg, was the First Sea Lord at the outbreak of war in 1914. Battenberg was an early convert to Laughton's approach, and a lifelong friend. When his ambitious project to develop history-based naval education was rejected Laughton shifted his focus to the narrower field of tactics and doctrine. He used two major texts in this field. The *Essay on Naval Tactics* written for the JNPA competition of 1873 combined maths, technology and history.[39] His second study was *Letters and Despatches of Horatio, Viscount Nelson* of 1886 and was developed in discussion with College President (1882–3), Admiral Hornby, the pre-eminent fleet commander and tactician of the age. Hornby, like Laughton, stressed that fleet evolutions[40] were only intended to develop ship- and fleet-handling skills. They were far too complex to be attempted under combat conditions. In his lectures Hornby used history to show the danger of rigid tactical systems.[41] Laughton had persuaded him that naval history would provide the basis for modern thinking. Laughton dedicated the *Nelson* book to Hornby, and demolished the myth that Nelson's tactical ideas could be summed up in Lord Cochrane's phrase 'never mind manoeuvres, always go at them'.[42] Elsewhere he rebutted the commonly held notion that a modern naval battle would rapidly degenerate into a mêlée.[43] Laughton stressed that Nelson's tactics were developed through personal study, past experience transmitted by senior officers like Lord Hood, and his own genius.

Laughton considered personal study to be the most important part of any officer's education. He wanted Greenwich to provide an intellectually stimulating environment where mid-career officers could prepare for the challenge of command. The *Nelson* volume would be the basic educational tool, conveniently assembling the raw material for a study of *the* naval career in a single volume.

The *Nelson* volume was the culmination of Laughton's work at Greenwich. After the failure of his initial attempt to develop a strong historical component to counterweight the dominance of mathematics, he had refined his approach. As history would only be accepted at Greenwich if it was 'scientific' he delivered 'The Scientific Study of Naval History' at the Royal United Service Institution on 22 June 1874. Although the Institution was the principal military forum of the era[44] Laughton pulled no punches. He declared that what little history the average naval officer knew was romantic, inaccurate and useless. Furthermore, 'an idea that the history of the past contains no practical lessons for the future, and is therefore a useless branch of scholarship daily gathers strength; and is, indeed, put prominently forward by those whose opinions on purely technical questions have a just claim to our respect'.

His message was clear: the Navy was ignorant of its past, and its officers had no business deriding the only discipline that could provide them with an education. It should be stressed that Laughton's naval history went far beyond mere battle narrative. In the hands of practised educators, history would be an essential study; it 'contained lessons of the gravest meaning', how fleets had been assembled and manned, the course of events leading to victory and defeat, as well as the principles of tactics. To reinforce his point he called for greater width of study, emphasising the danger inherent in limiting reflection to a single era. The easy victories of the Revolutionary and Napoleonic Wars, secured against ill-manned and badly-led opponents, were no guide for the future.[45] The paper was an extended argument for a naval history course at Greenwich, based on its relevance, and 'scientific' character.[46]

Significantly, Admiral Key, the College President, supported him from the floor of the meeting, and explained that when Laughton described his historical work as 'scientific' he wished to convey a particular meaning. It was 'accurate and exact knowledge, as distinguished from loose, vague, and empirical', basing his methods on those of the observational sciences. History was the 'only sound basis' for the study of tactics, strategy, organisation and discipline.[47] He recognised that this description was essential if he was to find an audience in an increasingly 'scientific' service.

Laughton was careful not to restrict his history to the age of sail, or to the Royal Navy. His message was consistent, but the context was flexible. His study of the battle of Lissa, 1866, the only ironclad fleet action, focused on the education of the victor, the Austrian Admiral Tegetthoff. Tegetthoff was a classic self-educated officer. The example was used to push home the critical role of history in the higher education of the Navy, not merely as an alternative to maths, but as the higher branch of professional study:

> There is a certain tendency in the minds of those who are most earnest in the cause of naval education to confuse the means with the end, and to imagine that all that is wanted is a competent knowledge of such sciences as mathematics, physics, geography, astronomy, navigation even, or pilotage, gunnery or naval architecture. In reality, and so far as the duties of a naval officer are concerned, all these are but branches, however important, each in its different degree, of that one science, the art of war, which it is the business of his life to practice.

The recognition that war was ultimately an art, however important the role of science, was a critical stage in the development of naval education. It could release officers from the dead-hand of routine, and encourage them to develop their own judgement. The basic building blocks of this art could be acquired by instruction, but the ability to use them, as Captains and Admirals, necessitated a different approach: 'Where the official instruction ends, the higher education really begins. From that time it is the man's own experience, and reading, and thought, and judgement, which must fit him for the requirements of higher rank'. In the absence of personal experience, 'the wise man will learn from the experience of others'. This method could be applied to seamanship and navigation, 'so also will he learn the art of commanding ships or fleets from the history of his great predecessors ... But this is a higher and graver study than all that has gone before'. For, unlike navigation and astronomy, 'the science of war is not one of mere rule and precedent, for changing conditions change almost every detail, and that too in a manner which it is often impossible to foresee'.

> The commanding officer who hopes to win, not merely to tumble into distinction, must therefore be prepared beforehand for every eventuality. The knowledge of what has happened already will not only teach him by precedent; so far as that is possible, it is easy, and within the compass of everyday abilities; it will also suggest to him things that have never yet been done; things in the planning of which he may rise to the height of genius, in the executing of which he may rise to the height of grandeur.

The educational system Laughton demanded would be based on history, because only history could contribute hard evidence to the process, making it, 'a study of real and technical importance'.[48] In the absence of personal experience the only way to learn the business of modern war was to profit from the experience of others, in earlier ages and other navies. Only by such preparation would commanders acquire the understanding and judgement required to meet the unknown, respond to changing conditions in wartime, and develop the capacity to think at a higher level. Laughton knew that Tegetthoff and Nelson were not made by education; sound education merely *facilitated* their development. This approach placed Laughton in the exalted company of the greatest military educators, men like Scharnhorst and Clausewitz.[49] As an experienced educator, mathematician and observational scientist Laughton recognised the intellectual limits of the existing naval system. He had pressed for adoption of a system of higher education to encompass doctrine development, strategic thought and leadership.

In 1885, just as Laughton's educational ideas were becoming widely accepted, he was retired from the College, because falling attendance on the voluntary courses had persuaded the Admiralty to cut the Greenwich establishment. While he regretted the loss of regular contact with the service[50] he retained the history lectureship for several years. Appointed Professor of Modern History at King's College London, he joined the small group of professional historians, and soon saw that they might be drawn into naval education.

His educational ideas had already secured a following among British and American naval officers. Admiral Stephen B. Luce USN, a frequent correspondent, relied heavily on Laughton's ideas to make the case for the United States Naval War College. Luce, the dominant intellect of late nineteenth-century United States Navy, recognised the inadequacy of the existing naval officer 'training' as the foundation for command when he came into contact with a first rate military mind. General William T. Sherman's instructions persuaded the hitherto pragmatic sailor that war should be understood at the level of principle.[51] Luce recognised that military thought could advance the intellectual coherence of naval education. His Naval War College was the first naval educational establishment anywhere in the world and the post-graduate education provided was intended to promote a deeper understanding of war.[52] The educational core of the War College was provided by a series of articles, written by Luce but almost entirely derived from Laughton's work, and a course of lectures linking this experience to a strategic system based on Jomini,[53] provided by Captain Alfred T. Mahan USN.[54] Where Laughton sought accurate understanding based on a wealth of detail, Mahan created a theoretical structure.[55] Both were essential to the development of professional naval education.

In the Royal Navy, Laughton's message was not adopted with such singleness of purpose or clarity of execution. While the Navy allowed Laughton to teach a small history course, it did not affect promotion, unlike seamanship, gunnery and navigation. Therefore promising officers, of whom Laughton taught many,[56] had to satisfy training targets if their careers were to advance. Naval education retained the personal character of the eighteenth century, the only difference was that the central figure was a scholar rather than a senior Admiral drawing on personal experience.

Laughton's closest friend, Admiral Sir Cyprian Bridge, shared his appreciation of the importance of the past in naval education, and of the Royal Navy in British strategy. Bridge would be the second Director of Naval Intelligence and his assistants and successors included many of Laughton's closest contacts in the Royal Navy, literally 'bridging' the educational-technical divide and providing the basis for serious war planning in the two decades before 1914.

In reality the Navy needed to think about its requirements for the higher direction of war before it could develop an effective educational system. At the most basic level this task required an intelligence-gathering and planning body, to replace the Hydrographer's Department. In the mid-1870s Hornby, now a Vice Admiral and experienced Sea Lord, called for a war staff to assist the Naval Lords with strategy, mobilisation and force planning. His efforts were rebuffed by politicians unwilling to incur the cost, and fellow Admirals who did not share his concern.[57] However, the 1881–2 Carnarvon Commission on Colonial Defence, influenced by John Colomb, revived the idea and by December of that year a Foreign Intelligence Committee had been set up to collect, analyse and disseminate information. Critically the new body was located inside the Secretariat. Within three years Captain William Hall had transformed his committee into a fully fledged Naval Intelligence Department (NID), recruited able juniors like Reginald Custance and Royal Marine George Aston, and filled the vacuum identified by Hornby, undertaking strategic planning. Later he would take a key role in the force planning process that underpinned the Naval Defence Act of 1889. By 1887 at the latest the Royal Navy had a War Staff, to which its best and brightest officers were appointed to consider all issues connected with preparation for war. It quickly set up naval manoeuvres to test new ideas.[58]

In addition to its planning role the NID also took a leading part in the key defence debates of the era. These were held at the Royal United Services Institution (RUSI), literally across the road from the Admiralty. To control the process one of the Deputy DNIs invariably sat on the Council of Institute. Here, and only here, officers of both services attended lectures and debated the key issues of the day, from smokeless powder to national strategy.

Before 1889 Britain took the Navy, and naval mastery, for granted. The tide turned in the early 1890s, following the 1891 Royal Naval Exhibition at Chelsea Hospital and Mahan's second *Sea Power* book in 1892. These events used history to make their point, and Laughton skilfully exploited the opportunity to enhance the role of history in naval education. In 1893 he and Bridge created the Navy Records Society from their friends, fellow scholars, serving officers, publicists and politicians. The Society was dedicated to the recovery, analysis and publication of historical evidence for education and doctrine development. It would serve Bridge's Naval Intelligence Department, the effective 'naval staff' of the era,[59] as an unofficial historical section. That RUSI was also the venue for Navy Records Society Council meetings reflected its semi-official character.

The link between the Naval Intelligence Department and the Records Society was maintained down to 1914 by a succession of educated officers, men like Reginald Custance, Prince Louis of Battenberg, Edmond Slade and George Ballard. An understanding of the past informed their thinking about the present, and they directed the publication programme of the Records Society toward studies of major campaigns, tactical thought, naval administration, strategy, blockade and the Navy in adversity. Such volumes were made available to serving officers *of both services* at members rates, while the Admiralty regularly made block purchases.[60] In the first two volumes, *State Papers Relating to the Defeat of the Spanish Armada*, Laughton exploded the myth that the Armada had been scattered and defeated essentially by the wind.[61] This was deliberate and timely, as the army was once again arguing that Britain could be invaded. Twenty years later Captain Herbert Richmond studied *The Loss of Minorca 1756*, examining the balance to be struck between a strong Grand Fleet and an adequate level of force in the Mediterranean.[62] This was no accident. Richmond was working on the contemporary aspect of this problem inside the new Admiralty War Staff.

The next question was how this wealth of material could be exploited in a formal programme of naval education. The first requirement would be sound preparation. By 1900, Laughton had recognised that Navy Records Society volumes would need to be supplemented by junior level textbooks and analytical monographs before history could become a key element in naval education. Working with Philip Colomb he had already produced a biography-based textbook for Greenwich.[63] When junior officers understood their past, a past Laughton used to stress the role of the individual in the transmission of understanding and doctrine, they would be ready for the study of tactics, strategy and administration. His friend Julian Corbett also worked at the entry level, as examiner in history at Dartmouth. Herbert Richmond stressed that the cadet entry needed to be trained, to make them useful, but they also had to be prepared for career-long education. The key subjects were technical and professional, save history which 'should be taught in such a manner which will lead to a strategical course'.[64] Corbett saw the need to provide a basic course dealing with the history of the Navy at this level, leaving the teaching of strategy to a later stage. He considered the current provision of half-baked strategic work, drawn from Mahan and Clowes, worse than useless.[65]

Once a sound basis had been created, officers would be ready for advanced study. To be useful at this level, history had to be analytical. To this end Laughton supported Mahan's attempt to write history,[66] but Corbett proved the better guide.[67] The provision of further expert civilian educators would require university-level education in naval history, which Laughton tried to establish at King's College. Unfortunately the initiative failed at his death.[68] After a lifetime devoted to the educational needs of the Royal Navy, Laughton clearly saw the need for advanced studies to be directed and conducted outside the service. His example was taken up and developed in Herbert Richmond's *Naval Review* of 1911, a forum for the critical discussion of non-technical issues by enquiring naval minds.[69] The new body shared the Junior Naval Professional Association's concern to address the intellectual aspects of war. Although the *Naval Review* came too late to help the Navy in 1914, it laid strong foundations during that conflict.[70]

It should come as no surprise that the Royal Navy only adopted a formal, historically based, education system after the Naval Intelligence Department had become an effective war staff and planning centre. The Naval War Course was set up in 1901 by DNI Reginald Custance, following an initiative from Admiral Sir John Fisher during an Admiralty visit to Malta in 1900.[71] The obvious link with the American Naval War College ensured that Laughton's ideas, albeit at one remove, were critical to the new course. The history element continued Laughton's Greenwich lectures. These had been taken over by Philip Colomb between 1887 and 1895, followed by Captain Henry May. While the American example was cited, the altogether more spacious Army Staff Course was ignored. Instead May, working alone, was expected to teach a basic curriculum of strategy, tactics, naval history and international law, with additional elements including navigation, compass adjustment, meteorology and foreign languages, in eight months.[72] The two glaring faults were undue compression of time, which allowed little or no time for the essential element of 'self-education', and the confusion of training and technical elements with intellectual work.

The Navy took a decisive step towards sustained educational improvement through the provision of civilian expertise. After two years working alone, May invited Corbett to provide a lecture course, which would combine history with tactics or strategy, with the emphasis on the latter. He also suggested that the basic approach should be 'the deflection of strategy by politics'.[73] Tragically May died in early 1904. His educational experience and high achievement led Fisher to select him as the next DNI, and a service still reliant upon a small supply of self-motivated, self-educated intellectuals did not recover his loss. After May's death Corbett worked closely with his successor as War Course Director and later DNI, Edmond Slade.[74] Another source of guidance was the navalist soldier and Secretary of the new Committee of Imperial Defence, Sir George Sydenham Clarke.[75] Clarke saw his role as the creation of a national strategy that combined the two services in a maritime programme, avoiding the twin dangers of 'blue water navalism' or conscriptionist homeland defence. This chimed with Corbett's thinking, as evidenced in the foreword to his *Successors of Drake*, where he declared 'The real importance of maritime power is its influence on military operations'.[76] The comment was a direct response to Laughton's criticism of the 'blue-water' excesses of Corbett's earlier *Drake and the Tudor Navy*. That his next book *England in the Mediterranean* of 1904 was developed from the war course lecture series of 1902, and credited Clarke with the key idea of showing how the Navy had exerted influence in a major theatre across a long period, neatly combined the twin strands of his career – historical scholarship and higher education. Inspired by the example of his friend and mentor Laughton, Corbett developed an elevated conception of his calling. His 1903 lecture notes for 'England in the Mediterranean'[77] and the War of the Spanish Succession, stressed 'object of course to direct & assist private study', because 'practical advantage of historical study is the chief value of a method of studying strategy'.[78]

Through his war course work and Records Society activities Corbett came into close contact with successive DNIs. Captain Charles Ottley (July 1904– October 1907) admitted that the routine business of DNI's office kept him from his 'proper function of war planning', which he passed to the war course. With that the war course became the effective War Staff of the Admiralty.[79] When Ottley left the NID in October 1907, to become the Secretary of the CID, he was replaced by Slade, whom Corbett already knew well. In November 1907 Corbett produced a major historical study of invasion, to refute the invasionist/conscriptionist case being made at a CID sub-committee. Corbett examined French eighteenth-century plans for the CID sub-committee, where his memorandum, focusing on the 1744 case, helped to re-establish the maritime basis of British strategy against the Army conscriptionist case. Inevitably Corbett used the same material to develop war course lectures. He also shared the paper with Herbert Richmond, who used it in his study of the war of 1739–48.[80] By this stage Corbett was also teaching strategy and taking part in the transformation of the war course into a proto-planning staff. The ideas and understanding that formed the basis of the 'Green Pamphlet' and later *Some Principles of Maritime Strategy* were first and foremost aimed at the higher education of the service. They defined fundamental concepts that senior officers would need to understand before they could explain their concerns to soldiers and statesmen, or take part in the inevitable debate on the direction of national strategy.

It would be difficult to argue that a service which provided mid-career officers with Corbett's carefully crafted and closely linked historical and conceptual lectures lacked education. The Navy might have been a little late making the provision, but there could be no doubt of its quality. Furthermore, the men who worked with Corbett (May, Ottley, Slade, Ballard, Aston, Richmond, Hankey and others) were well educated and intelligent officers. They shared Clarke's concern that national strategy should be maritime.

Two years after his first war course lectures Director Edmond Slade passed on a request for Corbett to lecture at the Army Staff College, Camberley, 'as I think it very important that sound ideas should be inculcated in the Staff College. They are quite ready to receive them.'[81] Colonel Rawlinson proposed a study of 'the Function of the Army in relation to gaining command of the sea, and in bringing war with a Continental Power to a successful conclusion'. The course delivered in November 1905 examined 'how we can confine enemy's strategy if we are acting with an ally as in 7 years war'.[82] This course was heavily influenced by the late Professor of Military History at Camberley, Colonel G.F.R. Henderson, for it was through the military educator that Corbett came to Clausewitz. Corbett's 1905 lectures to both naval and military courses, published as *England in the Seven Years' War*, used a Clausewitzian analysis of a major conflict as a template for the development of contemporary strategy. He also followed Henderson in explicitly stressing the primary importance of naval objectives in British combined operations. Corbett lectured on combined operations at Camberley or Aldershot in 1905, 1906 and 1907, and kept up his annual series with the Naval war course down to 1914. These lecture series, and the related monographs, met the educational agendas set by Clausewitz, by Laughton in the 1870s and by Henderson in the 1890s. However, their creation required a sustained research programme, much of it drawn from original archives.[83]

The link with Camberley reflected the rapid growth of education in the Army. Down to 1871 commissions had been sold, and only in 1875 was it made compulsory for officers to pass an examination before commissioning. However, the old gentleman amateur tradition was overturned by the disappointments of the Crimea. Giving evidence before the 1855 report on the cadet college at Sandhurst, General Sir Howard Douglas, chief promoter of the naval Gunnery School HMS *Excellent*, called for a course that was more practical and emphasised the study of history.[84] The new Senior College at Camberley adopted a two-year course to study war. Theoretical maths was quickly abandoned, leaving a programme of staff training and basic military education. It did not have a creative role because the Army did not have a strategic and planning department. This role was taken up by the new Intelligence Department in 1886, which would recruit the pick of the Staff College students.[85] The lack of focus was not surprising. There was no focal point for strategic debate at the higher levels of the state, which had no inter-service cooperative body, before the Committee of Imperial Defence was set up in 1904. The cabinet had been an effective strategic policy-making centre in the pre-Crimean era, but after the Second Reform Act of 1867 it was dominated by domestic and economic issues, and so detached from any experience of war as to be incompetent for the purpose.

In the late 1880s both services recognised the need for advanced study. One result was the Hartington Commission of 1890. While it concluded that the lack of inter-service co-operation was dangerous,[86] it missed the basic need for officers of the two services to be educated to communicate effectively at all levels. The need for higher level education was emphasised in Spenser Wilkinson's *The Brain of an Army*, an effective sketch of the German General Staff system published on the same day as the Commission report. Wilkinson's message was clear: 'The condition of success in higher education is that the teacher should be himself a student'.[87] Henderson used the Prussian/German system to stress the importance of history in training the judgement of mid-career officers.[88]

While this insight had long been familiar to Laughton's students, it was not shared with naval officers at Camberley, as none attended Staff College, although a handful of Royal Marines were admitted. The Corps was too small to bear the burden of transmitting understanding between the two services. Fortunately it did carry the germ of improvement, through the career of George Aston RM. Although the Army was providing education at a higher level than the Navy, this did not appear to be beneficial. Another poor performance in the Boer War of 1899–1902 suggested the Army officer was at an intellectual disadvantage to almost all other professionals, including naval officers. Little wonder Admiral Fisher was one of the three wise men selected to reform the War Office. While the Esher Committee did much to modernise the Army they left the development of a truly Imperial Staff to escape the control of the new CID, leaving the portentous title Chief of the Imperial General Staff to the Army.[89] This thoughtless aping of the German system ignored the reality of British strategy.

Many of the failings evident in South Africa, notably poor operational orders, failure to pass intelligence up and down the command chain and a lack of any concept of operations, would be evident in the Navy in 1914–18. This was in spite of increased inter-service links beginning in 1901. These revealed that the effectively uneducated naval officers had little understanding of strategic issues. An approach by George Aston inaugurated regular officer exchanges, two naval officers attending each course. Henry Rawlinson also extended the syllabus to cover naval strategy and inter-service issues like amphibious operations and imperial defence. He saw the College as a preparation for high command, and stressed that students should consider the impact of politics on strategy.[90] Julian Corbett had already developed this concept from Henry May's phrase, 'the deflection of strategy by politics'. While the Army was attempting to combine staff training with higher education for war, and the balance often shifted with a change of commandant, the two-year course recruited and developed the best minds the Army could offer. That it tended to the academic is suggested by the number of brilliant men who failed the hard test of war. George Aston and James Edmonds were not the only officers to collapse under pressure. The importance of the Staff College lay in providing an example to be emulated, and a basis for professional exchange in a more reflective atmosphere than the RUSI lecture theatre.

Through his friend Henry Newbolt, Corbett came into contact with Fisher, to whom he expressed his reservations about the poor quality of naval strategic thought evident in the papers submitted to him. Inevitably, he was asked to do something about this, by adding strategy courses to his existing history lectures.[91] This allowed him to build on the intimate connection he saw between accurate historical work, which he stressed was essential to any serious understanding of war, and the principles to be derived from such understanding. He faced an audience who knew little history, and as Laughton had pointed out 30 years before, much of what they did know was still romantic and inaccurate. Now the romance was Mahan's, and was taken rather more seriously than the lightweight stuff Laughton had been criticising. Nor were they ready for strategy in the abstract, an approach alien to their traditions and background. This was the core of the problem. The Royal Navy did not engage in speculative and lateral thinking, it did not teach philosophy or logic, and left mid-career officers with the impression that there were simple, correct answers to any problem they might face. Little wonder Corbett's carefully qualified approach to war, which followed Clausewitz in placing the emphasis on the higher direction by the political leadership, was so confusing. It was not that naval officers lacked brains, there were many fine minds in the service, but they were, as Custance demonstrated, not accustomed to being challenged by juniors, and especially not by civilians. Even so Corbett persevered, and the results were impressive.

It had also been intended that the course would provide the opportunity for a senior strategist to develop war plans in isolation from the administrative and technical demands that dominated the work of the Sea Lords at Whitehall.[92] However, Fisher did not adopt this approach, preferring to employ relatively junior strategic advisers, while retaining the higher role for himself. In effect the course acted as his war staff after 1906.

The course was intended to provide an education in war fighting and related issues for commanders and captains. Initially spread over eight months it was divided into two parts in 1903, to enable more officers to attend. More significantly it was compulsory from the outset, in marked contrast to the half-hearted and ineffective methods of recruitment adopted for the higher Naval College courses. This was the first full-time career path course for senior officers but, as Richmond observed, those attending lacked the prior education to make the best use of the opportunity.[93] After six years at Greenwich the course transferred to Portsmouth in 1906, and was expanded to include the special campaigns branch, which Fisher used, as the Ballard Committee, to plan for war with Germany.[94] In 1912 the Naval staff course for Lieutenants, Lieutenant-Commanders and Commanders was set up to provide trained staff officers.[95] By securing the course, providing it with the best brains in the service, and the most able civilians, Fisher created a system to educate senior officers and provide the resources for staff work. In addition it was critical to the creation of the first fully fashioned national strategic doctrine. *Some Principles of Maritime Strategy* was written at Fisher's request, to provide a maritime strategic alternative to the 'continentalist' model pushed by the Army General Staff. It has largely stood the test of time as a national programme. Like all of Corbett's major texts after 1900 it was developed from war course lectures and met Laughton's requirement for history as the basis for officer education.

The deliberately informal nature of the relationship between the war course, the Admiralty and the development of plans, enabled Fisher to make the best use of Julian Corbett. The more formal structures put in place by Churchill in 1912 could not incorporate Corbett effectively, and he was left on the sidelines, although he used his time to write a confidential history of the Russo-Japanese War for the DNI.[96] Only then did he realise just how much the development of doctrine and strategy would have been advanced by a thorough study of the wars of the nineteenth century, notably the Crimean.[97]

Conclusion

Throughout the nineteenth century the Navy continued to leave education to the commitment and interest of individual officers. Personal study, links with the leaders of previous generations and career opportunities encompassed the educational opportunities open to future Admirals. Despite the impact of the most profound 'revolution in military affairs', this system of 'self-education' provided a steady stream of capable Admirals. However, the Navy needed to work with the Army, and advise statesmen, and for these tasks a formal system of higher education in war-fighting was essential. Ultimately the requirement was addressed by the Naval War Course of 1901, inspired by the effective war planning staff, and the Navy's most dynamic Admiral. While educators would have preferred a comprehensive career system, the course was a major step forward, greatly enhanced by links with Camberley.

The course came too late to have a major impact on the higher direction of war before 1914 and the earlier opportunity created when the Naval College moved to Greenwich in 1873 was largely wasted on technical and narrowly professional issues. The failure to provide a historically based *education* at Greenwich denied senior officers a vital opportunity. The Naval War Course demonstrated what could be done, with enough impetus, yet its effect was limited by the lack of any serious preparatory education. The full implementation of the Selbourne scheme, at least in the version envisaged by Richmond, might have helped in the longer term, but the lack of an integrated educational package linking initial officer training, mid-career development and a staff course was a glaring failure.

The Navy had not taken John Laughton's work to heart. It preferred to work without a system, leaving the development and delivery of higher education to amateur scholars like Julian Corbett, relying on a handful of individuals to meet a critical task. Had Laughton's call for an advanced history course been adopted in the 1870s the Royal Navy would have had the basis of a modern professional education system in place a decade before anyone else. The Navy was not prepared to take such radical steps without the shock of catastrophic defeat. In 1914 it went to war intellectually ill-prepared, having failed to engage with experience of the past, trusting to a Nelson talisman rather than understanding the hard work and historical learning that formed the foundation of his genius. No amount of technical proficiency could compensate for the lack of 'insight' that crippled the higher direction of the war at sea. The salutary experience of war once again refreshed minds and improved understanding.

Much of the educational process was driven by those outside the naval system, notably Laughton and Corbett. These men had the time and the opportunity to develop a profound understanding of the Navy's requirements. It was in this role, as the academic outsider, working inside the system, that Bryan Ranft served the Navy so well. His insistence on the highest educational standards ensured that officers had the opportunity to think for themselves and found in his teaching a wealth of ideas to aid professional judgement. That he followed Laughton to King's College, and inspired another generation of naval educators, has ensured that his legacy lives on at Staff College and the university. This may seem a grand claim to make for one man, but the task facing naval educators has always been on a scale where individuals matter. The academic/service partnerships begun by Laughton, and sustained by Corbett, demonstrated the point. Bryan Ranft revived their legacy, opening the horizons of his students to a wider conception of their profession and to the world in which they might be called upon to act.

Notes

1 See the monumental Tunstall (1936c, reprinted 1990) for a classic study that reflects the sailing Navy's obsession with tactics, discussions of which effectively excluded strategy from the naval agenda. It should be noted that the text was actually written 40 years before, and that Tunstall was well aware of the higher, strategic level of war.
2 Bridge-Laughton 8.2.1887, in Lambert (2002) pp. 51–2.
3 Strachan (1984) pp. 198–9.
4 Rodger (2001) p. 10.
5 Colomb (1898) see pp. 3–9 for his time as a cadet, and pp. 324–76 for his time as Captain of the establishment.

Education in the Royal Navy: 1854–1914   57

6 Beeler (1997) esp. pp. 210–25 for a persuasive critique of the 'Dark Ages of the Admiralty' approach to contemporary naval policy.
7 For a contemporary account, emphasising the picturesque, see Moreby (1909) pp. 79–87.
8 Ibid. p. 87.
9 Ibid. p. 203. Moresby's reward was six years' on half pay.
10 Burrows (1908).
11 Ellison (1991).
12 Add MSS 34,919 f180 list of books sent to Nelson in June 1803.
13 After Jutland Jellicoe admitted that he had not even read Mahan!
14 James (2002) edition and intro. by Lambert.
15 Nicolas (1844–6).
16 Newnham Collingwood (1828). See p. 15 for his views on history.
17 Egerton (1896) p. 47.
18 For a strategic overview of this war as a maritime conflict see Lambert (1990).
19 Ibid. pp. 30–3.
20 Ibid. p. 4.
21 Lambert (2001).
22 Burrows (1869) pp. 27–8.
23 Chads to Sir James Graham (First Lord of the Admiralty) (Confidential) 1.10.1853: ADM 13/185 ff. 93–6.
24 Sulivan (1896).
25 See Lambert (1990) generally for these two officers.
26 Hornby and the Key compact. Egerton (1896) pp. 195–6.
27 Corbett (1911) p. 14.
28 Huntington (1957) p. 8.
29 Hamilton (1993) pp. 174–99 esp. pp. 188–9.
30 Lambert (1998a). See Lambert (1987) for the design history of this innovative ship.
31 For a broader perspective on Laughton's career and aims see Lambert (1998).
32 Laughton (1870) pp. iv–vi.
33 Laughton (1872) pp. v–vi.
34 Noel (1873) prints Laughton's essay with two others.
35 Lambert (1998a) Chapter 2, 'The Naval University'.
36 Admiralty Circular No. 28 14.3.1874 ADM 203/1.
37 Soley (1880), a work drawing heavily on Laughton's 1875 *RUSI* lecture.
38 Ballard (1976) p. 249.
39 Gieves, Portsmouth (1873).
40 See Gordon (1996).
41 Laughton (1885) pp. 234–64, quoting Hornby's lecture at p. 238.
42 Laughton (1886) pp. vii–xx. Corbett's handling of the 'Nelson Memorandum' in 1905 was strikingly similar.
43 Laughton (1885) pp. 239–40.
44 The range and quality of these discussions is best approached through the published *Journal of the Royal United Service Institution* but a good indication, drawn from military subjects can be found in Welch (1998) and (1999), papers in the RUSI Whitehall series covering the period 1829 to 1900.
45 Laughton (1875) pp. 283–4.
46 Laughton (1874) pp. 508–27.
47 Laughton op. cit.
48 Tegetthoff (1878) pp. 671–92. Reprinted in Laughton (1887) quote at pp. 148–50.
49 For a brief overview of these key figures see Lambert (2001) pp. 35–47.
50 Laughton to Stephen Luce USN 11.8.1889: Luce MS Library of Congress.

51 Hayes and Hattendorf (1975).
52 Huntington (1957) pp. 230–7.
53 Jomini (1838). Jomini reflected an older strategic tradition than Clausewitz. His work was widely used after 1815, notably in France and the United States. Mahan's father Dennis Hart Mahan taught his work at West Point. In 1886 Luce required Mahan to do for war at sea 'what Jomini has done for the military science'. Lambert (1998) p. 122.
54 Seager (1977). Sumida (1997).
55 Lambert (1998a) pp. 173–93.
56 The officers attending Greenwich between 1873 and 1885 included most of the best minds the service would produce in two generations. They are recorded in the pages of the *Navy List.*
57 Egerton (1896) pp. 192–3.
58 Mullins (2000). I am indebted to Dr Mullins for a copy of his excellent thesis.
59 Lambert (1998a) p. 224, from a speech by Prince Louis in 1916.
60 The Admiralty purchased over 200 copies of Julian Corbett's two volumes of tactical material.
61 London Navy Records Society 1894.
62 I am indebted to Prof. D. Baugh for this insight.
63 Laughton (1899).
64 Richmond to Corbett 31.12.1902: Partridge (1999) p. 8.
65 Corbett to Richmond 11.8.1909: RIC 1/8 National Maritime Museum, London.
66 Lambert (1998a) pp. 180–3, 195.
67 Schurman (1981). Lambert (1998a) pp. 150–8.
68 The College subsequently played the major role in reviving naval history in British academic life.
69 Hunt (1982).
70 Goldrick (1993) in Goldrick and Hattendorf (1993) at pp. 83–102.
71 Marder (1940) p. 390, quoting Fisher.
72 Schurman (1981) pp. 32–4.
73 Corbett (1916).
74 Slade had attended the first war course in 1901.
75 Schurman (1981) pp. 21, 26, 34.
76 Corbett (1900) p. vii.
77 The title of the published version, which appeared in 1904.
78 Corbett: War Course Lecture notes October 1903, Liddell-Hart Centre for Military Archives.
79 Schurman (1981) p. 43.
80 Corbett's paper is in Richmond's MS at RIC 9/1. See also Richmond (1920) Esp. vol. II pp. 74–93.
81 Slade to Corbett 22.8.1905 (Royal Naval College): Liddell Hart Centre.
82 Rawlinson to Corbett 25.8.1905 and Corbett notes on: Rawlinson to Corbett 30.8.1905: ibid.
83 Corbett's Trafalgar lecture includes a letter from Barham to Cornwallis, in Laughton's hand: ibid.
84 Bond (1972) p. 62.
85 Ibid. pp. 121, 171.
86 Ibid. pp. 143–4.
87 Wilkinson (1889) esp. pp. 173–91. Quote p. 173.
88 Bond (1972) p. 155.
89 Ibid. pp. 217–20.
90 Ibid. p. 264.
91 Schurman (1981) pp. 43–4.

92 Fisher to Lord Selborne (First Lord) 29 July 1901 in Marder (1952) Vol. I, p. 203.
93 Schurman (1965) p. 127.
94 Offer (1989).
95 Marder (1961) pp. 32–3, 265.
96 Corbett (1914). This was a major study of modern war, but it was too late for any educational value to be drawn from it before war broke out.
97 Corbett (1916) pp. 12–19.

4 Corbett and the emergence of a British school?

Geoffrey Till

At the end of the nineteenth century and the beginnings of the twentieth, there was a real explosion of British interest in maritime matters. As a result, there emerged a large group of naval thinkers, many of whom were indeed naval; their ideas developed just about enough internal coherence for them to be considered a 'school'. This did not mean that they all agreed with one another about everything, for they did not, but their differences were generally matters of degree and emphasis. They were a school rather in the sense that the Pre-Raphaelites 50 years before them were a brotherhood – united in general, disputatious in the particular but rather more enduring. After a short period of intense artistic co-inspiration the Pre-Raphaelites drifted apart 'to do their own thing'; the British maritime school, however, surged on, remaining 'the pens behind the fleet'.

Fin de siecle concerns

In their various ways, British navalists at the turn of the century were all reacting to a developing set of circumstances that they found worrying. These concerns echoed a general national anxiety, at odd variance with the golden glow in which the late Victorian and Edwardian ages is often perceived. Britain itself seemed to be entering a new, unfamiliar and potentially dangerous era with a marked increase in domestic dissatisfaction, with the country's industrial lead over everyone else seeming to falter and with the emergence of new rivals on the international scene. Perhaps the confident age of British imperialism was drawing to a close?

This led to a burst of romantic nostalgia for the glory days when that age began – the Elizabethan period, when thrusting mariners like Drake and Raleigh were boldly creating the basis for an empire on which the sun would never set:

> Nothing is more remarkable than the prescience and the instinctive grasp of naval conditions manifested by the great seamen of Elizabeth. To them was given the clear vision of a future in which the Navy of England, dominating the seas, would lay the foundations

of empire. That the rule of the sea was the natural heritage of the British people ...[1]

For many, the most immediate and potentially most dangerous manifestation of all this was that the Navy seemed to have lost its way and to be heading into danger. As a result, the country itself was in peril. This all may be said to have started with the publication in the *Pall Mall Gazette* of 15 September 1884 of the first of a set of articles by W.T. Stead entitled 'What is The Truth About the Navy?'

These articles reflected a growing concern that for much of the previous 50 years the Admiralty seemed almost deliberately bent on giving the impression that naval thought was a contradiction in terms. Its attention was largely concentrated on detailed imperial enterprises around the world and on the more practical consequences of the contemporary struggle between sail and steam. There was, it seemed to many, little real thinking about the future of maritime strategy, and certainly not the kind of thinking that was openly articulated in a form that the politicians and the public would find persuasive. This in turn played a part in the general loss of confidence in the Navy that characterised much of the middle part of the nineteenth century.

One result of this was a sudden obsession with the danger of invasion and a widespread fear that the Navy might be unable to do anything about it. These anxieties were greatly reinforced in 1844 when a French Admiral, the Prince de Joinville, wrote a truculent article in the *Revue des Deux Mondes* pointing out that the British fleet could be defeated in detail and, with the aid of steam, an invasion force could be rushed across the Channel in the darkness of one night. Against such a bolt from the blue, Britain would be powerless. For the rest of the century, the country was prone to bouts of panic about this. Richard Cobden identified three of these by 1862, and vainly pointed out the unreality on which they were based.[2] Steam, in Palmerston's view, had 'thrown a bridge across the Channel' and so seemed to justify the reallocation, as in 1888, of money from the Navy vote to coastal defence and the development of a home Army to guard the country against all manner of 'invasions' and raids. Worst of all, it resulted in the erection of expensive red-brick and stone fortifications along the coast and waterways of southern England; those on Portsdown Hill, above the great naval base at Portsmouth, were even intended to protect that Navy from the attentions of a French army advancing upon them from overland.

There was nothing new about this of course. In 1628, for instance, Viscount Wimbledon had written about the problem of 'How the coasts of Your Maj'tes Kingedome may bee defended against any enemye, if in case your royall Navie should be otherwise employed or impeached'. Nicholas Rodger has reminded us of the extent to which the Jacobite threat dominated British naval deployments a century later. It was, he concludes, '... the basic factor in British naval strategy in the first half of the eighteenth century'.[3] The same concerns arose in the Napoleonic era. Most naval officers then, however, were sceptical about the need for panic measures. The sole justification that Lord St Vincent could see for them was that they would 'calm the fears of the old ladies both in and out'.[4]

The accelerating press of new technology throughout the nineteenth century was unsettling too, for it raised many questions about the future conduct of naval battle and indeed the continued primacy of the Navy in national regard. In France this led to excited claims that the torpedo and the torpedo boat would so threaten conventional battlefleets that many of their normal operations, such as blockade, would be impossible. These, plus submarines, and perhaps in the longer term aircraft, would transform warfare at sea, and moreover, it was not clear that such a transformation would necessarily be in the interest of the Royal Navy. In the early twentieth century, Sir Jacky Fisher became an advocate of the new technology, not just in the shape of the *Dreadnought* battleship of 1904 and the battlecruiser/fast battleship, but also in the much more challenging notion of 'flotilla defence'. For a while at least, he was convinced that new technology, in the shape of the submarine, would make it impossible for hostile fleets to operate in such comparatively narrow waters as the North Sea. Accordingly it would not be possible for anyone to blockade Britain, or invade it once such a flotilla defence was in place. In 1904, and in 1914, he wrote:

> THE SUBMARINE IS THE COMING TYPE OF WAR VESSEL FOR SEA FIGHTING. And what is it that the coming of the submarine really means? It means that the whole foundation of our traditional naval strategy . . . has broken down! The foundation of that strategy was blockade. The Fleet did not exist merely to win battles – that was the means not the end. The ultimate purpose of the Fleet was to make blockade possible for us and impossible for the enemy . . . Surface ships can no longer maintain or prevent blockade . . . All our old ideas of strategy are simmering in the melting pot![5]

While, if true, all this might make the sea defence of Britain easier and cheaper, the same development also seemed likely seriously to inhibit the offensive operations, and therefore the value, of the British battlefleet.

Under such a battering, it was hardly surprising that British navalists should find it necessary to reconsider, review and if necessary amend, the ancient truths of maritime strategy, and to seek to articulate them persuasively to a more doubting world.

Leading figures in the school

Because there are so many good accounts of the leading figures of the British school,[6] it is only necessary here briefly to pick out its main and some of its minor players. In the late Victorian era, they were not, of course, starting from scratch – the school had its predecessors. Although these ancient truths might not have been explicitly gathered together and enunciated in the immediately accessible form of books and pamphlets, long maritime experience had given the Royal Navy some fairly clear guidance as to what needed to be done in warfare at sea. One form in which such ideas emerged, of course, were the *Fighting Instructions* that were periodically issued by the Admiralty – but these were almost exclusively tactical in their preoccupation.

Molyneux and Clerk

In the eighteenth century, some analysts did begin to elevate their concern more to what we would call the operational level of naval campaigns. The first Britons really to think about this and to put pen to paper in a really sustained way were Thomas More Molyneux with his *Conjunct Operations or Expeditions That have Been Carried on Jointly by the Fleet and Army, with a Commentary on Littoral War of 1759* and John Clerk of Eldin with his *Naval Tactics*, the first private edition of which was circulated privately in 1784.

Neither used the word 'strategy' in defining their subject and both had very many tactical things to stress. Nonetheless, Molyneux was certainly concerned with identifying some general principles that should govern the manner in which expeditionary operations by the Navy and the Army combined should be conducted. He attributed the failure of the Rochefort operation of 1758 to the '. . . little Regard the low Plight and want of System in the conducting of our Conjunct Armaments'.[7] Clerk was likewise concerned to guide fleet commanders in the disposition of their ships for battle. In their own ways, they were both seeking to proceed from the particular to the general, to lay down some ground rules that would help avoid the mistakes and the disappointments of the past. Both used the phrase 'system' to describe the body of recommended course of action based on logic and the considered analysis of previous experience they sought to develop. Moreover, they were both concerned to establish the importance of their subjects to national success. Thus Molyneux:

> We must tell our Countrymen, that a Military, naval Littoral War, when wisely prepared and discreetly conducted, is a terrible sort of War. Happy for that People who are Sovereigns enough of the Sea to put it in Execution! For it comes like Thunder and Lightning to some unprepared Part of the World.[8]

The Colomb brothers

In the late 1860s, after a gap of some 70 years, the two brothers, Captain Sir John and Vice-Admiral Philip Colomb took up the cudgels in the Navy's defence. Captain Sir John was the younger of the two, being born in 1838 on the Isle of Man. After a short uneventful career in the Royal Marine Artillery, he retired in 1869 and spent the remaining 40 years of his life writing about various aspects of imperial defence. He insisted that imperial defence needed to be seen as a whole and that it required partnership between the Army and the Navy. The House of Commons had the frequent benefit of his views as he was a far from silent MP for some 20 years. These views first saw the light of day in an anonymous pamphlet called *The Protection of our Commerce and Distribution of our Naval Forces Considered* (1867). Some of his later articles were gathered together in *The Defence of Great and Greater Britain* (1880). He generally ignored politics, economics, history and complexities of that kind, preferring to drive his message home by simple and forceful logic and the accumulation of statistics. He was very much the pioneer, blazing a trail for others. He was according to Azar Gat, 'possibly the first strategic analyst Britain had known'.[9]

His brother Philip was an early collaborator. Born in 1832, he was the elder of the two but a full, varied and active life in the Navy delayed his entry into the lists until 1873 when his *Slave Catching in the Indian Ocean* appeared. Although this was his first formal book, a batch of articles produced between 1871 and 1889 were published in *Essays on Naval Defence* (1896). This followed his successful *chef d'oeuvre*, *Naval Warfare* (1891). He retired from active service in 1886, but stayed on briefly to become an instructor in naval tactics at the Royal Naval College, Greenwich, and produced a prestigious biography of Admiral Sir Ashley Cooper Key in 1898. He died of a heart attack in the following year.

Philip Colomb's approach was quite different from that of his younger brother; his was not just a functional interest in the best method of imperial defence, but a concern for the principles of the naval warfare on which he put so much more stress than his brother. He believed there was too little thought about maritime strategy and was sure he could discover its principles: 'The science of Naval Tactics still remains in an exceedingly vague and unsatisfactory state: but the Author is now, as ever, persuaded that there are no difficulties in putting it on an absolutely sound basis in peacetime'. It was necessary to have a guide that would help naval officers distinguish between the possible and the impossible, the prudent and the imprudent, the wise and the foolish.[10]

He was convinced that the best way to discover the truth about naval warfare was by a combination of inductive reasoning, experience and 'a pretty thorough investigation of its history'. His attitude to the past was not that of the disinterested historian, studying it for its own sake. He acted more in the manner of a highwayman, expecting the muse of history to deliver the goods at the point of a pen.[11] Nevertheless, his *Naval Warfare* of 1891, actually a collection of essays written earlier for *The Illustrated Naval and Military Magazine*, was the first historically based survey of the principles of maritime strategy, and was his most influential book. It was very long (Admiral Sir Jacky Fisher with a typically atrocious pun called him 'a column and a half' from the length of his letters to the newspapers) and the reader was more bludgeoned than persuaded into agreement. The book analysed past struggles for command of the sea and identified the conditions under which attacks on territory succeeded or failed. It established general guidelines which recent wars seemed to confirm rather than deny, despite steam and other new inventions. There was, thought Colomb, 'no reason for believing' that these 'have modified the leading principles of naval warfare'.[12]

In *Naval Warfare* Colomb argued that real maritime strategy began 'with the Elizabethans for only then did ships develop the necessary sea-keeping qualities', and maritime endeavour became a really significant national activity. He analysed the development of the tactics of decisive battle, developed the notion of the fleet-in-being and identified the various types of blockade.

Both the Colomb brothers had a considerable influence on their times. They set people thinking about maritime strategy and they did much to rescue the Navy from the intellectual stagnation into which it had fallen. Sir John's prestige perhaps faded a little towards the end: 'he probably feels', said one critic unkindly, 'like a small dog whose bone has been taken away by a bigger one'.[13] Philip Colomb's work was not restricted to the analysis of the particular problems of imperial defence and so was of more general interest. He probably had the greater impact on contemporaries, and on subsequent events, and this not least because he made naval history a respectable and relevant subject of enquiry for naval officers.

In some ways, Philip Colomb was robbed of much of his due glory by the fact that his *Naval Warfare* came out in 1891 at the same time as Mahan's *The Influence of Sea Power upon History* – Colomb told Mahan, with charm and considerable modesty, 'I think all our naval men regarded it as the Naval book of the age, and it has had a great effect in getting people to understand what they had never understood before'.[14] Although scooped by Mahan in popular regard, Colomb provided a more systematic organisation of the concepts of the bluewater approach. His was a worthy essay in naval strategy, but Mahan's horizons were broader and, apparently, more generally appealing to the spirit of the times. For that reason even in Britain, Colomb was mainly eclipsed by his colleague from across the Atlantic.

Corbett

Sir Julian Corbett (1854–1922) came late to maritime affairs and associated with the great men ushering the Royal Navy painfully into the twentieth century. Deeply concerned about the poverty of contemporary naval thought, he sought to improve it partly through lectures at the Naval War Colleges at Greenwich and Portsmouth.

His teaching was supported by an impressive list of naval histories, including several on the Tudor and post-Tudor Royal Navy, a masterpiece on the Seven Years' War, a two-volume work on maritime warfare in the Mediterranean, a staff history of the Russo-Japanese War, another masterpiece on the Trafalgar campaign and *Some Principles of Maritime Strategy* in 1911, plus the first three volumes of the *History of the Great War: Naval Operations*.

Paradoxically, Corbett did most of his writing in that particularly interesting period just before the First World War, when Britain was actually moving away from the kind of strategy that he advocated. Nonetheless, his views dominated the British school.

Callwell

Major General Sir Charles Callwell, as he eventually became, was the other main figure in the British school. Born in 1859, Callwell eventually became Director of Military Operations at the War Office, but he was also a prolific author. Among the most significant of his works are: *Small Wars: Their Principles and Practice* (1896), *The Effect of Maritime Command on Land Campaigns since Waterloo* (1897), *Military Operations and Maritime Preponderance* (1905) and *The Dardanelles* (1924).[15] Of these the first is by far the most original but its main thrust is not on maritime strategy. The central tenets of Callwell's approach to this can be found, instead, in the second and third of these works, and an analysis of their practical application in the last. The most superficial skim through these works shows that Callwell provides an exact fit with Corbett over the core issue of the way in which sea- and landpower should be mutually supportive in a properly constructed maritime strategy. Callwell's basic theme was the mutual interdependence of sea- and landpower, especially for a maritime country like Britain.

Fisher and other minor players

The ideas associated with the Colombs were also increasingly explored by others of their time. As Andrew Lambert has already shown, Sir William Laird Clowes focused the public's attention on their Navy, its past and its future needs and Sir John Laughton made naval history the basis for rigorous maritime analysis, being happy to correct the historical inaccuracies of colleagues who let their enthusiasm to argue a good point run away with them. Both were convinced of the Navy's need to study the past in order to steer its way through an uncertain future. In Clowes' words:

> There is ... no study so vital to the welfare of her Empire as the study of the modern art of naval warfare; for only by study can a man become a master of that art; and only by producing masters of that art in the day of need can Britain hold her own upon the ocean. Ships, guns, and men will not avail unless there be brains behind them.[16]

Intellectual sailors like Admiral Sir Cyprian Bridge and Admiral Sir Reginald Custance (who sometime used the pseudonym of 'Barfleur') also wrote books, articles and gave lectures extolling the virtues of historical study and strategic contemplation. 'I hope', said Bridge in 1874, 'that the study of it [naval tactics] will soon become the common pursuit of the many, rather than, as now, the special occupation of the few'. In 1907 his *The Art of Naval Warfare* appeared. He hoped to show that 'naval history . . . ought to be studied not as a mere gratification of antiquarian predelection, but as a record of the lessons of naval warfare'.[17] For his part Custance produced *Naval Policy: A Plea for The Study of War* (1907). Custance, famous for his virulent dislike of Fisher, railed against the malign influence of the '*materiel* school' who dismissed the past, neglected the study of tactics and strategy and concentrated solely on the unthinking production of equipment. Over such things as the design of battleships, Custance thought:

> The naval mind is divided into two schools – the historical and the *materiel*. The adherents of the one appeal for guidance to the great masters of the art of war by sea and land; they hold that it is very important to study tactics and strategy by the light of history. The disciples of the other do not believe the lessons of the past are applicable to the present; they have neglected the study of tactics and strategy, and have devoted their energies to the development of the *material* – ships, guns, armour, etc.[18]

Custance was sceptical about the extent to which the latest technology had really transformed naval warfare as much as its advocates said it had. By 1907 though, he felt able to note, with some satisfaction, that the 'historical school' were slowly forcing 'the *materielists*' back into their lair.[19] As we shall see, Custance's study of naval history led him to adopt a maritime variant of the French '*guerre a outrance*' school in which an unremitting offensive in pursuit of the command of the sea should be the Royal Navy's default setting. He was to cross swords with Corbett over this.

The largely forgotten David Hannay deserves mention as well. Criticised by Laughton for his perverse reluctance to identify his sources, he was regarded as a publicist rather than a historian, and it is true that his two-volume history of the Royal Navy was clearly aimed at the popular end of the market. However his *The Navy and Seapower* (1913) is a thoughtful and unobjectionable short treatise on all aspects of seapower which ends with a clear sense of foreboding about the ability of the 'Great sea power' to maintain in itself as such in a more uncertain world.[20] Finally Lt. Col. George S. Clarke (who later wrote as Lord Sydenham) and J.R. Thursfield produced *The Navy and the Nation* in 1897, a large-scale but not particularly coherent survey of various aspects of naval warfare and imperial defence produced through the collaboration of, respectively, a politician and a publicist.[21]

Callwell was not alone in extolling the benefits of an amphibious approach for in his time other significant books were produced on the subject as well, although, sadly, these are largely forgotten now. They include Colonel George

Furse's *Military Expeditions Beyond the Seas* (1897) and *Letters on Amphibious Wars* (1911) by the Royal Marine, George Aston (1861–1938). Aston also wrote *Sea, Land and Air Strategy* (1914), the latter certainly among the first to seek to fold airpower into the equation.

It may seem strange to include Admiral Sir Jacky Fisher, one of the twentieth century's most noted sailors, only among the minor players in this cast, but for all his strengths, Fisher was not noted for the clear exposition of his views on paper. Forceful, even pungent, yes; clear, no. The bones of his approach to maritime strategy may nonetheless be picked out. In his *Memories*, he recalled pacing the sands of Scheveningen with Germany's General Gross von Schwarzhoff in June 1899, the latter complaining about the way in which '... the absolute supremacy of the British Navy gave it such inordinate power far beyond its numerical strength, because 200,000 men embarked in transports, and God only knowing where they might be put ashore, was a weapon of enormous influence and capable of deadly blows'. Animated by such observations, Fisher was quite clear that the Army should indeed remain a projectile to be fired by the Navy and optimised for coastal military expeditions; accordingly he was always on his guard against the insidious incrementalism of the continentalists – ineffectually as things turned out.[22] Fisher is still chiefly noted for his ultimate belief in the transformational effect of the latest technology on the manner in which future navies would perform their tasks and was violently opposed to, and by, sceptics such as Custance and Bridge. If there was a British school, Fisher and these two were on the far and opposing wings of it, on this matter at least.

Fisher's enthusiasm for transformational naval technology in the shape of fast battleships, submarines and later aircraft, made him wonder whether in future the performance of traditional naval roles, such as the defence of shipping, securing command of the seas in narrow waters and defence against invasion would need to be performed in entirely different ways although, in the event, when war came in 1914 he proved himself to be a good deal more conventional in his approach than some of his pre-war musings might have suggested he would be. He was certainly acutely aware of the costs of seapower and of Britain's increasing difficulty in bearing them, and so was predisposed towards any innovation, technological or otherwise, which might help solve this dilemma.

If these were the leading figures of a loose British school what, in fact, were they saying individually and collectively? How did they influence British naval thinking? Their message can be explored under six different but interconnected headings.

The need for, and value of, naval thinking

The first issue was about who should be doing the thinking. Some members of the 'school' were not scholars so much as lobbyists unashamedly focused on elevating thinking about maritime matters in the British government and amongst the attentive public. It was important to get the naval case debated as widely as possible. 'The people', remarked Hannay of an earlier time, 'were in terrible earnest about the navy, even when their earnestness was not according to knowledge'.[23] For that reason, probably his best book was a part of the 'Home University Library of Modern Knowledge'. Writers like W.T. Stead, Hannay and Thursfield were targeting the general public. In that their aim was to get the public thinking about the Navy, they were the intellectual shock troops of the Navy League and to judge by the 'We want eight and we won't wait' turmoil of the early twentieth century they were very successful in reawakening Britain to its maritime past, present and future. Laughton and Clowes on the other hand were principally targeting the smaller historical community, intent first of all on establishing the respectability of naval history *as* history. Neither, however, were at all averse to their publics drawing lessons for today from rigorous and well-crafted historical analysis.

Others, however, were mainly aiming at the education of the Navy itself and concerned to ensure that processed naval history was indeed seen as the essential means of inculcating the intellectual skills, concepts and knowledge that would make British naval officers better fighters and policy-makers. History, thought Admiral Sir Cyprian Bridge, can show us what to follow and what to avoid so that naval warfare is properly 'organised', 'based on plans devised in accordance with reasoned principles' and not a matter of 'violent and hasty conflicts'. Given the seductive but potentially misleading possibilities of modern technology, the identification of these principles was vital for properly educated naval officers:

> It is urgently necessary to give careful consideration to the extent to which we should attach value to speed of ships as regards both strategy and tactics. Owing to the deplorable influence which the modern habit of trusting to imposing material wins over the minds of those who neglect the study of naval history, there is danger of its being credited with a predominant importance to which it has no well-grounded right.[24]

Accordingly, it was appropriate that Laughton, Philip Colomb and Corbett all taught at the Navy's war courses at either Portsmouth or the Royal Naval College at Greenwich. Corbett also challenged the all too common preconception that lessons deduced from the age of sail were irrelevant to the concerns of the naval officers of the machine age. As Bryan Ranft justly observed, Corbett's defence rested on the way in which he defined such lessons and principles:

> Corbett did not claim that historical study would produce detailed rules for the future conduct of battles and campaigns. Its value lay in bringing to light the permanent characteristics of sea power and the specific nature of its contribution to national strategy; what it could achieve and

what were its limitations. Equipped with these insights, the contemporary naval commander would have a pattern of past experience, what had succeeded, what had failed, against which to assess his present situation and desirable course of action.[25]

Corbett's approach to this problem can be seen in his treatment of Drake. On the one hand he lamented the fact that 'in the Elizabethan age, the principles of naval warfare were as little understood as its limitations' and applauded the efforts of such as John Montgomery to produce a set of ideas in 1570 'so sound and so strikingly modern in its ring'. On the other hand, he admired Drake for his readiness, when applying such principles constructively, 'to break rules'. Corbett clearly took the principles of war to be a guide to thought rather than directives for action.[26] Accordingly, it was essential for naval commanders to have the knowledge and intellectual skills to navigate their way effectively through such treacherous waters. The study of naval history and naval strategy could only help.

The maritime approach at the strategic level

As a lawyer, Corbett had a more judicious sense than Mahan of the limitations of seapower, and quite crucially, therefore, of its place in the wider scheme of things. What is special about Corbett is his emphasis on the importance of putting naval operations in that broader context which does so much to explain their form and purpose, and which, in his view, was affected so much by their result.

Corbett emphasised that strategy needs to be consciously related to foreign policy. Having digested his Clausewitz, Corbett was well aware of the fact that war was a political act and that the first function of the fleet was '... to support or obstruct diplomatic effort'. He took an overtly *political* approach to seapower; maritime strategy should serve the interests of the state, and in war and peace the type of strategy a navy adopted should reflect national objectives. Corbett was particularly interested in *limited* maritime wars which were more political than most, but which allowed a country's rulers carefully to weigh the costs of war in order to compare them with the benefits. Because maritime operations were more controllable in the sense of being less prone to ruinous escalation, they were often particularly cost-effective when compared to ordinary, messy land operations.

Naval strategy has to be related to land strategy:

> Of late years the world has become so deeply impressed with the efficacy of sea power that we are inclined to forget how impotent it is of itself to decide a war against great Continental states, how tedious is the pressure of naval action unless it be nicely coordinated with military and diplomatic pressure.[27]

Naval strategy has to be seen not as a separate entity but simply as part of the art of war. Landpower and seapower were not in opposition, but their relationship with one another would be different for 'world wide imperial states, where the sea becomes a direct and vital factor' than it would be for those for whom geography makes the 'German or Continental School of strategy' more appropriate. Britain of course was pre-eminently just such a maritime state and had derived enormous benefit from developing a set of principles governing the conduct of war '... in which the sea is a substantial factor'. But this certainly should not mean the British neglecting the use of armies:

> Since men live upon the land and not upon the sea, great issues between nations at war have always been decided – except in the rarest cases – either by what your army can do against your enemy's territory and national life or else by the fear of what the fleet makes it possible for your army to do.[28]

Seapowers could not defeat landpowers on their own but, in conjunction with allies on land, they could determine the outcomes of wars and the nature of the peace. Although oddly, he did not list *The Principles of Maritime Strategy* among Corbett's books that he thought his students should read, Hannay echoed the point: 'It is a dream that power on the sea can dominate the land. It is valuable because it gives access to the land'.[29]

Even in the eighteenth century, the real debate between the Whigs and the Tories, the bluewater school and their opponents, was about the extent to which the maritime preference needed to be adapted in order to conform to the strategic realities of the time.[30] The essence of British strategy was the constant recalibration of the balance between sea- and landpower.

Britain, Corbett concluded, had been able to develop a style of maritime war which combined naval and military power in a uniquely beneficial way. It had allowed the British to '... become a controlling force in the European system' and to maintain and extend their interests by manipulating the balance of power in Continental Europe. This they had done by the controlled and careful application of maritime power in peace and in war. Because the secret of British success lay in the combination of land- and seapower, Corbett used the word 'maritime' when he reviewed the strategy of seapower rather than the much narrower term 'naval' that Mahan tended to use.[31]

Although most of the rest of his colleagues nonetheless continued to use the word 'naval', this was probably because the Navy, as an institution, was either their target or what they wanted their audiences to think about and nurture. It did not imply that landpower was unimportant for Britain or deny that a constructive balance between land- and seapower was a prerequisite for an effective British strategy and for operational success in 'joint operations'. As Bridge warned:

> Sea power, at any rate in the narrow sense of naval strength, has, as should always be remembered, its limits... Most maritime states are continental and are not likely to be conquered unless land forces are used against them... This brings out the importance of including plans for joint expeditions in a scheme of belligerent action. The mere act of looking at the problems raised will enforce the doctrine that in any great war in which an insular and maritime state may be involved, co-operation between the land and sea services must be frequent.[32]

Naval strategy was about the disposition, movement and immediate purposes of the fleet; these cascaded down from maritime strategy that decided the role of the fleet in relation to land forces. Accordingly, the exact balance to be struck between the naval and the land components of a maritime strategy would depend on general national circumstances (for some nations were clearly more maritime than others) and also on the particular strategic exigencies of the moment. Corbett was at his most interesting on this point when dealing with the Russo-Japanese War. This was a struggle involving one very maritime power, Japan, for the possession of a very maritime prize, namely the peninsula of Korea. Not surprisingly, therefore, the naval element of Japan's strategy would in many cases predominate in a situation in which '... everything turned on the sea factor'. Corbett approved of the way in which the Japanese evolved a joint staff, the detailed mechanics of which rested on this conclusion. He also pointed out that operational priorities between naval and military requirements in what was essentially an amphibious war often had to give precedence to the naval dimension even if this caused tensions with the Army.[33]

Nonetheless, Corbett did not neglect the legitimate demands of the land war, even in a maritime environment. Given the circumstances, he thought, 'it is obvious that a war framed on these lines demands a very accurate co-ordination of the land and sea forces. This is, indeed, the paramount necessity'. Once the Japanese fleet had concentrated,

> ... the movement of the two services goes hand in hand and our standpoint must be one from which the operations both on land and at sea can be kept in view as closely and clearly as possible. The war, in fact becomes essentially amphibious, and so intimately are naval and military operations knit together in a single theatre that the work of the one service is unintelligible apart from that of the other.

Equally obviously, in less maritime conflicts, the land element could be expected to predominate, but in this case the important naval element might need to be articulated and defended.[34]

Like Corbett, Callwell pointed to the American War of Independence, the Crimean campaign of 1856 and the Russo-Japanese War of 1905 as demonstrating the extent to which land campaigns may depend on command of the sea. In the many cases where the military balance ashore depended on reinforcements and supplies coming across the sea, maritime preponderance was essential. But rather more explicitly than did Corbett, Callwell paid equal attention to the help that land forces could offer navies, especially by conducting territorial operations against coaling station bases where an inferior and blockaded fleet had taken refuge. Over and over again, Callwell emphasised how important it was for sea and land forces to cooperate effectively, and if air forces had existed at the time he, like Corbett, would undoubtedly have included them too:

> It has been the purpose of this volume to show how naval preponderance and warfare on land are mutually dependent, if the one is to assert itself conclusively and if the other is to be carried out with vigour and effect. There is an intimate connection between command of the sea and control of the shore. But if the strategical principles involved in this connection are to be put in force to their full extent, if the whole of the machinery is to be set in motion, there must be co-ordination of authority and there must be harmony in the council chambers and in the theatre of operations ... 'United we stand, divided we fall,' is a motto singularly applicable to the navy and army of a maritime nation and of a world-wide empire.[35]

Corbett and his colleagues generally argued that navies and their supporters should accommodate themselves to the simple fact that in the last analysis it was upon the land that mankind's destiny was decided. But, very definitely, this should not mean acceding to the more voracious demands of the Continental school. Corbett and indeed all of the British school approved of the fact that with the paradoxical exception of much of the nineteenth century, the Navy tended to be best favoured in British defence spending.[36]

Maritime vulnerabilities and command of the sea

And it needed to be, for the costs of seapower were high. Seapower is often represented as uniquely cost-effective in that its constituents come naturally and easily from the existence of a large and profitable merchant marine, a prosperous empire and the sophisticated financial system that these both encourage.[37] Indeed, navalists argue that a virtuous circle is at work in the generation of maritime resources. Maritime trade, they point out, produces maritime resources which help create naval strength, leading to maritime supremacy and even better terms of trade. Seapower requires, they say, fewer human resources than large continental armies and greatly reduces the prospect of the homeland being ravaged by foreign invaders. This reinforces the impression that maritime powers can command at sea and dominate foreign shores with a kind of Olympian ease that their less fortunate landbound competitors might envy.[38]

In fact, gaining and maintaining sea control demanded huge resources. Britain's maritime power in the eighteenth and nineteenth centuries depended on an enormous infrastructure. When, in June 1692, Admiral Russel brought 64 English ships of the line and 24 fireships into Torbay, his crews totalled 24,000 men. The effort to support such a vast endeavour can be deduced by the fact that at that time the population of Exeter, the county town of Devon, was a mere 14,000 souls. In the eighteenth century, 'the Navy was by far the largest and most complex of all government services, and indeed by a large margin, the largest industrial organisation in the western world'.[39] In 1809, the Royal Navy comprised 755 ships totalling 500,000 tons but depended on the biggest shipbuilding industry in Europe by far, and a merchant fleet twice the size of the French, four times the size of the Dutch and ten times the size of the Spanish. The Navy's manpower strength peaked at 142,000 in 1810. Seapower may be considered cost-effective, in the sense that it regenerates itself in the long term; in the short term, however, it does not come cheap, and this was generally recognised.

Sometimes Britain's balance of advantage in naval resources was in fact worryingly small. The American War of Independence was an example; in 1782 the Royal Navy comprised 94 ships of the line while its adversaries deployed 146, although they were, admittedly, not concentrated. Britain's inability to maintain an adequate Western Squadron at this time meant that all the naval battles of that conflict were fought in the western hemisphere and this played a significant part in Britain's defeat. The naval balance in the decade before the First World War caused concern too, necessitating new alliances with Japan, France and Russia, and played an important part in the British acceptance of a Continental commitment.

The extent to which the increasing need for massive naval expenditure conflicted with the financial pressures bearing down on 'the weary Titan' and the consequence of this for British naval design, strategy and tactics have recently been authoritatively documented by Jon Sumida[40] who makes the point that Fisher hoped that technological transformation in the shape of fast battleships and, perhaps, submarines, torpedo boats and mines mustered into some kind of 'flotilla defence' could solve the problem.[41] Unfortunately technological developments could also make this problem worse. The advent of sea denial weaponry such as torpedoes, submarines and aircraft (the first two at least then essentially weapons of sea denial) challenged the traditional primacy of the Navy's main weapon system, the battleship – together with its supporting units – in a way which made the struggle for sea control more costly still, at least until the Navy learnt how to absorb this new technology in ways that added to, rather than subtracted from, its offensive capabilities.

The problem of maritime vulnerability was still further aggravated by the fact that the Navy had also to defend the country from potentially ruinous attacks upon its shipping and indeed upon its coast, its naval bases and its possessions overseas. It was the threat to imperial shipping that most exercised the Colomb brothers and the rest of the school, rather than the prospect of invasion. 'The Navy is the 1st, 2nd, 3rd, 4th, 5th . . . *ad infinitum* Line of Defence', proclaimed Admiral Sir Jacky Fisher in 1904. 'If the Navy is not supreme, no army, however large, is of the slightest use. It is not *invasion* we have to fear if our Navy is beaten, it's *starvation!*'[42] This was Sir John Colomb's main message too:

> If the heart and citadel of the Empire is alone protected will it surprise us to hear that, when the Empire is attacked, our enemy prefers cutting our unprotected communications and appropriating our undefended colonies and possessions, to a direct assault upon a 'small island bristling with bayonets'.[43]

Corbett agreed. As far as he was concerned, command of the sea was really about the control of maritime communications; operations aimed at securing them therefore lay at the heart of naval strategy. All of them were well aware of how difficult and profligate in resources the defence of shipping could be. Worse, because the forces required to protect trade or indeed to offer point defence of threatened coasts and bases were largely distinctive, these strategic necessities drained resources away from the main struggle to maintain sea control on the open ocean. Forces had to be kept back or specifically designed against such threats. In Erskine Childers' opinion, Germany before the First World War had this one great advantage over Britain: 'Her hands are free for offence in home waters since she has no distant network of coveted colonies and dependencies on which to dissipate her defensive energies'.[44]

Nonetheless, maintaining sea control was the best and ultimate defence against both types of threat. It remained the only real safeguard against invasion on a large scale. An invasion would require such obvious preparation on the part of the enemy that no British fleet would allow itself to be decoyed away from the main theatre. It would be hazardous indeed for anyone to throw an invasion force across the Channel without first securing command of the sea. Pushing troop transports through waters swarming with enemy torpedo craft and submarines, thought Mr Balfour (the prime minister) in 1905, would be simply 'the enterprise of a lunatic'. Of course a defending army on the British coastline was necessary, but its strength should be based on the assumption that the Navy was the first line of defence and not on the desperate alternative that the Navy did not exist or was somewhere else at the critical time.[45] Sir John's views on this were powerfully reinforced by the historically-based observations of his brother. Philip Colomb showed that some form of blockade had always been the main defence against invasion. Furthermore, in the whole period from 1690 onwards the supposition that a substantial invasion could be successfully mounted without first securing command of the sea had constantly showed itself to be a dangerous error.[46] Denying the enemy the capacity to develop

76 *Geoffrey Till*

that degree of command was therefore the best way of securing the country against invasion.

Command of the sea was also seen to have the same beneficial consequences for the protection of shipping. Apart from a brief and rather unsatisfactory analysis of the relative merits of convoy,[47] Philip Colomb does not deal directly with the challenges of the defence of shipping. His brother, however, was almost obsessed with the need to stimulate the Admiralty into constructive thought and policy on the issue. He argued that Britain's expanding overseas trade and overseas possessions meant that the country was highly vulnerable to such attack and that it was supremely important to do something about it.[48]

In consequence of growing public alarm the Admiralty did indeed devote increasing attention to the problem but started from a very low intellectual base characterised by woolly thinking and a set of assumptions which Bryan Ranft called 'breathtaking in their complacency'.[49] The problem was that naval policy was dominated by a set of unquestioned conclusions, namely that offensive measures were more effective than defensive ones, that trade routes needed to be protected rather than the ships that moved along them and that the main problem of the future would be French or Russian surface commerce raiders. Mahanian thinking was bowdlerised into the assumption that the possession of command of the sea would resolve all the issues.

But, to be fair, the Admiralty were not alone in that assumption. Corbett also started with the assumption that the ultimate defence was the maintenance of command of the sea since this would force an adversary to take the ineffective route of a direct *guerre de course* rather than the much more powerful commercial blockade based upon sea control. Accordingly, he maintained that 'A plan of war which has the destruction of trade for its primary object implies in the party using it an inferiority at sea. Had he superiority, his object would be to convert that superiority to a working command by battle or blockade'.[50] Maintaining command of the sea would therefore reduce the level of threat to manageable proportions and provide cover for the forces engaged in the direct defence of shipping from enemy forces that managed to leak through the British blockade. Corbett advocated the patrolling of terminal areas rather than hunting commerce raiders on the open ocean: 'Where the carcase is, there will the eagles be gathered together!' He was sceptical about the value of the traditional convoy-and-escort means of direct defence in the new conditions of steamships, writing, 'It now comes doubtful whether the additional security which convoys afforded is sufficient to outweigh their economical drawbacks and their liability to cause strategical disturbance'.[51]

The same uncertainties may be seen in Bridge, for after a long and quite thoughtful discussion of the balance to be struck between the (offensive) cruising warfare means of defending shipping against marauding commerce raiders on the one hand and traditional convoy-and-escort on the other, he concluded that in the days of steam and iron ships, 'we have no evidence collected

The emergence of a British school? 77

under modern conditions on which we can base a conclusion; and preference for one method rather than another will to a great extent be dictated by circumstances, some of a military, some of a commercial character'.[52]

It is hard to resist Bryan Ranft's own conclusion on this matter: 'The near-defeat of 1917 was due not to previous lack of thought or to the allocation of inadequate resources to the protection of trade, but to the poor quality of the thought and consequent misuse of the resources'.[53]

Clearly British maritime strategists of this period were at their least effective in this area. Far from helping avert the Royal Navy's difficulties in handling the U-boat threat of the First World War, they may arguably even have contributed to them.

Limiting liability and increasing cost-effectiveness

One of the great advantages of sea power as an arm of national strategy, Corbett thought, was its particular utility in situations of limited conflict. Where the protagonists were not neighbours, where distance made retaliation difficult, and where geography helped isolate or at least contain the extent of any fighting, any conflict could be limited. The nation with command of the sea was in the best position to choose how much or how little of the conflict it wanted. Maritime powers could limit their liability in ways that others could not, for as Sir Francis Bacon remarked, '... this much is certain, that he that commands the sea is at great liberty, and may take as much and as little of the war as he will. Whereas those that be strongest by land are many times nevertheless in great straits'.[54]

As far as Corbett was concerned, eighteenth-century experience showed that power at sea provided opportunities for the British to make limited interventions for limited objectives in unlimited wars. Through this capacity to exert influence on the continent of Europe from outside, the British, unlike many of their more land-bound competitors, had been able to develop a uniquely businesslike approach to the otherwise messy and wasteful processes of war. They generally tried to avoid expensive large-scale military commitments to the continent of Europe, and its ferocious wars, but there was always the danger of getting sucked into Continental conflicts anyhow. Thus Smollett, at the beginning of the Seven Years' War:

> [M]any friends of their country exclaimed against the projected army of observation in Germany, as the commencement of a ruinous continental war, which it was neither the interest of the nation to undertake, nor in their power to maintain, without starving the operations by sea, and in America, founded on British principles.[55]

'British principles' centred on the acceptance of limited objectives. Their aim was merely to act as a balancing power, and not for the country to be major protagonist in Continental struggles fought for ideological aggrandisement or territorial expansion in Europe. Vainglory and total objectives, especially on the continent of Europe, were to be avoided for the British were manipulating, not transforming, the European balance of power. To be effective, seapower had to be exercised with restraint, just because in the words of Eyre Crowe, the Senior Clerk in the Foreign Office in 1907, 'Sea power is more potent ... No one now disputes it'. However, it was 'but natural that the Power of the State supreme at sea should inspire universal jealousy and fear, and be ever exposed to the danger of being overthrown by a general combination of the world'.[56] Only moderate behaviour would keep that possibility in check.

Outside Europe it was a question of limited operations for limited gains at, hopefully, limited cost. Indeed, in many cases, though mainly in the eighteenth century, there was the hope of actual profit, through the acquisition of other people's ships, colonies and commerce. Although this could be presented as a strategic assault on the enemy's war-making capacity, eighteenth-century British society still looked on war, at least partly, as a matter of profit and loss. There was something very commercial about the appearance, in monthly editions of *The Gentleman's Magazine*, of lists of British ships lost and French and Spanish ones taken, complete with details of their cargoes. There was nothing reprehensible about this, since mercantile prosperity and everything that went with it was what Britain stood for, after all.

Usually, the landpower necessary for the defeat of Continental foes was provided in the main by equally necessary Continental allies. Preferably, it was a case of fighting the war in Europe to the last Prussian, or Russian, or Frenchman, as the case might be. This would leave the British free to conduct their maritime and expeditionary campaign outside Europe. Maritime power was usually a balancing, perhaps compensating, factor, rather than one which could decide the fate of empires in its own right. Thus Pitt in 1796:

> While the violence of France has been over-running so great a part of Europe, and everywhere carrying desolation in its progress, your naval exertions have enabled you to counterbalance their successes, by acquisitions in different parts of the globe, and to pave the way for the restoration of peace to your allies, on terms which their own strength might have been unable to procure.[57]

Of course this was not always possible. Indeed the period under review was an example of a time when the British could not find enough Continental Europeans ready and able to do their fighting for them. As the campaigns of Marlborough and Wellington both demonstrate, this had also happened before.

Generally, though, the aim of British maritime strategy was a combination of the financial support of Continental allies and the exertion of maritime pressure through blockade, the threat of amphibious landings, attacks and raids on threatened coastlines and through the seizure of their adversaries' far-flung colonies and bases. The British preferred their main theatres of operation and their objectives to be essentially maritime in character: ports, peninsulas, colonies and bases. These were desired for the commercial value their retention would provide, for the damage their loss would do to the adversary's war economy, and sometimes, as in the 1801 Treaty of Amiens, as end-of-war bargaining counters that could be traded back to offset comparative failures in Europe. These 'British Objects' were carefully distinguished from the Continental preoccupations of William III, and the first two Georges. They were, usually, distant rather than close, finite and containable, and so an expeditionary approach seemed entirely appropriate for their achievement.[58] The maritime strategy that Corbett advocated therefore required the kind of Army that could work with the Navy to conquer overseas territories and to outflank landbound adversaries with amphibious operations, '... more or less upon the European seaboard designed, not for permanent conquest, but as a method of disturbing our enemy's plans and strengthening the hands of our allies and our own position'.[59] Corbett considered this an immensely cost-effective approach to the business of war. Command of the sea, and the opportunities it provided, explained how it was after all, '[t]hat a small country [Britain] with a weak army should have been able to gather to herself the most desirable regions of the earth, and to gather them at the expense of the greatest military Powers . . .'.[60]

Command of the sea and decisive battle

The advantages of command of the sea were summarised by Admiral Sir Cyprian Bridge like this:

> It enables the nation which possesses it to attack its foes where it pleases and where they seem most vulnerable. At the same time it gives its possessor security against serious counter-attacks, and affords to his maritime commerce the most efficient protection that can be devised. It is, in fact the main object of naval warfare.[61]

While command of the sea was ideally won or maintained by decisive battle, this was often not easily or quickly achieved against a reluctant enemy; in such cases, a blockade could be imposed either to neutralise that enemy or to force him to battle. High levels of such command greatly facilitated the strategic use of the sea, but were not always possible and sometimes were not necessary.

Command of the sea implied its control as a medium of communication; the enemy's commercial and military shipping could be attacked, and yours protected. Your military forces could be moved about in safety and his attacked.

The obvious method of achieving command of the sea was to *force* a battle on the enemy's naval forces, destroy them and decide the matter once

80 *Geoffrey Till*

and for all. The Royal Navy was always attracted by the notion of the decisive battle as the optimum means of winning command of the sea. Their view just before the First World War was usefully summarised for the benefit of the 1902 Colonial Conference:

> The primary object of the British Navy is not to defend anything, but to attack the fleets of the enemy, and by defeating them to afford protection to British Dominions, supplies and commerce. This is the ultimate aim ... The traditional role of the Royal Navy is not to act on the defensive, but to prepare to attack the force which threatens – in other words to assume the offensive.[62]

But Corbett warned that this 'old British creed', although generally admirable and effective, could be taken to excess. In some circumstances, it could lead to a distraction from the real aim of the war. He also pointed out that Britain's adversaries, whose naval forces were normally weaker, often sensibly sought to avoid battle with the Royal Navy. This being so, the British needed to be on their guard against the danger of trying too hard in this direction, lest such purist aspirations undermine their practical capacity to use the sea as fully as they often needed to in the meantime.[63]

Over and over again, Corbett sought to remind sailors that command of the sea should not be seen as an end in itself, and that it was a relative concept. Absolute command of the sea was little more than a Kantian ideal; high levels of command of the sea were extremely difficult to achieve – and to a surprising extent unnecessary. Even in a profoundly maritime war, all sorts of useful military manoeuvres could be conducted without it. In 1903, the Russians decided '... they could succeed without getting the command. By merely keeping it in dispute they would gain time enough to bring their vastly superior military strength to bear'. It was equally proper for the Japanese to conclude that in such circumstances they could conduct amphibious operations without securing command of the sea first.[64]

Corbett was concerned about the unremitting pursuit of command-through-battle for four reasons. Firstly it might well prove nugatory in those all too common situations where a weaker adversary declined the invitation to his own execution. Secondly, it might not work for good operational reasons. Thirdly, concentrating on the rigorous requirements of securing command could easily damage a navy's capacity to exploit that command, particularly through amphibious operations, but also through campaigns against, or in defence of, shipping. Command of the sea in itself did not win wars or decide political outcomes, but being able to exploit (or sometimes deny) that command very well might.[65]

Fourthly, and perhaps most importantly, the pursuit of the decisive battle could so easily make it difficult for sailors and others to see what seapower was really about. Thus:

We require for the guidance of our naval policy and naval action something of wider vision than the current conception of naval strategy, something that will keep before our eyes not merely the enemy's fleets or the great routes of commerce, or the command of the sea, but also the relations of naval policy and action to the whole area of diplomatic and military effort.[66]

All too often, he thought, the simple-minded (in uniform and out of it) confused the incidence of dramatic battle with the role and importance of seapower. They were not the same thing at all.

It is important, however, not to exaggerate the extent of Corbett's scepticism about command of the sea and decisive battle. He acknowledged that the concerted pursuit of these two central objectives of 'Mahanian' maritime strategy was usually valid. It was only his willingness to say that sometimes it might not be that was later to get him into trouble with the Admiralty.[67]

In the same way it is too easy simply to condemn the views of the *guerre a outrance* school often said to be represented by Custance. In fact Custance warned against the Admiralty's picturing, '... to themselves one particular sort of war in which great fleets and squadrons are alone to bear a part, whereas ... there have been in the past various sorts of wars, each having its peculiarities and requiring special treatment'. He was concerned that there was so much concentration on preparing for the decisive battle that insufficient steps had been taken to handle the threats that might well emerge in the meantime from smaller forces able to escape blockading forces, for example to prey on British shipping. Although the concentration of force was 'a first principle in strategy' it needed to be applied with imagination.[68] Custance criticised the Fisher Admiralty for its preoccupation with too few, big, fast battleships, because he thought making them fast undermined their individual fighting power and indicated '... an attitude of mind defensive rather than offensive' that was 'destructive of the true spirit ... and traditions of the Navy'. But this was a tactical point, not an operational one. Custance was not saying that the pursuit of battle was the only thing that mattered – far from it.[69]

Some particularly important contributions to this debate were also made by Philip Colomb, in his exploration of the idea of the 'fleet-in-being'. This concept arose largely in connection with the debate about the seriousness with which the prospects of invasion were to be taken. One issue here was the *degree* to which an invasion would need to depend on command of the sea. Continentalists, arguing for substantial defensive army forces ashore, doubted that absolute control was necessary for an invasion and that temporary and geographically very limited forms of control might be sufficient. Accordingly an invasion force might well be rushed across the Channel while the Navy was asleep in its hammocks or away doing something else. The bluewater school rejected this possibility. Colomb went furthest arguing that an invasion would be impossible, even if command of the sea was in dispute. Accordingly, even an inferior British naval force kept 'in being' would deter an invasion. He argued that it had done exactly this in the famous and controversial 1690 example provided by the unfortunate Lord Torrington, and that there were other examples of the fate of would-be invaders who tried to invade somewhere whilst fighting for sea control at the same time. Colomb cited the Spanish Armada and the 1866 battle of Lissa as examples of this and, had he been able to, would no doubt have pointed to the Battle of Midway as well.[70]

Corbett, ever the proponent of the judicious compromise, was concerned that this argument could likewise be taken too far, but built on it to point out the potentialities of an active and imaginative naval defensive.[71]

Amphibious operations, the projection of power ashore and the joint approach

The capacity to project power ashore (and of course the ability to prevent the enemy from doing the same) was the real payoff for the effort to secure or maintain command of the sea. Based on evidence such as the capture of Havana in 1762, Wolfe's Canadian operations in the Seven Years' War, Wellington's Peninsular campaign – surely the quintessential combined operation – and the Crimean War, Corbett and his colleagues argued that properly conducted amphibious operations could indeed be the means by which sea powers could help decide the outcome of wars. Accordingly, it was essential that the conduct of amphibious operations be thoroughly studied and understood, but, lamented Aston,

> Amphibious strategy, or the combined strategy of fleets and armies, treated as a special subject, has not yet received the attention which its importance deserves, and the Japanese have so far been the only exponents of the art on a large scale under the conditions of modern warfare.[72]

It was particularly important for the British to get to grips with the subject since their war strategy '... must always be "amphibious" in the sense that it must consider the armies and the fleets of both sides'.[73]

Maritime supremacy allowed strikes at the enemy's weakest points with strategic and potentially war-winning effect. So, thought Sir John Colomb, once the Navy had secured command of the sea, then the nation's main weapon of offence – the Army – could be set for action. A small but highly-trained force striking out of the blue at a vital spot could, it was believed, produce a strategic effect out of all proportion to its size. The Navy would provide the necessary maritime conditions for such enterprises and would act as the 'shield to guard'; the Army, properly supported, would be the 'spear to strike'.[74]

Projecting power ashore, to use modern terminology, could take any number of forms. It could be in support of economic blockade. It could be

The emergence of a British school? 83

characterised by naval bombardments – or simply the threat to conduct one. It could mean limited raids to destroy irritating forts on Chinese rivers. It could mean the conduct of expeditions against exposed parts of the enemy's coastline or his distant possessions. At the top end of the scale, it could even mean large-scale assaults intended to determine or reverse the course of a major continental war. The common element in many if not all of these was that they depended on dominance of the sea, and so were a means by which a maritime power like Britain could seize the strategic initiative and dictate the course of play, even against far stronger land powers.

Few members of the British school therefore made serious objection to Bridge's central point, that whatever some soldiers from Continental countries might think, it was still true that, '... the strategic principle that command of the sea is an indispensable preliminary to over-sea invasion'.[75] But the success of this approach also depended on the development of a specialised amphibious capacity. Callwell and others, particularly in the Army or the Marines, were well aware of the challenges posed to amphibious operations by modern military technology in the shape of heavy machine-guns, coastal artillery, fortifications and improved land communications (roads, railways, the internal combustion engine) which allowed for rapid responsive movements by the invaded adversary. These issues were all thoroughly investigated in the course of the debate about the feasibility of landing operations against Germany.[76] Callwell's own hesitations about contested landings against first-class opposition were clear. Modern difficulties did not necessarily imply that:

> Opposed landings are now impracticable when the force which can be disembarked at one time is greatly superior to that drawn up on shore. If the attacking army is prepared to accept heavy loss, it may succeed. But the operation is not to be ventured on with a light heart, or one to be undertaken without counting the cost and without accepting the risk of disaster.[77]

Accordingly it was essential that the Navy afford all the help that it could, particularly in making the landing operation itself as fast as possible. Speed was essential. Building on his analysis of the 1891 Chile war, Aston was quite clear about this since '... every minute lost may increase the strength of the opposing force, and the improvement of modern weapons has rendered a landing in the face of serious opposition almost an impossible task'.[78] Such concerns were not of course new. Molyneux after all had devoted much thought to an exploration of such issues as the best command arrangements, the advantages of tactical if not strategic surprise, the value of deceptions and feints and the tactical handling of the landing operation itself, and so forth.[79]

Modern conditions were however thought to give these issues a particular salience and emphasised the need for amphibious forces to develop the means to cope. Embarkation and disembarkation operations were complex and required special skills, training and equipment. Aston emphasised the value of portable artillery, and clear communications and signalling between all parts of the force. Furse made the point that:

> An expedition across the seas differs from other military operations, inasmuch as an army does not step over a frontier or advance from a selected base of operations, but is thrown into a hostile country, and all the combatants, materials and stores have to be conveyed thereto from a distance in ships. Operations of this nature demand very thorough preparations.[80]

The real point was that supply, logistics, strategic transportation and all the rest were either specialist requirements for amphibious operations, or general military ones that took on particular force in an amphibious context.

The Navy needed to take all of them seriously. For instance, Callwell and Aston emphasised the need for the Navy to take along shrapnel rather than their standard armour-piercing shells, because the latter would not be much good against fortifications. Again, the need for speedy and protected disembarkation, they thought, might well require small armoured gunboats able to close the beaches, but these were exactly the type of vessels likely to be neglected by a Navy totally preoccupied with the task of securing command of the sea against first-class opposition. The implications of this were clear. But would Fisher and his colleagues take these requirements sufficiently to heart? The unavoidable tension between the two requirements of securing command of the sea and supporting an amphibious operation explains why the British school accepted the notion that it was best for the Navy first to win command of the sea and then concentrate on helping the Army.

This pointed to the need for close cooperation and understanding at every level between the Army and the Navy (and Aston added air forces to this as well). This aspiration echoed Molyneux's earlier comment that, 'The Fleet and Army, acting in consort, seem to be the natural Bulwark of these Kingdoms'. This quotation is very familiar and often quoted (nearly always wrongly!) but is held nicely to exemplify a British way in warfare that worked best when there was a synergistic relationship between the Navy and the Army. Strategically, the two services were seen as complementary; both could serve the interests of the other. Historically and strategically the Army could be used to protect the Low Countries, preventing their vital ports from falling into the hands of hostile navies – an imperative ranging from Elizabeth's war against Spain in the sixteenth century to the Passchendaele campaign in the twentieth.[81] Indeed, interventions on the mainland were occasionally justified on the grounds that this would protect Britain's position at sea by preventing the emergence of a hostile power or coalition strong enough to generate a dangerous *maritime* threat.[82]

The emergence of a British school? 85

The same could be true at the operational and tactical levels too. In the eighteenth century success in 'conjunct operations' depended on a:

> ... perfect harmony that has uninterruptedly subsisted between the fleet and the army from our first setting out, indeed it is doing injustice to both to mention them as two corps, since each has endeavoured with the most constant and cheerful emulation to render it but one.[83]

It wasn't always like this of course, but it happened more often than Michael Howard's famous denunciation of such operations might lead one to suppose.[84] Such successes led Callwell and Corbett to argue strongly that the country needed both a strong Navy and an effective Army, for offensive and defensive purposes. Callwell put it like this:

> The gladiator who enters the arena equipped with nothing but a shield may fail to win the plaudits of the amphitheatre ... When a nation appeals to the final tribunal of actual combat with any confidence of securing a favourable verdict, it must set up for itself some loftier ideal than that of merely averting a catastrophe or warding off the blows of its antagonist. It may assume a posture of defence; but it must be prepared to strike, and if the struggle is to be brought rapidly to a satisfactory conclusion, it must be prepared to strike hard. The ability of amphibious force to inflict grave injury upon the foe is usually immense. The capabilities of purely naval force to cause the adversary damage is often limited.[85]

Even when it came to defending against invasion, Corbett emphasised:

> ... the Navy may give an emphatic repudiation to the idea that it regards resistance to invasion as a purely naval problem. It regards it essentially as a problem of combined strategy, and desires nothing so much as a thorough and reasoned understanding between the two services as to their respective functions in that behalf.[86]

So, whether it was a question of defending the country against invasion, or of invading other people, success depended upon a degree of mutual understanding and cooperation of course that needed to be developed in peacetime, not improvised in war.[87]

This had implications for the kind of Army the British school thought the country needed. It was not the static, heavy Army devoted to the defence of the homeland advocated by the 'bricks and mortar school,'[88] but neither was it one that could only garrison India. Instead, the Army truest to the British expeditionary impulse was of a light and expeditionary sort, sensitive to the need for the closest cooperation with the Navy.

The vision of German grenadiers in the British service standing stiffly to attention as they were conveyed in little boats across the Hudson to seize

New York in 1776[89] suggests that the Army was not always prepared to adapt its standard operating procedures to expeditionary realities however – and this often led to difficulties. With the mechanisation of war at the end of the nineteenth century moreover this problem got a good deal worse as the proportion of 'heavy metal' (machine guns, large calibre artillery, ultimately tanks) steadily rose. Awareness of the increasingly heavy requirements of Continental war together with growing differences in view of the strategic situation in Europe made for a growing tension between this model of the Army and the older, lighter, expedition-capable version favoured by the maritime school.

Notes

1 Clarke and Thursfield (1897) p. 2.
2 Cobden (1862).
3 Rodger (2004) p. 207.
4 Quoted in Colomb (1896) p. 134.
5 Fisher (1919b) pp. 74, 182–3.
6 The first that needs to be consulted is still Schurman (1965) and also (1981). See also the editorial introductions in Corbett (1911) by Eric Grove and Callwell (1996a) by Colin Gray.
7 Molyneux (1759) Part 1, pp. 2, 3–4.
8 Ibid.
9 Gat (1992) p. 205.
10 Colomb (1896) p. vi and (1899) p. v.
11 Ibid. p. 197; the highwayman analogy is in Schurman (1965) p. 55.
12 Colomb (1899) p. 452.
13 Lord Carnarvon quoted in Schurman (1965) p. 32.
14 Quoted in ibid. p. 52.
15 See Colin Gray's introduction in Callwell (1996).
16 Clowes (1902) p. vii.
17 Bridge (1907) p. viii.
18 Custance (1907) pp. vii–viii.
19 Ibid. p. 290 and preface.
20 Hannay (1913) pp. 246–7.
21 Schurman (1965) pp. 13–14.
22 Fisher (1919a) p. 212.
23 Hannay (1913) p. 173.
24 Bridge (1907) p. 212.
25 Bryan Ranft 'Sir Julian Corbett' in Till (1984) p. 40.
26 Corbett (1917) Vol. I, pp. ix, 345–7 and (1988) pp. 3–9.
27 Corbett (1907) Vol. I, p. 5.
28 Corbett (1988) pp. 15–16.
29 Hannay (1913) p. 249.
30 Rodger (2004) p. 178.
31 Corbett (1917) Vol. I, p. 6. Corbett (1988) p. xxv.
32 Bridge (1907) pp. 174–6 ff.
33 Corbett (1914) Vol. I, pp. 17, 174–5, 328.
34 Ibid. pp. 68, 187.
35 Callwell (1996) p. 444. Colin Gray's introduction is very useful.

The emergence of a British school? 87

36 Some interesting statistics on the balance between spending on land and sea forces may be found in French (1990) p. 227.
37 This is the burden of Padfield (1999).
38 This is the 'naval myth' explored in Rodger (2004) pp. 48, 178, 235–6.
39 Duffy (1992a) p. 66. Rodger (1986) p. 29.
40 Sumida (1989) esp. pp. 329–39.
41 This latter is the burden of Lambert (1999).
42 Quoted in Marder (1940) p. 65.
43 Colomb (1880) p. 41.
44 Childers op. cit. p. 282.
45 Colomb ibid. pp. 54–5.
46 Colomb (1896) pp. 194–229.
47 Ibid. pp. 230–58.
48 Gat (1992) p. 206.
49 Ranft (1977) p. 4.
50 Corbett (1911) p. 236.
51 Ibid. p. 245.
52 Bridge (1907) p. 145.
53 Ranft (1977) p. 1.
54 Corbett (1988) pp. 53–8.
55 Smollett (1760) p. 423.
56 Cited in Tracey (1991) pp. 101–2. For a similar view in 1763 by the duke of Bedford, see Rodger (2004) p. 287.
57 W. Pitt, speech of 6 October 1796. Pitt (1806) Vol. 2, p. 429.
58 Baugh (1988a) p. 42.
59 Corbett (1988) p. 66.
60 Ibid. pp. 57–8.
61 Bridge (1910) p. 84.
62 Cited in Kennedy (1989) p. 168.
63 Corbett (1988) p. 167.
64 Corbett (1914) Vol. I, pp. 46, 73; Corbett (1988) pp. 103–4.
65 Ibid. p. 91.
66 Ibid. p. 164.
67 See the infamous Admiralty disclaimer inserted into Vol. III of Corbett. Ranft (1993) provides the background. See also Clarke (1931) and Anon (1931) pp. 242–3.
68 Barfleur (1907) pp. 113, 124, 130–1.
69 Ibid. pp. 189, 228.
70 MS 59 PP 136.
71 MS; FN 59, on p. 137 SP FN 41 on p. 182.
72 Aston (1914) p. vii.
73 Ibid. p. 167.
74 Marder (1940) p. 70.
75 Bridge (1907) p. 167.
76 'British Military Action in Case of War with Germany' August 1905, W.O.106/46/E2/6, PRO. These matters are thoroughly discussed in the excellent Massam (1995). See also Gooch (1974) p. 279. I am indebted to Thomas W. Crecca for reminding me of some of these issues.
77 Callwell (1996) p. 360.
78 Aston (1911) pp. 37–8.
79 I am grateful to Christian Liles for reminding me of Molyneux's operational focus.
80 Furse (1897) Vol. 1, p. 84.

81 But for an interesting challenge to this view see T124 (1940) pp. 44–73.
82 Kennedy (1983) p. 5. For scepticism that this was really a sustainable argument, see Rodger (1992) pp. 39–55.
83 Rear-Adm George Pocock, quoted in Rodger (2004) p. 288.
84 Howard (1972) p. 172. For an opposing view see Syrett (1983) p. 51.
85 Callwell (1905) pp. 168–70.
86 Corbett, 'Memorandum on Invasion' presented to the CID Sub-Committee on Invasion, 4 Dec 1907. Corbett MSS, Box 6. NMM. I am indebted to Thomas Crecca for this reference.
87 Callwell (1905) p. 5.
88 Marder (1940) pp. 68–9.
89 Hibbert (1990) p. 121. Admittedly, the British themselves sat down, bayonets fixed!

5 1914–18: the proof of the pudding

Andrew Gordon

The task of measuring the Royal Navy's success in the war which started on 4 August 1914 must be situated in the context of the sort of war that was expected and planned for, and in the light of the Service's two related but specialist seapower tasks: firstly, achieving fleet v. fleet dominance, preferably by decisive battle; and secondly, behind the shield of fleet supremacy, maintaining the free flow of British communications with the Empire, with allies, and with trading partners in general. If the Navy failed in either of those tasks, Britain could be assumed to lose. In both the fields of decisive fleet battle and of defending the sealanes, the Royal Navy had matchless historical experience, but in 1914 that experience had been lying fallow for 100 years, and in the intervening generations the naval seascape had been transformed by far-reaching technological and strategical changes, and by the small-scale peacetime mundanities of servicing a global maritime empire. The issue in 1914 would be: how far would the old 'creaking timbers' methods and doctrines be appropriate in this new world of H.G. Wellsian war machines, and would the Navy be hazarding its supremacy more by remembering them or by forgetting them? Was it even conscious of the choice?

By 1815 the Royal Navy had been at war for 50 of the past 75 years. Its main fleets were the benchmarks by which naval power was measured. Its officer corps had come to understand, through long, and sometimes painful, trial and error, that combat by its very nature requires a degree of judicious extemporisation. They had learnt to exploit the vagaries of battle as *ad hoc* force multipliers, instead of fearing them as obstacles to central control, and therefore to be resisted. Admiral Sir John Jervis ('the great and good Earl of St Vincent', in Nelson's words) said that 'The great talent is to take prompt advantage of disorder in the enemy fleet, whether caused by shifts of wind or accidents, or his deficiency in practical seamanship'. What he meant was: 'never miss a chance to throw grit in the enemy's machinery'; and behind this statement was the towering assumption that the British Fleet would be less dependent than the enemy on adherence to a precise plan, could extemporise more casually, and would be less compromised by – indeed would be better able to exploit – the disruption of plans once battle had commenced. In the light of this doctrine we can easily see how Jervis's approval of Nelson's famously disobedient manoeuvre at the Battle off Cape St Vincent falls into place – indeed its disobedience is diminished by knowledge of Jervis's doctrine (although not all his subordinates shared in the 'community of thought', a notable dissenter being Jervis's own flag captain). In musical terms, the fleet with the confidence to play jazz was much better equipped for the chaos of battle than one that tried to follow a scripted score. It makes perfect, timeless sense.[1]

But in terms of doctrine, the fleet was at risk of becoming a victim of its own catastrophic success. St Vincent's hard-earned doctrinal insight had little relevance to the Operations Other Than War which occupied the Navy for the next 90 years. With Britain's global maritime security secure, the Royal Navy set about suppressing slavery, punishing warlords, relieving disasters, charting coastlines, exploring the polar extremities and supporting expeditionary warfare – that is, no fewer than 235 'out of area' projections of military power from the sea in Queen Victoria's lifetime.

As naval officers, these men were less concerned with the application of naval force at sea than with the maintenance of authority ashore. They were the *inheritors*, rather than the *winners* of dominance, and the criteria by which they were rewarded inevitably changed, just as the cultural context within which the Navy had to exist and prosper was also very different. The Military Division of the Most Honourable Order of the Bath was created by Henry IV as an Arthurian reward for prowess on the battlefield. By the 1890s they were scratching about to find enough people to keep the thing going. In 1893 a KCB was offered to the C-in-C Mediterranean, who modestly demurred, on the grounds that to give one to an officer who had not fought a battle would be to 'drive a coach and horses'[2] through the regulations (anyway, he had a baronetcy already). The First Lord of the Admiralty, Earl Spencer, told him that the Duke of Cambridge feared that the military division would die out if the rules were not bent, and that the Prince of Wales wanted him to have a KCB.[3] In the end they settled for a GCB (a Civil Division upgrade).

That cameo exchange of letters illustrates the dearth of senior combat experience in the mainstream fleets and army units towards the end of Victoria's reign. A happy circumstance, of course; but a symptom of the difficulties officers were having in distinguishing themselves in the traditional warrior manner, and of the fact that the rules for professional advancement were no longer governed by the harsh integrity of combat.

In fact a large fleet in peacetime can be so busy just existing that the reasons for its existence keep getting pushed to the bottom of the Admiral's pending tray:

> The complex problem of running an army [= fleet] at all is liable to occupy his mind and skill so completely that it is very easy to forget

what it is being run for. The difficulties encountered in the administration, discipline, maintenance and supply of a fair-sized town are enough to occupy the senior officer to the exclusion of any thinking about his real business: the conduct of war.[4]

So then as now, there was plenty to keep Victorian senior officers focused on their immediate foregrounds, and with which to measure their supposed efficiency, without an enemy in the offing. And seismic changes in culture were taking place. The role of officers was 'urbanised'. Historically a sort of nautical squire with patrician obligations towards almost familial followers, the naval officer now had to manage a relationship increasingly defined by contract and by complex legalities – and whose keynote was standardisation.

Meanwhile, and most obviously, there occurred the Revolution in Military Affairs which came with industrialisation. Within 40 or 50 years the Service assimilated staggering material changes – changes which made obsolete the former technologies of sea warfare. First iron, then steel, compound engines, water tube boilers, electricity, locomotive torpedoes, breech-loading rifles, and ultimately turbines and wireless telegraphy were all absorbed into the Fleet. Instead of lapsing into decline, as the laws of chance might have dictated, Britain's industrial maturity enabled the Navy to ride the switchback and even reaffirm its superiority.

The mechanisation of propulsion prompted the development of 'Steam Tactics', which came to be widely known in the Service as the 'goose step'. Geometrical fleet evolutions, choreographed by a stupendous array of flag, semaphore and later wireless signals, all but supplanted the old fashioned casual ideas of combat. Among other unNelsonic criteria (such as paintwork and ceremonial), ships became graded by how efficiently they could perform the 'goose-step'. As early as 1861 a Captain could write to his Admiral father: 'It is no use imagining that steam ships can only form as sailing ships used to do . . . for by adhering to those old ideas . . . we are throwing away the advantages that steam has given us'.[5] *The Manoeuvring Book* of 1874 actually contained the assertion that 'To work a Fleet at speed in the closest order is now admitted as the chief aim of the naval tactician'[6] – a conceit which (if its applicability can be stretched so far) could be said to shed light on the management of the Grand Fleet at Jutland in 1916.

Taking advantage of the enormous fallow capacity of the alphabetical *Signal Book*, the Victorian tacticians tried to ritualise the Fleet's concept of battle in the way that ballroom dancing was intended to ritualise courtship: they were trying to regulate the naturally erratic. The Fleet's preparedness to dispense with the inexact methods which had served it well in the (now) distant past, the sophistication of its signalling and its systematisation of fleetwork were universally admired. It dovetailed easily into Victorian social mores of deference, obedience and tidiness; and notwithstanding some dissent from within the Service, was advanced by three colossus-like

Commanders-in-Chief of Britain's showcase fleet – the Mediterranean: Sir William ('Pincher') Martin in the early 1860s, Sir Geoffrey Phipps Hornby (who wrote the above-quoted letter to his father) in the late 1870s, and Sir Michael Culme-Seymour in the mid-1890s – the latter of whose subordinates included most of the future trainers of the Edwardian Navy. By 1890 or 1900 the Navy was the world's exemplar in how to embrace technological change and harness industrialisation.

The assumption that the newly mechanised fleet – the sublime product of rational, scientific, cutting-edge technology – must be managed in combat by rational, scientific, 'Newton's Clock' methods, was easy to believe and difficult to resist. One may reflect that the advent of new technology in peacetime appears to discredit existing empirically-learned doctrine, and any officer who harks back to the 'old' ways of combat – in this case to the winning ways of the old wooden Navy – risks the charge of Luddism and Flat Earthism, and might even endanger his career prospects. Still, naval officers are an irascible lot, and needless to say there were dissenters who feared that combat doctrine was being commandeered and corrupted by systems lobbyists. They saw the communicators as being allowed to define fleet practices in the light of the capacity of the *Signal Book* and no longer by the realistic limits of signalling in the confusion and dislocations of combat; and we all know that unless restrained, volume always expands to meet capacity. Captain John Arbuthnot Fisher predicted that in battle 'the *Signal Book* will be practically useless. In fact the use of signals at such a time would be fraught with danger. They would fetter the action and diminish the responsibility of the captains'.[7] The most deep-thinking critics perceived that there is an inverse law between robust doctrine and the need for communicating, that heavy signalling must be a symptom of doctrinal deficiency, and even that the mere promise of signalling is likely to foster a neglect of doctrine. In the dozen years between Hornby and Culme-Seymour, the dissidents found a leader, nearly secured reform, and then imploded in spectacular disaster.

The man who emerged as the champion of the would-be fundamentalisers was Vice-Admiral Sir George Tryon. He was an old friend and shipmate of Jacky Fisher, and they used each other as sounding boards over a period of years. He had an instinctive understanding of the problems associated with signals intensity and was the first to try, in a slightly disorganised way, to articulate them. There were two particular practical handicaps which triggered his interest in tactical reform. First, he saw that 'it would be impossible to maintain an adequate staff of signalmen in exposed conditions'; and second, 'the delay occasioned by having to wait till signals were repeated and answered, even supposing it could be done, would be unendurable'.[8]

Shortly after taking command of the Mediterranean Fleet in 1891 he sent to the Admiralty three memoranda on 'A System of Fleet Manoeuvres With and Without Signals', for distribution around seagoing flag officers, and attached his covering explanation. Here are some keynote extracts:[9]

3   Signal masts and halliards, signalmen, helm signals and speed signals are all liable to be swept away, and to my mind it is clear that at the very outset of an engagement at least some of the ships will have suffered in the above respects with a result . . . that embarrassment might be expected; and, clearly, the movements of a fleet would be greatly delayed, and probably even an opportunity to obtain an advantage . . . would be lost; again a signal might be made executive at a wrong time, should the halliards be shot away while the signal is flying.

4   It is necessary that a fleet should be able to move in any direction, with all the rapidity that is consistent with safety to its component parts, so that a leader may be able to manoeuvre against another who may have adopted quite different methods based on a different system; in other words the system . . . should be such as to leave the fleet in the hands of its chief, plastic, and free to move in any direction without delay.

5   It is also desirable that signals should be so few and so simple that it would rarely be necessary for officers to refer to a book, save when there is time and the opportunity to do so.

6   It is apparent to me that a fleet that can be rapidly manoeuvred without having to wait for a series of signal repetitions and replies will be at a great advantage [compared] to one that cannot manoeuvre with signals rapidly because it is subject to the restraint they impose.

George Tryon set about teaching the Mediterranean Fleet to manoeuvre with an absolute minimum of signalling; and while he met initial opposition from Captains accustomed to regarding initiative within signalling distance of a superior as tantamount to mutiny, he nursed, cajoled and bullied the fleet into manoeuvring remarkably well and remarkably fast without the convoluted song and dance of the *Signal* and *Manoeuvring Books*. The Awkward Squad gladly took up station astern of him; and one can surmise, with a high degree of confidence, that the great Admirals of the eighteenth century would have warmly applauded.

Confidence in him and his shorthand system was riding high in the summer of 1893, when HMS *Camperdown* rammed his flagship, HMS *Victoria*, in the approach to the anchorage in Tripoli Bay, Lebanon, on 22 June. The kinetic details need not concern us here, but it is clear that Tryon made a mistake. He issued an order which was impossible to execute without a collision. His informal manoeuvring system was *not* being used (and could not have been, for a formation anchorage). If it somehow *had* been in operation, his second-in-command would have known that he was expected to manoeuvre clear of the danger. But he did exactly what he had been told by signal, and collided. *Victoria* sank and Tryon drowned along with 357 other officers and men.[10]

The loss of the ship, the loss of so many men, was bad enough, but the Royal Navy lost far more that midsummer afternoon, for those vested interests who had been affronted by Tryon's rejection of *Signal Book* manoeuvring successfully managed the travesty of linking Tryon's informal methods with the disaster, and it was the end of tactical reform. Tryon's successor, Sir Michael Culme-Seymour, returned the fleet to the *Signal Book*, and retrained it in the goose step. He and his successors expunged manoeuvring without signalling from the corporate memory. Serving on his staff were the key officers who would command and train the dreadnought Navy before 1914,[11] and in his orbit were a dozen future flag officers of Jutland.[12] John Jellicoe, his flag commander, belongs to both groups.

So, over a period of perhaps 30 years the technocrats, with their Victorian sense of deference and order, reasoned with Trenchardian logic and grandeur that the Navy's distant warfighting experience had been rendered spectacularly irrelevant, and that the new warfare of machinery and science could only be managed in battle by equally scientific, systemised techniques of command and control – by comforting processes of tabulation and regulation. The attractions of this to an officer corps deprived of real war experience and armed with largely untested technology, in a long period of peace, are obvious. As an article in the *Saturday Review* on 'The over-regulation of the Navy' put it in 1894: 'It is convenient for some men to have a nice book of arithmetic to save them the trouble of thinking and the responsibility of acting for themselves'.[13]

Tryon's campaign to restore tactical fundamentals having met with disaster, the next potential reform torchbearer, who had both the vision and the power of four-star position, was that dangerous and volatile First Sea Lord and former Tryon collaborator, Sir John Fisher.

After leaving the Mediterranean, Fisher's heretical views about the command and control of fleets in battle disappear off the historical radar screen, after 30 years. I am not aware of any further direct reference to it after 1902. Did he happen to undergo some sort of 'netcentric-warfare' conversion or did he, having moved ashore into the Navy's highest administrative posts, no longer care? It could be said that he had 'form' in abandoning interests when his career moved on: he had dropped his hands-on involvement in gunnery and torpedo development once technical expertise had served his career purpose.[14] But his 'awkward squad' dissidence about the signals-intensive doctrine of fleet command in vogue in the Navy had never promised career leverage – more likely the reverse – and the attainment of four-star rank. In 1904, the First Sea Lordship removed any possible motive for reticence.

In fact the explanation is, typically, much more dramatic: he planned to use his position as the professional head of the Navy to get rid of the battlefleet and replace it with quite different means of ensuring maritime security.[15] So why should he bother crusading about fleet tactics? Even today, nearly 20 years after we first understood his Carthaginian, secretive, agenda, it still has the capacity to shock; and we can see why Fisher was so feared and disliked. The panoramic scene of Grand Harbour, Valletta, on the day Sir John Fisher left the station in his flagship *Renown*, with serried rows of magnificent black-hulled pre-dreadnoughts dressed overall to see him off, seems to represent the epitome of naval supremacy. Britain's lead in battleships appeared sublimely unassailable, almost a divine right. And just two years later the new First Sea Lord was proposing to consign it to oblivion.

As far as he was concerned, the Navy would merely be jumping before it was pushed by technological progress and by sheer cost. The combination of factors which were pushing the battlefleets towards irrelevance must have appeared compelling to him and need only be glimpsed here: they were locked into short-range gunnery by their multiplicity of calibres (which made central direction of fire impracticable); they were threatened by the growing reach of torpedoes and the coming of age of small, fast, torpedo craft; they could not catch the new, faster French armoured cruisers which were expressly designed to interdict British trade on the sealanes; and they were hugely expensive in men and money (as indeed were the armoured cruisers which we now had to build in reply to their French prototypes).

Fisher's solution was that home defence would be entrusted to 'flotilla craft' (destroyers and submarines), while the safety of the sealanes would be overseen by a few enormous, fast, armoured cruisers with turbine propulsion and a single-calibre armament of the largest guns, giving enormous reach. They became known as 'battle cruisers', and, as they were conceived as antidotes to armoured-cruisers, they need not be armoured against their own big-gun calibre of shellfire. No more battleships would be built.

But here, where the 'dreadnought revolution' was born, our proof of the pudding analysis of the British Fleet in the First World War reaches a fork in the road, for Fisher was unsuccessful in his radical aim of abolishing the battlefleet – so unsuccessful that, by letting the genie of 'all big gun' capital ships out of the bottle, he ironically ended up fathering the most impressive battlefleet of all: the wartime Grand Fleet of Jellicoe and Beatty. His agenda was just too radical for the Admiralty, who inserted one battleship into the 1904 programme of four 'all-big-gun' ships; that ship was completed well ahead of the battle cruisers, was named *Dreadnought* and astonished the world. So there are two strands of policy to things to be tested in the 1914–18 establishment of capital ships: the battlefleet itself, of whose command and control flaws Fisher (among others) had been aware since the 1870s, and which now assumed a surreal 'dreadnought' manifestation; and Fisher's intended nemesis of both the battlefleet and armoured cruisers, the battle cruiser, whose delivery was overshadowed, and limelight stolen, by the early completion of *Dreadnought*.

One can easily see why, when *Dreadnought* was launched in 1906, there could be no going back to pre-dreadnoughts, and why there was relatively little interest in the battle cruisers which belatedly appeared in 1908. The mathematics are simple and startling. If a government wished to field a battle line with a broadside of (say) 32 guns of the heaviest calibre, it could either be done with (using British data) eight pre-dreadnoughts, costing £13,250,000 and manned by 6176 officers and men. Or, it could be done with just four dreadnoughts costing £7,200,000 and manned by half as many people. And that takes no account of the in-service savings of maintaining half as many ships. And once battle had commenced, the faster, more compact dreadnought squadron could dictate the range and concentrate fire. It was a 'no-brainer'! In his all-big-gun revolution, Fisher had attached the jumpleads to a monster which even he was not strong enough to control.

Dreadnought had particular appeal to a Navy whose rate of expansion was constrained by the rhythms of its career structure, but no financially responsible naval power was going to go on building cost-ineffective pre-dreadnought battleships, and after the arrival of *Invincible*, nobody was going to go on ordering armoured cruisers. In the sense of their original terms of reference, the overshadowed battle cruisers were spectacularly successful: they rendered armoured cruisers obsolete at a stroke and ended their building. While world attention was diverted to the new 'dreadnought' building race which now ensued, the *guerre de course* threat, crafted by the French '*jeune ecole*', was quietly snuffed out. The revolution in capital ship types appeared (to anyone other than Fisher) to be comprehensive and complete.

But just as we had built many armoured cruisers in reply to those of France, it should not have taken advanced staff work to predict that others – perhaps potential future enemies – might be prompted by *Invincible*, *Inflexible* and *Indomitable* to build their own battle cruisers. Perhaps the assumption was made that battle cruisers were so obviously a defensive weapon for a global maritime empire that countries which did not share that particular security problem would have no need of them. But several countries partially shared that problem, and some had aspirations for more of it. By 1910 (at the latest) it was clear that the Imperial German Navy was embarking on its own variants of *Invincible*, and that more were likely to follow. And the first German ships (*Moltke*, *Goeben*, *Von Der Tann*) were built with hypothetical combat with *Invincibles*, and certainly not with armoured cruisers, in mind: they were substantially more heavily armoured that their British prototypes.

The question of what would happen to our battle cruisers, if and when they were confronted by their own big-gun kind, was not fully asked – an officer doing so 'would have injured his professional prospects'[16] – until no fewer than ten had been built: the last four with armour plate increased from 6" to 9", but still less than the 'battleship-scale' 12" of the Germans. The issue of exactly what the *Lion* class and *Tiger* were built for is a tricky one: they were thoroughly armoured for fighting armoured cruisers, but still inadequately so for their fellow battle cruisers. Thus is illustrated the ephemeral nature of Fisher's original battle cruiser theory, which logically became obsolescent – or, at least, backed into a niche – with the decline of the armoured cruisers they so impressively eclipsed. After *Tiger*, the hybrid type was mercifully merged into the battleship type with the *Queen Elizabeth* class of the 1912 programme.

As the dreadnought battlefleet grew and grew, with the Germans a neck behind, the issue of its combat doctrine remained unaddressed. There was some Tryonic discontent about the unreformed *Signal Book* but not from anyone senior enough to force the issue through, and one of Sir Michael Culme-Seymour's former flag-captains, Admiral Sir William May, jousted with the idea of reform while he was C-in-C Home Fleets. He was troubled that in fleet exercises, even without gunfire, signals could hardly been made out because of all the funnel smoke. But in the end he dropped it. The task of centrally controlling a huge fleet was so daunting that voluntarily downgrading one of the few (theoretical) means of central control seemed to be a counter-intuitive step.

The outbreak of the Great War was not unexpected, even though its greatness and longevity certainly were. For 20 years or so, Europe had been a simmering arena of national grievances, posturing statesmen, huge conscript armies and feverishly-built fleets. It was only a matter of time; indeed, before some respected establishment figures welcomed the prospect: 'Give us war, O Lord, For England's sake, War righteous and true, Our hearts to shake'.[17] Therefore, notwithstanding the fact that a century had passed since the last conflict at sea between great powers, the Royal Navy cannot claim to have been caught by surprise by the opening of hostilities, and nor was it.[18] But a century after the British Fleet had accomplished so much by harnessing precisely opposite methods, its doctrinal tone was set by a fraternity of senior and greatly respected officers who immersed themselves in detail and control at the expense of their clarity of view of principles, and who measured efficiency by the devices of accountancy management.

As Churchill famously wrote, of 1914, 'we had more captains of ships than captains of war'.[19] And nowhere was this regrettable state of affairs more prevalent than in the Grand Fleet, under the anxious, centralising Jellicoe. The famous photographer Henri Cartier-Bresson coined the phrase 'decisive moment' to explain his art. He would wait sphinx-like (one imagines), observing events around him, watching for a moment in which his subject's character and significance would be betrayed at their most pronounced. He would then press the shutter. There is a useful concept parallel here, even if it cannot be stretched very far; and the factor, I would suggest, which separates the captains of war from the captains of ships must be the disposition to recognise when a *decisive moment* has arrived, and the preparedness (if necessary) to 'take their orders from providence'[20] to initiate the necessary exploitative or preventive action. But only in the battle cruiser squadron, under the command of the charismatic, careless, Sir David Beatty, was such a philosophy tolerated in the 'dreadnought' Grand Fleet with which Britain went to war.

By early 1915 there was no more work for battle cruisers on the sealanes of empire. Von Spee's elite armoured cruiser squadron had been sunk at the Falklands battle in the prescribed manner by *Invincible* and *Inflexible*, and Germany's clutch of marauding light cruisers had been hunted down and eliminated.[21] One squadron had returned from the Mediterranean. The two 'Falklands' units and *Princess Royal* returned from sealane deployments. What was to be done with Fisher's favoured brainchildren now? There were plans afoot to split up the squadrons and allocate battle cruisers in one and twos to light cruiser squadrons to help them to push home a reconnaissance. But the balance between the two battlefleets was too close to forego recruiting those heavy guns in a fleet action, and the battle cruiser squadrons were brought together and ennobled into a 'battle cruiser fleet' under the senior squadron commander, David Beatty. They thus entered the trap which had been lying in wait for them almost since their completion.

There were three conspicuous features of the Battle of Jutland – the only fleet encounter of the Great War – which took place on 31 May 1916. The first was the easy destruction of three British battle cruisers when in receipt of big-gun shellfire from their German notional equivalents. Given their original, specialist design requirements as the antidote to armoured cruisers, this should have been predictable: if 6" and 9" armour had been good enough against 11" and 12" shells, then battleships would not have been burdened with heavier belts. The second was the dependence on orders – which seniors might not be in a position to send and which might not get through if they were – of the Grand Fleet's flag officers and captains, the focusing on station-keeping and the lack of proactive interest in the detailed movements of the enemy. 'Decisive moments' came and went, and there was no clear decision. The third was the Germans' success in gaining the refuge of home waters in spite of the Grand Fleet's seemingly unassailable initial advantage of position.

The post-mortems and recriminations were protracted and painful, but something had to be done. At length, in November 1916, Jellicoe was succeeded by Beatty as commander-in-chief, and the process of revising, reforming and in some cases discarding the stifling accretion of battle orders began. It had taken the terrible lessons of Jutland and three years of war to bring the Fleet to the doctrinal condition that men like Sir George Tryon had sought a generation earlier. That new, old doctrine may be said to have carried the British Fleet into the Second World War.

When the Earl of St Vincent was told of the 'submarine' invention of Robert Fulton, in 1804, he allegedly said: 'Don't look at it, and don't touch it. If we take it up other nations will; and it will be the greatest blow at our supremacy on the sea that can be imagined.'[22] He was, in truth, being a little alarmist. A hundred years later not much progress had been made in the submarine's threat to naval supremacy. But it was seen mainly as a *defensive*, almost immobile weapon, and Fisher envisaged it picketing Britain's coastline and lying in wait for attacking or invading enemies. The Germans had built their first submarines, *U-1* and *U-2*, contemporaneously with *Dreadnought*, and for several years they (at best) kept station, rather than blazed trail, in submarine experiment;[23] and even 1914 saw the U-boat in an unadventurous light.

The very first 'war cruise' of the U-boats, on 2 August 1914 was a defensive positioning of submarines on sentry duty to seawards of Heligoland, but in the ensuing weeks and months the range and reliability of the boats were explored and established. The torpedoing of armoured cruisers *Hogue*, *Aboukir* and *Cressy* on 22 September by Otto Weddigen in *U-9* turned preconceptions upside down. And as the 'envelopes' of endurance and operational capability (and sometimes ethical behaviour) were being tested to the limits into 1915, the Germans realised that they possessed a weapon with the range and endurance both to harry the Grand Fleet outside its bases, and to interdict Britain's transatlantic trade.

The French had redoubled their frigate *guerre de course* efforts after Trafalgar, having nowhere else to go, and after Jutland the German naval high command similarly turned to the U-boats. Even as Scheer was being acclaimed as the victor of '*Der Skagerrakschlacht*', he was arguing his way out of renewing the battle: 'even the most successful outcome of a fleet action will not force England to make peace' he told the Kaiser, with opaque reasoning which had not seized him before the Jutland experience, 'a victorious end of the war within a reasonable time can only be achieved through the defeat of British economic life – that is, by using the U-boats against British trade'.[24] This despairing, evasive document would have shocked the German public. It was a tacit admission that the British Grand Fleet was undefeatable, and that the High Seas Fleet was actually incapable of furthering Germany's war aims. A useless waste of money, in other words – after just one shadowy, twilight, half-cocked brush with Jellicoe. The U-boat would have to be the saving of the German Navy and, perhaps, the war.

The U-boat arm had had a year's grace to develop and define their own operational potential after the curtailing of the first '1915' bout of unrestricted war against trade; and now, in the autumn and winter after Jutland and the High Seas Fleet's near-escape from the Grand Fleet in August, they were properly let off the leash in defiance of international protest. The consequences were devastating. By the time Beatty succeeded Jellicoe in high command, merchant-ship sinkings were three times higher than at the time of Jutland, and the strategic focus of the naval war had shifted from the North Sea to the 'Western Approaches' of the Atlantic (the focal areas of shipping lanes north and south of Ireland). By April 1917 a dozen ships, Allied and neutral, were being sunk every day. At this rate the war would soon be lost.

Jellicoe had gone to the Admiralty partly to bring a blast of salt air to its musty corridors, and to grapple with the burgeoning U-boat problem. He failed. His administration set its face against the old answer to *guerre de course*, convoying, partly through doubts that merchant ships (to whom sailing in close company was anathema) could keep station, with their limited means of fine-tuning speed, but partly because of an obdurate quest for a technological rather than an organisational solution. After all, the armoured cruiser *guerre de course* threat had been kicked into touch by radical new technology, so why not the U-boats?

In fact, in the end, the new threat proved highly susceptible to the old solution, once the logistical and prejudicial obstacles to convoying had been surmounted. Convoying subjected the terminal ports to famine and glut cycles which degraded the operational efficiency of a merchant fleet by, say, 25–30 per cent (depending on the size of the convoys), but if that burden were accepted as the lesser of two evils, it was strikingly effective in tactical terms. For a start, an escorted convoy made it necessary for the U-boat to risk the proximity of one or more warships, if it was to press home an attack. That compelled the U-boat to attack submerged, depriving it of the use of its gun – by far the cheapest method of sinking a tramp steamer – and forcing it to expend one or more of its small outfit of torpedoes. The best attacking positions were as well known to the escorts as they were to the U-boat, and the need to remain submerged (and on waning battery power) meant that if the first salvo missed, there would probably be no second chance. Meanwhile the development of towed explosive sweeps, depth charges, hydrophones and destroyer tactics placed U-boats in ever greater danger. Almost 180 were sunk and, at the war's end, a similar number meekly surrendered to the Allies.[25] No wonder that, in the subsequent 'interwar' years, the U-boat was assumed to be a discredited weapon of the past – more especially in the light of the invention of Asdic.

By the end of the war some 12 million tons of shipping had been sunk by U-boats, some 7 million of it British (ten times more than by mine, the next most frequent cause of loss). But the curve of sinkings had taken a decisive downturn with the belated introduction of convoying and other countermeasures, and in 1918 the rate of losses fell by 71 per cent from its peak in the terrible spring of the year before, as successes came harder to U-boats, and the aces were progressively eliminated.

How far is blame appropriate for the near loss of the Great War to the U-boat? In operational, if not quite technological terms, submarine warfare progressed between 1914 and 1918 every bit as much as aerial warfare, and posed a threat of far greater strategic significance. That threat, seemingly, came from nowhere. Had the conflict which broke out in August 1914 been over as quickly as was widely expected, it would never have been discovered – at least in this war.

The cruiser *guerre de course*, on the other hand, had been long imagined, and catered for; and, after some initial confusion, was dealt with more or less within the pre-anticipated timeframe of hostilities – assisted by Fisher's all big-gun revolution which had been conceived with that purpose expressly in mind. One must fairly acknowledge the difficulty of investing in an antidote to a mode of warfare whose practicability had scarcely been imagined, still less demonstrated, and which was specifically banned by international conventions. But in the current era of apparently unassailable western military superiority, it is sobering to reflect that Britain and her Allies came so close to losing the Great War because of an offensive weapon which scarcely flickered on the radar screen of human awareness at the outbreak.

The institution of the wrong doctrine in the Grand Fleet, and the near-fatal delay in adopting convoying in answer to the U-boat threat appear to be unrelated, and were quite different in the timescales involved. The first was the osmostic product of two or three generations of peacetime sailoring, and the second was an obtuseness lasting just a few months. But they had this in common: they both represented a cutting edge technocratic dismissal of old concepts as potential solutions to challenges brought about by radical technology. In both cases, the technical evangelists were too tightly focused on 'transformation', and in both cases what proved to be the appropriate doctrine was handed down from the classic, combat-intensive unscientific days of sail – an era which they assumed had been confined to the museum, lock, stock and barrel.

The truth is that to impose its will, every military force has to deal with the 'real world' of all the circumstances bearing upon its effective output, and in which the enemy may be only one shifting circumstance among several. Some of those circumstances may lie internally, in the realms of leadership, structure, personnel, technology, training or doctrine. The Royal Navy fought the Great War with some major self-assumed handicaps, and in the end surmounted them. Across the North Sea, by the time the U-boat campaign was obviously defeated, the German High Seas Fleet had lapsed into irretrievable operational obsolescence, even dereliction. Its best young officers and technicians had been siphoned off and expended in the U-boats, while the Grand Fleet, by contrast, had quietly grown in strength and stature: Beatty had driven through reforms which had restored the feared 'Nelson spirit' to its tactical doctrine, and it had been swollen by a squadron of American battleships. A new fleet encounter would have been a hopeless, suicidal business for the Kaiser's demoralised *Luxusflotte*. It was going nowhere, other than to Scapa Flow to open its sea-cocks.

Notes

1 Most of this chapter is distilled from Gordon' (1996) and subsequent reprints.
2 24/10/93, Althorp Papers, K437.
3 9/11/93, ibid.
4 Michael Howard (1962) pp. 9–14.
5 Egerton (1896) pp. 81–2.
6 *Manual of Fleet Evolutions* (aka. *The Manoeuvring Book*), MLN/198/4B10, NMM.

7 Quoted in Mackay (1973) p. 88.
8 Covering letter to his Temporary Memoranda A B & C, 21/11/91, ADM1/7057.
9 Ibid.
10 These were men on the Navy payroll. There were others onboard, uncounted: Chinese laundrymen, Maltese stewards, Italian bandsmen.
11 Wilson, Bridgeman, May, Battenberg, Jackson, Jellicoe, Milne.
12 Jellicoe, Evan-Thomas, Burney, Archibald Moore, Leveson, Heath, Napier, Alexander-Sinclair, Halsy, Brock, Goodenough, Everett, Le Mesurier, Dreyer.
13 *Saturday Review*, 21 July 1894.
14 Andrew Lambert paper to Fisher Centenary Conference, JSCSC, 29 Sept 2004 (pub. pending).
15 See Lambert (1999).
16 Bellairs (1919) p. 53.
17 Lord Tennyson.
18 See Goldrick (1984).
19 Churchill (1927) Vol. I, p. 93.
20 In 1940 Australian Captain John Collins confessed to Admiral Cunningham that he had taken his orders from providence. Cunningham invited him to carry on doing so.
21 *Leipzig* and *Nurnberg* were sunk at the Falklands battle. *Dresden* was caught in Patagonia, and *Emden* in the Cocos Islands in the Indian Ocean. *Karlsruhe* is thought to have been destroyed by an internal explosion in the West Indies. *Konigsberg* was safely bottled up in German East Africa and *Breslau*, along with the battlecruiser *Goeben*, in Turkish waters.
22 Gibson and Prendergast (1931), frontispiece.
23 *U-1* and *U-2* were built contemporaneously with *Dreadnought*.
24 Translation in ROSK/3/5, CC Archives.
25 Gibson and Prendergast (1931), appendices.

6 Richmond and the faith reaffirmed
British naval thinking between the wars

Geoffrey Till

Introduction: British naval thinkers of the interwar period

Naturally enough, there was a good deal of reflection about the naval lessons of the First World War, aptly described by Archibald Hurd at the time as 'the supreme contest in our history'.[1] But, although hugely influenced by the experience of the First World War, the naval thinking of the interwar period was not, of course, distinctive and discrete in intellectual and conceptual terms. Some naval thinkers were newcomers to the field but they usually were well aware of, and were much influenced by, the views of those who had gone before. Many of the thinkers of the pre-war period were still active and therefore able to review their own initial conclusions against the background of four years of war at sea.

Richmond

These latter included the likes of Corbett, Aston,[2] Callwell plus Clarke, Thursfield and more popular writers such as Archibald Hurd himself. But, in this period, Admiral Sir Herbert Richmond dominated the field. Before the war, Richmond, singled out for accelerated promotion, had served as Naval Assistant to Admiral Fisher in 1906 and been promoted to Captain in 1908, taking command of *Dreadnought*, flagship of the Home Fleet and the first of Fisher's revolutionary all big-gun battleships. But after this bright start, his career entered choppier waters; he was relegated to command of second-class cruisers attached to the Torpedo School at Portsmouth. From February 1913 to May 1915 he served as Assistant Director of Operations at the Admiralty.

During this whole period, however, he became increasingly disenchanted on the one hand with what he took to be the 'materialist' preoccupations of the Fisher school and, on the other, with the sheer amateurishness of the Admiralty's approach to an offensive naval strategy. For their part, he was increasingly regarded by those he tended to criticise, perhaps too freely, as that dangerous kind of naval officer who read and thought too much. By founding, with other choice spirits such as Admiral W.H. Henderson, the potentially subversive *Naval Review* he had already raised doubts about his general trustworthiness and was soon after exiled by Winston Churchill to a minor role in the Mediterranean.

Admiral Beatty's rise in prominence after the Battle of Jutland helped resuscitate Richmond's career. He came back to the Admiralty in 1917 and got involved in fleet planning and in the revision of Grand Fleet Battle Orders at a time when the strategic situation in the North Sea still seemed, to the more offensively minded, to be in a state of unsatisfactory stalemate while the German unrestricted U-boat offensive was alarmingly successful. Richmond tried to show how the Admiralty's preoccupation with maintaining the numerical superiority of the Grand Fleet was tying down flotilla resources and denying any possibility of effective offensive measures against the enemy. He put forward his own proposals for limited offensives in the Mediterranean and Adriatic to draw off U-boats and for a more aggressive use of naval airpower against the High Sea Fleet under whose influence the U-boats sheltered. Nonetheless, Richmond, like most professionals, distanced himself from the more extreme *guerre a outrance* critics of Admiral Jellicoe, believing instead that unless the Germans themselves offered battle, Britain's best course was to maintain strategic superiority in the North Sea, trusting to the long-term effects of the blockade, and to limiting the U-boats' effectiveness through convoying and realistic complementary offensives against their bases.

But to some extent a familiar pattern re-emerged as Richmond became increasingly disenchanted, in turn, with Admiral Beatty's postwar naval policy, especially over the priority to be accorded the construction of a new round of large, fast battleships. Richmond was appointed Admiral President of the Royal Naval College Greenwich, reflecting acknowledgement of his strong interest in staff training; he later assumed command of the Imperial Defence College. He was frustrated in what he wanted to do at both these places, and when he decided quite consciously in 1929 to publish a direct attack on the Admiralty's battleship policy in *The Times*, he was right to anticipate that this was likely to terminate his naval career. Afterwards, Richmond found a new role for himself as a full-time academic, writing extensively, and being appointed to the Vere Harmsworth Chair of Imperial and Naval History at Cambridge in 1934. Following this, he became Master of Downing College, where he remained until his death in 1946.

Richmond was unusual in being able to combine an active, if not always happy, service career with a great deal of academic work on naval history and policy. He wrote his first book, *The Navy in the War of 1739–1748*, with the encouragement of Corbett, while commanding HMS *Dreadnought* and as already remarked, founded the *Naval Review* in February 1912. Inevitably, though, he was at his most productive after he left the Navy. He used his new freedom to finish his *The Navy in India, 1763–1783* and to write *Economy and Naval Security* (1931) which summarised his earlier disarmament and small ship arguments. That same year, he delivered the Lees

Knowles Lectures at Cambridge, published in 1932 as *Imperial Defence and Capture at Sea in War*. In 1934, he returned to the theme of economy and collective security in *Sea Power and the Modern World*. In 1943 he delivered the Ford Lectures at Oxford, which were published in 1946 as *Statesmen and Sea Power*. Finally his unfinished *The Navy as an Instrument of Policy 1558–1727* was completed and published in 1953, seven years after his death.

The diversity of his interests and the intertwining of his roles as naval officer, planner, reformer and scholar makes it difficult to summarise his approach. While he may have wanted to define a 'British doctrine of war', his concepts of naval operations were never systematically developed and so need to be extrapolated from his writings. His fundamental theme, however, has been aptly summarised by his biographer like this:

> Richmond's purpose was to educate politicians and sailors alike on the abiding realities of naval greatness, the inter-relationships of political and military strategy, and the connections between Britain's developing overseas influence and the utilization of her maritime strengths.[3]

While most at home at this grand strategic level, however, he was equally interesting, if not always unassailable, as a thinker at the operational and tactical/technical levels of his profession as well.

Liddell Hart

The other major thinker of the period was Basil Liddell Hart. Although only a small proportion of his work centred on maritime issues, he knew Corbett and Richmond well, associated with other maritime figures of the time and produced in the *British Way of War* a proposition that the maritime school found generally seductive. He first raised this argument in a public lecture at the RUSI in 1931 and followed it up with a book of that title in 1932. He suggested 'that there had been a distinctively British practice of war, based on experience and proved by three centuries of success'. Unfortunately, this experience had not been translated into an intellectual framework strong enough to withstand the pressures that took Britain into a Continental war in 1914.[4] The result was a monstrous aberration from Britain's standard practice which had resulted in a terrible war, the loss of countless lives and the depletion of Britain's financial resources with lasting effect. He advocated an immediate return to normal policy and the steadfast rejection of any repeat of Britain's experience in the First World War.

Normal policy meant the avoidance of a large-scale Continental commitment and a heavy reliance on Britain's naval superiority to provide unremitting economic pressure on the adversary in the form of an economic blockade and the capacity to attack exposed points through the 'mobility and surprise' that derived from command of the sea. Seapower in short was the key to the British way of warfare:

This naval body had two arms; one financial, which embraced the subsidising and military provisioning of allies, the other military, which embraced sea-borne expeditions against the enemy's vulnerable extremities. By our practice we safeguarded ourselves where we were weakest, and exerted our strength where the enemy was weakest.[5]

In the First World War, Britain had indeed imposed a crippling blockade but many of its other opportunities to fight a hard-headed cost-effective war had been swept away by the romantic image of the glory of Continental engagements. It had led the British, Liddell Hart claimed, to throw away the opportunities of the Gallipoli campaign by the half-hearted and faltering way in which this most imaginative of campaigns was conducted.

Liddell Hart could be, and indeed was, both at the time and subsequently, criticised for presenting a dubious version of the past and a set of recommendations for the future that hardly suited the emerging conditions of Europe in the middle to late 1930s.[6] After a talk by Liddell Hart at the RUSI, the Chairman, Lord Ampthill, who in the past had been active in the promotion of the national conscription that a Continental commitment required, took the unusual step of saying that he disagreed with everything his speaker had said. Nonetheless, Liddell Hart's arguments had a natural appeal for sailors. Richmond pointedly clapped him, and the dark blue members of the audience were supportive. Some soldiers supported him too, for the revulsion against the experience of the Western Front was widespread at the time. But appealing though they were, Liddell Hart's theories on the British way in war were highly generalised, nebulous and abstract. They were never 'operationalised' into anything approaching a doctrine.

The lesser lights of the interwar period

A perceptive but unassuming treatment of what could perhaps be called the orthodox British line on these and other maritime questions in modern conditions came out just before the Second World War, when Commander John Creswell published his *Naval Warfare: An Introductory Study* in 1936. Creswell, an evident believer in the power of history, intended his study to be of special benefit to junior naval officers: 'to put before them the lines of thought most likely to lead to sound strategy and tactics'.[7] Unlike Richmond, Creswell focused largely on the operational level of war, being mainly concerned with the question of how the Navy could best perform the duties expected of it, rather than with the role of seapower in national grand strategy. Of course, he was well aware that 'naval problems do not stand by themselves', needing to be seen in context, but thought 'it is practicable to discuss naval warfare as a distinct, though not an independent, activity'.[8]

Creswell argued that battlefleet supremacy still exerted as decisive an influence on naval warfare as ever. This supremacy would continue to be best established by winning victory in battle, on the 'immense importance and predominance over all other acts of warfare' on which he laid great stress. Neutralisation by blockade, although occasionally necessary, was a much less satisfactory way of gaining this maritime supremacy. He explored the possibilities available to a weaker Navy and concluded that a defensive strategy had much scope if tackled in a skilful and enterprising way. Despite recent advances in submarines and aircraft, the battleship, he felt, remained the backbone of the battlefleet. He dealt fully with battle tactics, the defence and attack of trade, and the mounting of overseas expeditions.

Commander Russell Grenfell's *The Art of the Admiral* (1937) was another similar survey, but although he covered much the same ground as Creswell and came basically to the same conclusions, his was a much more conceptual approach. Grenfell was an instructor at the Naval Staff College at Greenwich and was later, like Creswell, to prove himself to be a more than competent naval historian. He identified his subject in his very first line: 'this is a book about naval strategy'.[9] He sought to educate a public increasingly involved in the operations of war through a 'plain statement' of his subject.

A particularly interesting part of his survey, however, was his attempt to distinguish between the gaining of command of the sea by the destruction of the enemy, and the control of sea communications. The first was more than just the means to the latter, he thought: in many cases fighting for the sake of the moral ascendancy that actual victory gave was justified in circumstances where strict logic showed it to be unnecessary. His book, commented one reviewer, 'exudes the spirit of the offensive . . . if talking will do the trick our next opponents should stand no chance'.

The views of Richmond, Liddell Hart, Creswell and Grenfell together with the surviving and/or amended work of the prewar thinkers such as Corbett, Aston and Colomb, provide a fair cross-section of the assortment of ideas that the Royal Navy took with it to war in 1939. They will now be considered under three headings.

The maritime case

The Continental school of British strategy fell into public disfavour after the bloodbaths of the Western Front. Archibald Hurd summed up the Royal Navy's achievements in ringing tones:

> We have been saved by our Navy, built under the influence of panics, from the worst consequences of war – the invasion of these islands, the disintegration of the empire, and the strangulation of our ocean-borne commerce, which is the life-blood of the British peoples, distributed over the world's seas. The Fleet has also enabled us to save Europe and, it may be, the world from the domination of Germany. Behind the screen provided by the Navy we have trained and equipped new armies, constituted ourselves, in some degree, the paymasters of the Allies, and placed at their disposal the industrial resources of the United Kingdom

and, in large measure also, of the United States, besides assuring to them and ourselves supplies of raw material which have been readily obtainable, owing to our command of the sea, from British Dominions as well as distant foreign countries.[10]

All well and good, but could not these aims have been achieved at less cost? Was there not a case for a return to the kind of maritime strategy advocated by Corbett, Callwell and their colleagues before the First World War?

To many, the gruesome experience of the land war merely confirmed the advantages of maritime powers being in many cases able to avoid this approach to conflict. Richmond was certainly so persuaded. Like Corbett, Richmond wanted the Royal Navy to move on from its obsession with battle, to concentrate on securing its sea lines of communication, to prepare for expeditions against the exposed interests of any adversary and to integrate the Navy's contribution to national strategy effectively with that of the other two services. Such was also the aspiration of Sir Basil Liddell Hart. Both concentrated on the role of maritime power at the level of grand strategy.

In *The Navy in India*, Richmond was concerned to examine the connections between national objectives and what naval commanders did at sea in the various interconnected theatres of war. The Indian theatre, he thought, demonstrated how power at sea led to power from the sea and it would not take the 1930s reader long to spot the contemporary implications of this.[11] When Richmond arrived at Downing College in 1936, he told Pollen:

> I am working on an outline of British strategy from Elizabeth to 1918, with special reference to the Statesman's problem and how he must use the sea and land forces he had at his disposal, and how the strategy worked out in practice – the perpetual clash between the two schools of thought, maritime operations and land operations in the main theatre on the continent.[12]

But his real emphasis was on the closest cooperation between these two approaches. Grenfell for his part pointed out the strategic muddle of the prewar period when the work of the two services had not been properly coordinated and when in effect 'it was possible for the Navy and the Army to be preparing their own war plans without the one knowing what the other was doing'.[13] So, as George Clarke remarked, what Richmond was really advocating was a considered philosophy of 'British warfare' in which a 'major strategy' of the sea, the land and the air was welded into a national policy of imperial defence. Sea, air and land power should be seen not as competitors but as complements. The strategic circumstances of the early twentieth century, he thought, demanded service interdependence. At a time when relations between the RAF and the Admiralty were as bad as they could be over everything from defence priorities to detailed disputes over aircraft design, pilot training and ownership of the Fleet Air Arm and Coastal Command, these were indeed challenging aspirations, obvious though they might sound now.[14] Richmond also argued strongly for a much more professional and considered approach to the conduct of war at the highest level than seemed to have been possible last time. The country's leaders needed to be more prepared in policy formulation and execution.[15]

In this proposition Richmond found welcome, if sometimes dangerous, support from Liddell Hart. After the war, Liddell Hart denounced the slaughter of the Western Front and the unthinking abandonment of the traditional British strategy which he thought had led to it. Liddell Hart strongly opposed any national defence policy that might lead to another such 'Continental commitment' in the future. Richmond was never so extreme. For him 'maritime' and 'Continental strategies' were not mutually exclusive but for Liddell Hart, it seemed, they were, or at least could be.[16]

Based on his understanding of 400 years of British history, and a simplifying synthesis of the work of Corbett, Callwell, Aston and Richmond, Liddell Hart produced the concept of 'The British way in warfare', an approach to strategy that emphasised:

- the importance of securing command of the sea;
- the effectiveness of sea-based economic pressure;
- the need to avoid Continental commitments while securing the aid of allied landpowers;
- generous expenditure on the Navy;
- a focus on maritime areas of operation;
- developing synergy between the Army and the Navy;
- the value of expeditionary operations;
- limited, modest objectives, cost-effectively attainable;
- the need to project power ashore.

Although the British had not always followed their own rules in this matter (particularly in spending money on the Navy), Liddell Hart concluded that by such means a maritime power like Britain could defeat a Continental adversary while avoiding a direct confrontation on the European mainland. It was an example of 'the indirect approach' for which he has become famous.

Not everyone was impressed by the concept or the effectiveness of 'the British way in warfare', however. Some doubted the strategic effectiveness of maritime pressure through blockade on a Continental power with access to the resources of extensive national and/or conquered territory. Others pointed to the difficulties of amphibious operations on the periphery and wondered about their real impact on the correlation of forces in the centre. And there is also the obvious point that the approach's manifest deficiencies have several times led to Britain's taking a leading role in warfare *on* the Continent of Europe as well as around it.

The Royal Navy had performed a wide array of functions in support of British grand strategy during the First World War and naval thinkers during the interwar period considered them all:

Maritime power projection

The Navy's capacity to influence events ashore was clearly at the heart of the notion of a British way in warfare. First the Navy had safely and speedily transported the British Expeditionary Force to its operational theatre. 'The Navy', remarked Hurd in 1915, 'must always be the lifeline of the Expeditionary Force, ensuring to it reinforcements, stores and everything necessary to enable it to carry out its high purpose'.[17]

Corbett did not believe that the disastrous outcome of the Gallipoli campaign had invalidated the amphibious approach he had advocated before the war. In his semi-official history, he concluded that although its implementation in the campaign left a good deal to be desired, the basic conception of the indirect strategy in general and its particular application in this case was basically sound. He rehearsed the basic argument behind the inception of the campaign. By the end of 1914, it seemed likely that the situation on the Western Front would for the time being degenerate into stalemate. At this juncture, there was a 'stirring of the old instinct':

> Looking back upon it against the background of our past war history, we seem to see in what prompted our action at this time, a first indistinct warning that the old influences, which had never permitted us to concentrate in the main European theatre of a great war, were about to reassert themselves.

Sending more British troops to that main theatre seemed unlikely to have significant strategic effect in the present circumstances. The possibility of sending them to do more useful things elsewhere therefore arose, and, 'the Dardanelles was the spot where the naval and military arms could act in closest co-operation, and there too we could hope to achieve the largest political, economic and financial results'.[18]

This was, of course, exactly the kind of strategy that Corbett had advocated before the war. Although Richmond had his doubts about the practicalities of operations against the Dardanelles he too was a firm believer in such an approach. In 1915, he lamented that:

> We are conducting the war on purely Continental lines, trying to beat them at their own game, at which we can develop only half of our peculiar strength, and the enemy can develop the whole of theirs. We are fighting Germans with German weapons and conforming like sheep to their strategic plan.[19]

He argued that Fisher was too fixated on achieving a decisive battle in the North Sea. In fact, British command in that area was sufficiently secure to allow new and imaginative campaigns in the Mediterranean. 'We have now', he wrote in 1915, 'a more complete command of the sea, so far as the waters outside the range of submarines are concerned, than we have possessed in any previous maritime war, and yet we are making less of its special advantages than we ever did'.[20] Seapower and landpower working together, however, should be able to outflank the strength of the Central Powers on the Western Front. This was the general consensus both of the practitioners and the policy-makers of the time and continued to be the conclusion of most naval thinkers afterwards.

The problems arose when the *scale* of the commitment to the Gallipoli campaign and its possible consequences for the landpower balance on the Western Front and the maritime balance in the North Sea began to sink in. Concerned about this, Kitchener and Fisher respectively were unwilling to deploy the level of concentrated force at the beginning of the campaign that with the wisdom of hindsight now seemed to be the prerequisite for the kind of decisive success the advocates of the scheme expected.[21] This was a campaign in which many of the main policy-makers were only willing to commit forces to a campaign if it 'permitted of the operations being broken off at any stage without loss of prestige if insurmountable difficulties were encountered'. 'There can be no doubt that this was at the time the consideration which more than any other had appeared to limit the danger to a justifiable risk, *and had been the chief factor which had turned the scale for accepting it*'.[22] At the highest level such issues had not been properly thought through. In Corbett's measured conclusion, 'Owing to our imperfect machinery for bringing together the naval and military staffs for intimate study of combined problems, such failures in council were inevitable'.

Neither did Callwell see the Dardanelles experience as in any way invalidating his prewar opinions. The strategic approach was right and the objectives for which the campaign had been fought were sound. It had been worth trying, but it had been done badly. Part of the reason for this was the total lack of experience of an amphibious operation of this scale in contemporary conditions:

> There was no precedent to point to and no example to quote. The subject had been studied tentatively and as a matter of theory, and certain conclusions may have been arrived at, but few works treating of the art of war concerned themselves with the matter at all, and the problem involved had hardly received the consideration to which it was entitled either from the point of view of the attacking or of the defending side. Still, all soldiers who had devoted attention to the subject were in agreement on one point. They realised that an opposed landing represented one of the most hazardous and most difficult enterprises that a military force could be called on to undertake . . .[23]

While this amphibious approach was an attractive option for the British at the grand strategic level, Creswell also pointed out that it could pose unpleasant choices for both the services. The Navy faced the dilemma of deciding the priorities for allocating its assets to this function, rather than the struggle for sea control or the protection of trade. The potential dilemma was heightened by the fact that expeditionary task forces, being full of soldiers, military equipment, ammunition and fuel, would always need a higher level of security against attack than 'ordinary' convoys.[24] Moreover while it was easy enough to provide sufficient protection for the British Expeditionary Force crossing the Channel (and indeed close escort was not generally provided), reaching a more distant expeditionary theatre of operations could be more problematic from this point of view.[25] Creswell focused on the various types of threat such an amphibious force could face and identified 'the concentrated attack of the enemy's main force' as the most dangerous.[26] The protection of the force at sea was part of the 'virtual command of the surface of the sea in the area of operations' without which 'the landing of a large body of troops in hostile territory is scarcely possible'.

Interestingly, Creswell's analysis of the naval contribution to the conduct of such expeditionary operations moved on to less familiar topics. He was a clear advocate of 'the outstandingly British doctrine of combined responsibility' when it came to command and control. Here he echoed Corbett's argument that the nature of command at sea and on land was so different that it would be unwise to put either component commander in charge of the whole operation. However, he conceded the notion of the 'predominant partner':

> It will sometimes be convenient to come to an understanding that in a certain operation, or during a particular phase, one of the services is playing the predominant part. Combined responsibility still exists, but it is tacitly admitted that the requirements of one service are of outstanding importance at the moment.[27]

Creswell used the Gallipoli campaign as a case study for the examination of such questions as the necessity for beach reconnaissance, the relative advantages of day and night landings, the need for intense naval gunfire support, the desirability of tactical surprise and the likely impact of aircraft and modern armoured vehicles on the conduct of amphibious operations in the future. His judicious and considered conclusion was that:

> It is clear, then, that the problems of an opposed landing in the future are likely to be more complicated than they were in 1915, and from some points of view such an operation may seem well-nigh impossible. But against this there are other factors which may be on the side of the attackers.[28]

Such concerns were widespread. Both Callwell and Aston remained concerned about the difficulties of opposed landings against first-class opposition and indeed, this was one reason for their interest in deception, surprise and night landings. Callwell even wondered whether, in the age of mass armies, command of the sea could 'be turned to account to such good purpose in connection with land operations as was formerly the case'.[29] By 1939, Liddell Hart was concluding that airpower would make a seaborne invasion almost impossible. Carrying out a 'new "Gallipoli" expedition . . . might not merely end in failure, but meet disaster at the outset'.[30]

Recent scholarship, however, has established that the extent to which the failure at Gallipoli depressed amphibious aspirations for years afterwards until strategic circumstances required their re-animation in 1942 has been considerably exaggerated. Corbett spoke for more than had been realised. The campaign had failed, he thought, not because of faulty conception but simply because it had been badly conducted. Nor were those fatal failings unavoidable. Indeed, during the campaign huge lessons were learned, as its conclusion paradoxically demonstrated in December 1915 and January 1916:

> In that marvellous evacuation we see the national genius for amphibious warfare raised to its highest manifestation. In hard experience and in successive disappointments the weapon had been brought to a perfect temper, and when the hour of fruition came to show of what great things it was capable, it was used only to effect a retreat.[31]

By the end of the following year ambitious amphibious operations against the heavily defended coast of Belgium were being actively considered.[32] The general view was that the Gallipoli campaign remained a good idea, but one that hadn't come off; the problem had been one not of conception but of execution. Accordingly, the emphasis given to combined operations and the manouevrist approach by the likes of Philip Colomb and Sir Julian Corbett survived largely intact. The fact that progress in the development of equipment and doctrine was slow during the interwar period was mainly the consequence of the apparently sensible view that with defence resources being tight and any new Western Front being defended by the Maginot Line, Britain could afford to concentrate those resources on maintaining command of the sea rather than on exploiting it – at least for the time being. Given the loss of a clear naval lead over the United States on the one hand and Japan, Germany and Italy on the other, it would have been surprising, indeed even irresponsible if, in such straitened circumstances, the Admiralty had *not* chosen to accord the requirements of sea control the highest priority.

Sea control and the decisiveness of battle

Although in order to avoid the men with blue pencils, Corbett's account of the Battle of Jutland in the semi-official *History of the First World War* that he wrote with Sir Henry Newbolt was a subtle matter of nuance, some members of the Admiralty Board who read the draft did not like it, even if they did not quite know why. They had inserted in the final volume a note to the effect that, 'Their Lordships find that some of the principles advocated in the book, especially the tendency to minimise the importance of seeking battle and of forcing it to a conclusion, are directly in conflict with their views'.[33] The controversy over this and the Admiralty's arrogance towards Corbett and his colleague Sir Henry Newbolt damaged the former's health and profoundly shocked Richmond. But it did at least indicate that analytical history of this kind was at last being taken sufficiently seriously by the Navy to be regarded as a possible threat. Naval history, in other words, had begun to matter.

Afterwards, Corbett's 'sea heresy' continued to be attacked by members of the *guerre a outrance* tendency. An anonymous contributor to the *Naval Review* of 1931 said of him that:

> He had a legal training and mind, which was shown in his preference for getting the better of the enemy in some other way than coming to blows ... his teaching did not preach that to destroy or to neutralise the enemy's armed force was the primary military aim leading to a military decision. As an example one may look at his 'Principles of Maritime Strategy' and see, out of 310 pages, how many are devoted to 'Battle'. ... Is it too much to say that Lord Fisher's Baltic Scheme, Mr Churchill's naval Brigade, even the Dardanelles Expedition, were instances of 'ill digested Julian Corbett's "Seven Years' War"'?[34]

This perhaps shows that it was where Corbett most irritated some of his naval audiences that he should have done them the greatest good. But, as far as he was concerned, the experience of the First World War confirmed his views on command of the sea and the pursuit of battle. Accordingly he bravely stuck to his guns.

Corbett was not alone in making this point. Archibald Hurd likewise attacked the *guerre a outrance* group. Jutland, he thought, was a sufficient victory:

> If the Battle of Jutland had resulted in the annihilation of the High Seas Fleet our position would not have been greatly altered: Germany would still have possessed in her destroyers, submarines and minelayers the only active element of her naval power; her coast defences – which she believes to be impregnable – would have remained. The great ships would have gone, and to that extent our great ships would have been set free. For what purpose could they have been used after the German High Seas Fleet had been destroyed? ... It must be apparent that the naval situation would not have been greatly changed if the victory which Admirals Jellicoe and Beatty achieved had been so overwhelming as to wipe out every battleship and battle-cruiser under the German ensign.[35]

Hurd bolstered this argument with some sceptical observations about the decisiveness of previous encounters, including Trafalgar.[36]

Aston was also concerned with the profoundly unhistorical and total preoccupation with perfecting *materiel* simply and solely with a main battle in mind. Last time, he thought, too many people in uniform as well as out of it entered the Great War 'with a sort of general impression, with no historical backing, that a war at sea opened with a decisive battle in which both sides fought to a finish'. The experience of the First World War demonstrated the need for a more sophisticated approach, one less absorbed by the immediate search for – in Callender's phrase – 'glory': 'There is no national wish for it, as a factor in our foreign policy'.[37] Instead, in an era when British naval supremacy could no longer be taken for granted, naval policy should be guided by sober calculations of national interest and national security.

Nonetheless, and responding to those who doubted the value of victory in a fleet battle, Richmond was clear about the advantages that it could produce,

> Much has been done by the destruction of the enemy's capital ships. Concentration of our own units is no longer necessary: in the past, the battleships were set free to act as escorts: today it is the cruisers and destroyers. Your defending force is multiplied, your powers of exercising pressure by blockade are increased. If the enemy possesses oversea bases, your powers of affording escorts to expeditions sent to capture them are increased instead. The dangers of invasion are removed and ships and men and material are set free for protection of trade, or attack upon trade. The whole experience of war tells the same tale – a great victory is followed by a dispersion of the ships that had concentrated for it.[38]

All the same, Richmond, like Corbett, stressed that however advantageous a full-scale victory might be, its pursuit was not the be all and end all of maritime strategy that some of the 'fighting blockheads' of the time thought it was.[39] He also argued that a fixation on the requirements of decisive battle could easily, and in the First World War indeed had, sucked resources away from the defence of trade and the conduct of overseas expeditions that was the real contribution to victory that navies could make.[40]

The Admiralty's policy on decisive battle and command of the sea was, however, assailed from the opposite quarter as well. Creswell was far from being a fighting blockhead but he did, nonetheless, advocate a more offensive approach, operationally and tactically. Jellicoe had been too cautious.[41] Creswell argued that a more decisive victory at Jutland had been tactically and operationally possible and represented a missed strategic opportunity because this had been a rare chance to catch a cautious and inferior adversary out in the open, away from the security of its bases. The moral effect of total defeat on Germany might have been considerable.[42] Grenfell added his support to this view:

> And what of the moral effect? We cannot doubt that, as with the Battle of Trafalgar, the moral effects would again have been prodigious. In addition to the glamour of victory and the appeal it would have made to the imagination of the world, it would, I believe, have convinced all nations that the final victory was bound to be with the Allies, and it might easily have shortened the war by a year.[43]

Again the 'materialist' Fisher group was blamed for the decline in the Nelsonic spirit and the over-cautiousness that went with it.[44] The most extreme expression of this came from Admiral Custance, who was still hammering away at his prewar themes. He complained that basing the Grand Fleet in the far north at Scapa Flow, rather than down south where it could more easily get to grips with the High Sea Fleet, 'accorded with the mistaken doctrine that the military aim should be to control communications rather than destroy the enemy's armed force'.[45]

The fact that the German fleet escaped meant that the Grand Fleet had to continue with its laborious 'neutralisation' strategy. In discussing this however, Creswell made the distinctive and important point that superior intelligence meant that the Grand Fleet had only to go to sea when there were indications that its adversary was about to do likewise. This considerably reduced the difficulty of maintaining a distant naval blockade at a time when the battlefleet faced new technological threats in the shape of submarines.

Despite the difficulties, however, Creswell concluded that:

> As had usually been the case in the past, so it was in 1918: the Navy whose battlefleet had maintained a dominant position achieved at last an almost complete mastery of affairs at sea. The doctrine of battlefleet supremacy was once again justified by results; but it had not had too easy a passage, and there were times when many wondered whether this doctrine was really as unassailable as it had been in the past.[46]

This was particularly important for the British because, unlike other countries less dependent on their maritime communications, they really *needed* to be superior at sea.

Captain Bernard Acworth put the matter in particularly trenchant style:

> The main strategical lessons of the late war are not difficult to apprehend. It is clear that the primary mission of the British fleet, the mission for which its component parts should be definitely planned and constructed, is not, as is now almost universally preached, the patrolling of the trade routes for the protection of trade. Rather it is the decisive and

Richmond and the faith reaffirmed 117

overwhelming destruction, incapacitation or capture of the enemy's main fleet, an action which carries in its train certain automatic consequences of which the principal fruits are strategical initiative in the land campaign and the now comparatively simple business of trade defence, and the more effective blockade of the enemy's ports.[47]

Delays and restraints in getting to this happy state were the product of the preoccupation with keeping the fleet in being, 'a fleet of great material superiority, was to be regarded as an acceptable substitute for a decisive victory at sea ... safety became, perhaps for the first time in England's maritime history, a naval doctrine of war'.[48]

Not totally unsympathetic to this view, Creswell was pleased to see the increase in the extent to which the battlefleet of the interwar period was becoming more flexible through the adoption of divisional tactics and more delegated command authority. The fleet was more prepared to fight at night and was making use of new weaponry, especially in the shape of naval airpower to 'fix' a fleeing adversary.[49] Grenfell also was keen to identify the way in which an encounter at sea could be turned into decisive engagement, but in his case this exploration of the 'techniques of victory' took the form of an exploration of the way in which what were in effect the principles of war could be applied to the conduct of battle.[50]

Trade protection

In the interwar period, after the shocks of 1917 and despite the advent of ASDIC at the end of the war, there was very little complacence about the requirements of trade protection. 'The defence of trade', remarked Creswell, 'has always bulked large in British naval strategy and never more so than in the present century'.[51] Events had demonstrated the truth of John Colomb's observations about the need for a chain of overseas bases and for a serious effort to defend the British Empire's all-important sea communications.

Creswell covered all aspects of Britain's trade protection campaign of the First World War but emphasised that '[t]he success of the convoy system as a counter to submarine attack on trade was one of the outstanding features of the war'. Experience had shown that almost anything was preferable to ships sailing singly. Grenfell explained why, in a deceptively simple section which deserves some attention:

> Besides the greatly increased protection which it gives to shipping, the convoy system possesses another important advantage in that it renders the seas relatively much emptier than is the case with individual sailings, and thus reduces the mathematical chance of the attackers finding anything to attack. If we assume a ship to be visible at sea from ten miles away, a vessel on the ocean will be represented by a visibility circle of ten miles radius, which visibility circle will move along with the ship as

she alters her position. If, say, twenty-five ships are pursuing separate tracks through an area out of sight of each other, they will present twenty-five separate ten mile visibility circles moving through the area. Those twenty-five ships, if formed in convoy, will, however, present a visibility circle of little more than one ship; perhaps one of twelve miles radius . . . it can be seen that the chances of a convoy being sighted by hostile warships are very much smaller than of a similar number of ships sailing separately.[52]

Of course, convoy had disadvantages, in terms of assembly and arrival delays, the problems of diverse ships sailing in formation at the speed of the slowest ship and the 'all the eggs in one basket' syndrome – that is the ever-present danger that a raider might chance across a vulnerable convoy and be able to sink the lot, or a large proportion of the ships it included. There were complementary activities such as offensive patrolling, the defensive arming of merchant ships, decoy ships and so forth, but after the experience of the war, they were all presented as essentially ancillary.

The fact that the Navy had been caught by surprise by the advent of the U-boat threat and was slow to adapt to its presence, thought Grenfell, was directly attributable to the lack of a proper naval staff and the lack of a study of war amongst pre-war naval officers. In this he was echoing some of Richmond's most strongly-held views. Richmond had been intimately associated with the push to introduce convoys in 1917 and blamed delays on the faulty conceptions and amateurish administrative procedures of his seniors.

Grenfell, however made the balancing point that, with the best will in the world, even those who did study the subject of trade protection could get things egregiously wrong. He singled out Corbett for criticism on this front. While most naval officers of the prewar period were vaguely aware of the traditional advantages of convoy, Corbett had produced 'the standard book on naval strategy' but arrived at the erroneous conclusion that convoy was now of doubtful value, especially on account of the arrival of steam: 'It is by no means unlikely that the seeds of doubt as to the value of convoy, which were probably sown in the minds of any officers who turned to Sir Julian's book for inspiration, were responsible for the Admiralty's antipathy towards convoy in 1917'.[53]

But these were essentially avoidable errors. The Royal Navy's basic confidence in its capacity to defend British trade was robustly summarised like this by one commentator in 1940:

Suffice it to repeat the general verdict of history that the attack made direct against commerce by a navy that has not fought for and gained the command of the sea ought never to be fatal. It can be annoying, it may at times be disquieting; but, provided the appropriate countermeasures are taken, it should not be decisive. As a means of plunder the *guerre de course* may be gratifying: as a method of overthrowing an enemy it has so far always failed.[54]

Conversely Richmond and his colleagues remained convinced that Britain's capacity to strangle German overseas trade was a major cause of its victory in 1918. From the start, Hurd claimed, the war had demonstrated the crippling power of the British blockade:

> In the history of sea power, there is nothing comparable with the strangulation of German overseas shipping in all the seas of the world. It followed almost instantly on the declaration of war. There were over 2,000 German steamers, or nearly 5,000,000 tons gross, afloat when hostilities opened... Some... were captured, others ran for neutral ports, the sailings of others were cancelled, and the heart of the German mercantile marine suddenly stopped beating.[55]

Whatever the more considered view of historians long after the event might be, at the time and in Germany too there was little doubt that in the imposition of the commercial blockade on Germany British seapower had one of its most effective strategic weapons, and this was a verdict that Richmond and others were quick to accept, though not all would have gone quite so far as Michael Lewis:

> The economic blockade was beyond question the primary cause of her [Germany's] collapse. The interlocked armies, loudly slaughtering each other over shell-pocked battlefields, held men's gaze to the last. But the war was not really decided there. It was lost and won on the misty sea approaches to Britain and Western Europe.[56]

Acworth was equally bullish: 'The expulsion from the sea of every German merchant vessel for four years', he wrote, 'provides perhaps the most striking demonstration of sea power that has ever been presented to the world'.[57]

Grenfell was much more cautious than this, pointing out that the strategic effectiveness of the commercial blockade was a slow acting business and that a quick military victory with forces in place might finish the war before such economic pressure had begun to take effect.[58] Nonetheless, this sense of the importance of this kind of power from the sea led Britain's Navy and its government to do everything it could in the interwar period to defend the concept of the commercial blockade and belligerent rights. In this they were urged on by a set of thinkers, before and after the war, for whom blockade had almost ideological significance. As MP and publicist T. Gibson Bowles had written in 1910, 'The lesson of all history is that, whether in peace for trading or in war for fighting, the sea has always dominated the land; that in war most especially, navies are more potent than armies, the Trident a mightier Weapon than the Sword'.[59]

After the war, his son argued that for geographic and preeminently commercial reasons, Britain was the archetypal sea-centred state, in the middle, literally and figuratively, of a global sea-based trading system for the defence of which it was primarily responsible:

> Upon England accordingly, as a matter not of choice but of urgent necessity, devolved the business of freeing the main roads of the earth from the deadly obstruction of piracy and from the almost equally deadly obstruction of the national monopolies of shipping attempted to be set up in turn by each one of her rivals. For both purposes force at sea was evidently needed.[60]

On the other hand, because seapower was essential to Britain, conceding limitations on the country's capacity to blockade its adversaries at and since the 1856 Declaration of Paris effectively meant giving in to a 'conspiracy against British naval supremacy' started by the Dutch in the seventeenth century and which had continued in various guises since then.[61] The concessions mistakenly made on belligerent rights before the war needed to be recovered if at all possible – and should certainly not be developed. Richmond did not take quite such an impassioned view but nonetheless regarded the matter as sufficiently serious to make it the subject of the Lees Knowles lectures at Cambridge in 1931, under the title of 'Capture at Sea in War'. In these lectures he provided a reasoned and authoritative justification for the British consensus of the development of belligerent rights and the international law of the sea. He argued:

> To abolish the power of investment at sea, while leaving it untouched on land, is the negation of logic. Moreover to take from a maritime power the right to exercise pressure in this manner leaves her with no offensive weapon except for the only alternative measure of enforcing pressure – assault.[62]

Creswell for his part went more into the mechanics of blockade, explaining the various dimensions of the British commercial blockade and noting that in addition to the maintenance of the northern patrol it involved a sophisticated legal and diplomatic campaign. When deciding the way forwards, the government would need to 'take into consideration the economic conditions of all countries, our own, allied neutral and enemy; the tenets of international law; and the influence of neutrals'.[63] The capacity to inflict this kind of damage on the enemy's war economy was a crucial advantage of seapower at the grand strategic level and it was a particular area of naval activity that needed consciously to be fitted into the broader national strategy.

Perhaps thinking of the potential problem of dealing with Japan, Creswell also considered circumstances where the physical location of an enemy's ports and trade routes were so situated that the Navy would perforce have to resort to a policy of 'raiding' as other countries had against Britain. This was clearly a second best: 'A policy which, without being able to inflict vital damage, may still have a restricting influence on the enemy's trade, and under some conditions a disturbing effect on the disposition of his forces'.[64] Such faint praise for the policy of commerce raiding was an indication of a general confidence in the Navy's capacity to contain an enemy's attack on shipping and, by way of contrast, of the crucial strategic value of a well-mounted British commercial blockade. Events in the Second World War were to show that this level of confidence in both aspects of trade protection was overdrawn.

The impact of new technological challenges

But whatever their verdict on the strategic efficacy of seapower during the First World War, British naval thinkers of the 1920s and the 1930s knew they lived in a world facing major technological change that some believed would transform the nature of warfare at sea – so much so, in fact, that the old verities of maritime strategy might themselves be entering a period of substantial challenge. Thus Aston in 1927:

> The march of scientific discovery, accelerated by the impetus of war, has wrought radical changes in the sea service. Material has changed. Everything has speeded up. Progress in wireless telegraphy and telephony has revolutionised speed of communication, or information, orders and instructions. Guns and torpedo ranges have increased beyond recognition. The art of human flight, still in its infancy, already affects naval problems, both of strategy and tactics.[65]

Jellicoe agreed, claiming, '[a]t no previous period in our history have such radical alterations been effected in so short a period, and it is only natural that they should have exercised a marked influence on naval tactics'.[66]

But a number of radical naval officers and observers of the time went much further than this, suggesting that technological change would affect not only naval tactics but would also transform the size, shape and functions of the fleet and indeed the fundamental principles of naval strategy. Much of this tended to focus on the future role of the battleship in the face of the technological challenges posed by aircraft and submarines, a proposition put most forcefully by Admiral Sir Percy Scott and S.S. Hall, who by so doing took further the arguments sometimes advanced by Admiral Fisher before the First World War.[67] In effect, they argued that such capital ships were now so vulnerable to these new aerial and sub-surface threats that they would no longer be able to take their ancient place in the line of battle, that the defence of the country, its overseas bases and possessions and its trade would need to be performed instead by a host of much smaller vessels and by aircraft. These views commanded widespread support even among opinion-formers. Thus Lord Esher describing Churchill's book *The World Crisis*,

> I think the book shows the folly of going on building these great armoured castles that you have to keep in harbour and protect as though they were Dresden china. No battleships did a single thing in the whole war. They just 'menaced' each other at a safe distance. Jellicoe was terrified the whole time, unless he was protected by every sort of device and in harbour.[68]

At the Capital Ship Enquiry set up to investigate such claims and chaired in 1921 by Bonar Law, Richmond however rehearsed the traditional argument for the role and importance of the Navy's capital ships. In his view, and despite all the new technological threats, 'The Battle Fleet played the same vital part, in the same manner, with the same results as battle fleets have played in the past and ... without battleships on our side, the war would have been lost by the Entente.[69] In effect, the argument was that sea control had been won by the Grand Fleet and that this had underpinned the British blockade of Germany, the transport of military equipment and personnel around the world, the defence of British trade, and the defence of Britain and its overseas possessions from the fear of invasion. The fact that this had not required a Trafalgar-scale victory in battle was immaterial.

Referring, for example, to Scott's views on the campaign to defend Britain's sea communications in the First World War, Richmond remarked:

> He does not appear to know what part a fleet of battleships plays in war. He says that our Grand Fleet, supported by the fleets of our allies, was 'impotent to help us while we hovered on the brink of disaster'. He does not seem to understand that the small craft acting as escorts, patrols or hunting were able to operate freely without any appearance of force, solely by virtue of the cover afforded by the Grand Fleet. If an earthquake had closed the mouth of Scapa Flow and the fleet had been shut up inside, there would have been nothing to prevent heavy German ships in company with lighter vessels from going to sea and sweeping away all the small vessels that constituted the defence of trade.[70]

Later, Grenfell usefully developed this idea still further by exploring the notion of 'cover'. He pointed out the difference between the battle and control fleets, the former securing or defending command of the sea, thereby allowing the latter to exercise it through blockade and the defence of shipping. The Grand Fleet in short provided the conditions in which the control fleet of escorts could prosecute the war against the submarine, either through a strategy of convoy and escort or offensive patrolling.[71]

If Richmond's conclusion was that in the First World War the battlefleet had so far dealt with the technological challenges that had already taken place, he was nonetheless well aware of the technological challenges that still lay in the future. As a guard against them, he argued for a balanced fleet able to meet a variety of threats and somewhat displeased the First Sea Lord, Admiral Beatty, by urging more resources for research and development than for the immediate battleship building programme, which the Admiralty were requesting in response to the evident ambitions of Japan and the United States. Through the 1920s, this agnosticism increased and by the end of the decade Richmond, concerned about the mindless acceptance of technological possibility in the shape of ever bigger, valuable and more expensive capital ships, became an advocate of restraint. The bigger battleships became, the less strategically mobile and useful they would be: 'The policy of always outdistancing our competitors in size and armaments has done more to weaken our power at sea than either submarines or aircraft'. It was his public declarations in support of an international agreement for smaller battleships, of about 6–10,000 tons, that, in effect, terminated Richmond's naval career under what he bitterly described as the 'idiot dead weight of the materielists'.[72]

More generally, Richmond echoed Custance and others in believing that the prewar preoccupation with ship design, weapons performance and the procurement of material had stifled creative intellectual thinking. In 1912 and in connection with the setting up of the *Naval Review*, and concerned about the damage this was doing, Richmond had confided to his diary:

> We are going to have a try to stir up interest in what Kempenfelt called the 'sublime' parts of our work – strategy, tactics, principles . . . What I hope to develop is the mental habit of reasoning things out, getting at the bottom of things, evolving principles and spreading interest in the higher side of our work.[73]

There had been, and still was, the tendency to associate the production of new material with cautious and unimaginative strategies and operation designed to conserve it through the avoidance of risk. Creswell likewise opened his book with a preface by Admiral Sir Roger Keyes lamenting the fact that:

> A school had sprung into existence, and flourished exceedingly, which concerned itself mainly in the production and development of *materiel* in peace time, and its preservation in war. The importance of seeking battle, and forcing it to a conclusion, was lost sight of in a preconceived determination to run no risks of impairing our immense superiority.[74]

The pursuit of the offensive was, as we have seen, a major theme of the lively and controversial writings of Captain Bernard Acworth, who was extremely hostile to those who put *materiel* before policy. Although Acworth was absolutely clear that 'the battleship is still, as always, the citadel of all

124 *Geoffrey Till*

effective sea power, a citadel from which all classes of vessel derive their power to range the sea steadily and consistently',[75] he was hostile to the construction of large battleships, worried about the Navy's going over to oil, sceptical about the value of speed and the menace of aircraft, submarines and the torpedo: 'Perhaps the most vital need of the Navy today is to take up the torpedo by the gills, so to speak, and to look this pretentious bugbear squarely in the mouth'. Above all, he was opposed to what he termed the 'safety first' school of thought. Although Acworth's commentaries frequently verged on the libellous, he made for a lively and worthwhile read. As one critic concluded, 'Those who can refrain from throwing the book across the room will still obtain considerable amusement and instruction, as well as mental exercise in sorting out grain from chaff'.[76]

The problem was that as diverse representatives of the anti-materialist tendency, Richmond, Acworth and others of their historical bent not infrequently turned out to be wrong technologically, not least in regard to thinking through the consequences of airpower. Custance, as Hurd pointed out, had gone seriously astray on submarines, torpedoes and the all big-gun ship.[77] Richmond was manifestly uninterested in new technology and was indeed irritated by the 'new era' advocates; when he descended from the grand strategic level to the tactical and procedural some of his arguments were based on 'remarkable unsound technical premises'.[78] In reviewing one of Acworth's books, Richmond described aircraft carriers as 'costly and very weak' and grossly underrated the threat of land-based aircraft.[79] Grenfell likewise argued that the contemporary power of aircraft was conjectural, was dismissive of 'ship-borne aircraft [which] cannot drive the warship off the seas', but was much more alert to the future impact of shore-based airpower.[80] Seduced by the attraction of having more smaller ships, Richmond and Acworth both rejected the notion that large battleships were in fact less vulnerable to air attack than much smaller vessels, thanks to their greater resilience, defensive firepower and supporting units. Certainly, contemporary scholarship now tends to rehabilitate the reputation and insight of 'the authorities' in their responses to the new technology of the time.[81] It would seem that they were more often right than many of their critics.

Evidently effective balances need to be struck between the materialist and historical schools, neither of which had a monopoly of intellectual virtue. At the least, while strategic wisdom can indeed be derived from the scientific analysis of historical experience, its conclusions for the present and future also need to be disciplined by sufficient familiarity with technological reality. This balance had also to be struck in naval education and staff training.

History, education and the need for independent thought

Many were inclined to attribute the failings of the Royal Navy in the First World War to the claim that it had not prepared for war intellectually:

It should be remembered, however, that the study of naval history was not particularly encouraged in the pre-war Navy. It enjoyed no official encouragement and earned no official recognition in the way of early promotion or other material benefits. Rather the reverse. An officer who was known to study the higher branches of his profession was often looked on askance.[82]

The place where this kind of thing, it might be thought, should have been going on was the Royal Navy Staff College at Greenwich. As briefly referred to in Chapter 1, Bryan Ranft's department at Greenwich was founded in 1922, but neither this nor the founding of the Staff College in 1919 led to an explosion of interest in naval history and strategic thinking. Professor Sir Geoffrey Callender was the first to take the chair, but he was then really more of a preparatory school house master needing to be transferred from the College at Osborne in 1921, when it closed, than a first-rank naval historian. Nonetheless he was committed to the encouragement of interest in naval history both inside and outside the Royal Navy. Indeed, he played an important part in the establishment of the Society for Nautical Research and left the College in 1934 to become the founding Director of the National Maritime Museum.

Callender was absolutely clear on the importance of his subject:

> The written word was a driving force as mighty as that of a steam turbine, and in the stored up volumes of recorded history are to be found unchanging principles which will decide the wars of the future as they have decided the wars of the past.[83]

In order to advance the cause of naval history, Callender wrote a series of works on Nelson and Trafalgar and a book, specifically aimed at impressionable 12–13-year-old cadets, called *The Sea Kings Of Britain* which was hugely influential in shaping the attitudes of a whole generation of naval officers. It has since unfortunately become notorious for its uncritical approach to British naval history, and indeed for arguably damaging the standing of the subject.[84]

'Naval History' Callender thought '... is fairly easy to understand; and demonstrating, as it does, the finest and most characteristic achievements of the race, should be instant and widespread in its appeal'. *The Naval Side of British History*, published in 1924, from which this remark is taken, is a better book, clearly aimed at a more sophisticated clientele, but was still deeply imbued with romantic conceptions of the 'island race' instinctively taking to the sea in pursuit of national glory. The tone is didactic, uncritical and assertive:

> ... the battleships of Britain ... were the guarantee of integrity in word and deed; and the British sailor came to be regarded by races of every

colour and every creed as a warrior, capable of dealing trenchant blows, but preferring always in any one of a thousand ways to lend a helping hand.[85]

While a good deal of this may be ascribed to the patriotic values and propensity for purple prose characteristic of the time, it was designed to inspire rather than challenge its readers. It confirmed their prejudices rather than made them think. More dangerously, it substituted fine words and rhetoric for substantive evidence. Richmond criticised Callender's approach for ladling out a 'dead mass of inert facts'. 'You never saw such drivel as he pumps into [the students]' Richmond unkindly remarked.[86] Callender, a professional educator in the sense that Richmond wasn't, retorted that it was up to the student to draw the lessons not the teacher. The problem appears to have been that it was not always clear to the students what they were supposed to be drawing their conclusions about.[87]

Callender's immediate successors, Michael Lewis, John Bullocke and Christopher Lloyd, were better scholars and certainly more in tune with modern conceptions of what history is for. Lewis was old-fashioned in his approach, even in his day, but wrote extensively after he left RNC Greenwich producing a large number of accessible books and pioneering naval social history, especially in his best book, *A Social History of the Navy 1793–1815*.[88] Although a good scholar and by all accounts a riveting and sometimes outrageous lecturer who brought his subject alive, Bullocke was not primarily a naval historian and left little permanent mark on naval thinking. Christopher Lloyd was more ambitious, used original documents and took a broad view of the place of the Royal Navy in world events. He too was primarily interested in the social history of the Navy, indeed calling himself a 'social historian' and going into other such less familiar waters as naval medicine and the suppression of the slave trade. In addition, he wrote a number of eminently accessible campaign histories.[89] Arguably he came nearest to raising the standards of naval history as serious scholarship.[90]

Nor should the sensible, balanced and down-to-earth work of Brian Tunstall, who lectured at Greenwich from 1925–37, be forgotten. His *The Realities of Naval History* was a level-headed review intended to demonstrate that there was much more to naval history than ships, heroes, the smoke of battle and the lure of glory. He was worried that what happened at sea, and why it mattered, was not being explained properly. 'No wonder', he remarked, 'that a generation accustomed to looking at national achievements with a critical eye turns in disgust from such tawdry bombast'.[91]

Because British history could not be properly understood without a mature appreciation of the role of the sea, it was important to get that naval history right. In acknowledging his debt to Sir Julian Corbett, his father-in-law, Tunstall remarked that, 'It is no exaggeration to say that his writings and teachings not only created an entirely new outlook on naval strategy and tactics, but have exercised a very considerable influence on naval policy'.[92]

Here analysis of the naval past is seen as a means of better understanding the naval present. This was another reason to get the analysis right.

To do this, Tunstall sought to put naval operations into their social, economic, administrative and political context. He could be quite critical of the simplicities of some of his predecessors, doubtless including Callender.[93] His approach to naval history was comprehensive, including everything from the grand strategic to the tactical, technical and procedural. His *Naval Warfare in the Age of Sail*, for example, shows deep understanding of how the Royal Navy's complex flag-signalling system worked and the purposes it served. His *Anatomy of Neptune* likewise demonstrates deep familiarity with sources – another characteristic of the professional historian.

But paradoxically enough, and as remarked in Chapter 1, the historian now most remembered of what might be called the Greenwich set was probably not a standard academic but a naval officer – Admiral Sir Herbert Richmond. As his biographer shows, Richmond completed and extended the earlier efforts of Mahan and Corbett by raising the general awareness of naval history's significance both as a distinct field of serious academic endeavour and also as a vitally important process in the education of officers. This was 'history with a purpose'. Richmond was using its 'lessons' not to inform a general theory of maritime strategy, as Mahan and Corbett did, but simply to explain the complex role of seapower in Britain's security past and present. Some of his works were tracts of their times, but his last two books, *Statesmen and Sea Power* and the unfinished *The Navy as an Instrument of Policy 1558–1727* (edited by E.A. Hughes, 1953), stand apart and have survived as his best remembered. In these broad surveys, he sought to explain to both political and military leaders their joint responsibilities for defining national objectives and for developing strategic policies to best serve them in peace and war.

As a historian, while Richmond could not perhaps claim a direct line of his own disciples, he nonetheless hugely influenced the likes of Professor Arthur J. Marder and Captain Stephen Roskill, whose careers touched upon his in various ways. Richmond's mind and pen dominated the field after the First World War but his influence lasted long after that.

Educational consequences

One problem with this otherwise distinguished group of scholars, however, was their principal focus on the history of the Navy of wood and sail.[94] While no period of history is better or worse than any other in encouraging the development of the analytical skills so necessary for commanders at sea and naval policy-makers at home, this absorption in what many of their naval contemporaries regarded as a mildly interesting but distant and essentially irrelevant past did not help their cause. Concerned as they were with the unrelenting impact of new technology in the shape of aircraft, submarines, radar and later missiles and atomic bombs, it was all too easy for modern sceptics to regard this kind of naval history largely as a means of socialisation for younger members of the profession and a relaxing hobby for their more civilised seniors. For the latter at least, naval history was worth doing for its own sake. In many ways, this non-utilitarian sentiment was wholly admirable of course, but it was a weak basis for the inclusion of rigorous naval history in staff training syllabi.

Only a minority of naval officers took naval history that one step further, by regarding it as a means of developing analytical naval thinking. Richmond was a leading proponent of this view, however. He started from the proposition that the Navy needed people capable of breaking free from orthodox opinion and making up their own minds about what needed to be done:

> It is not the 'wearisome reiteration of type' that we require in the Navy but the freshness of outlook which results from the association of men with widely varied and differently acquired experience; men whose minds are free from the clogging influences of living from their early youth within a ring fence. Orthodoxy has its merits but blind orthodoxy such as is liable to result from cramped early association which accepts without question certain traditions, sayings, customs or dogmas, is one of the most dangerous of all conditions in a fighting service.[95]

This had been the reason for his creation of the *Naval Review* before the First World War. He wanted to develop the capacity for independent thought in the staff and war courses at Greenwich while Admiral President there from 1920–3. He emphasised the need for reading and self-study, rather than formal training, and he put special emphasis on the value of history. He was clinically exact about what he meant by the term 'naval history':

> In my interpretation, Naval History is a record, as accurate as it is possible to make, of the manner in which the Navy has, up to the present day been used by Statesmen of all the several periods to achieve the national ends; of the methods of the employment of the naval weapon in pursuance of those ends; and of the conduct of the operations which resulted from that employment.[96]

Richmond argued that the study (not the mere reading) of naval history was useful to three sets of people – the general public, statesmen and sea officers. Without it, the first would have but an incomplete understanding of their own past, the second would be less likely to exercise their strategic responsibilities efficiently in pursuit of the national interest and the third, less able to learn from the mistakes of others, would be more likely to make their own.

Aston was particularly concerned about the need to educate the general population in the more sceptical atmosphere of the 1920s and 1930s: 'It would be an inestimable boon to our responsible sea officers if, in times of emergency, they had behind them the force of a public opinion acquainted with the nature of sea warfare'.[97] The result should be a population properly supporting the Navy on the one hand but not one unreasonably expecting an instantaneous Trafalgar as they had last time.

Common sense, whilst a theoretical and alternative defence against error, had all too often proved to be far from common. Creswell, who aimed his book at young naval officers, made the point that the detailed analysis of naval history was a way of compensating for an individual's lack of operational experience, and it could also provide a reality check for theory.[98] For all these reasons, it was essential, he thought, to remedy the British failure to develop an official organisation both to research the naval past and to spread a knowledge of naval history through the Navy and the country as, Richmond argued, other countries did.

Richmond did his best to remedy these deficiencies when, both at Greenwich and as Master of Downing College, he wrote some of his very best books. Progress was certainly made, but as a 1935 study conducted by Vice Admiral William James, Deputy Chief of the Naval Staff, demonstrated, its overall impact on the Navy as a whole was constrained by the fact that the best officers were kept at sea rather than put through the staff training system.[99] This was their and the Navy's loss, since, the report concluded, with their intellectual needs un-catered for, such officers would be less likely to reach their full potential. Richmond's views were nonetheless not always understood or sympathised with, and he found the Greenwich experience 'interesting but saddening'.[100]

The beginnings of jointery

In 1926, after a period as Commander-in-Chief, East Indies, Richmond was made the first Commandant of the new Imperial Defence College (IDC) in London. He played a considerable role in the creation of the IDC and in its subsequent progress on a course which made it, its successors and Commonwealth sister colleges, vital institutions for the higher discussion of national defence issues.

As has been discussed earlier in this chapter, this failing had had serious consequences both at the level of grand strategy and when it cascaded down to the operational and tactical levels. The fatal difficulties in securing and expanding the bridgeheads at Gallipoli for example can be directly attributed to weaknesses in joint thinking around the council tables of London. Such examples had demonstrated the need for a body of senior officers able to fit their single service perspectives into 'the problem of war as a whole'. This aspiration was not advocated merely in the name of organisational expediency; it represented the beginnings of a recognition that especially with the advent of mass industrial-age warfare on the one hand and of airpower on the other, the nature of warfare itself was changing, growing more complex and more demanding of those responsible for the formulation and execution of military policy.

Accordingly, the aim of professional military education was to correct such dysfunctional practices by encouraging the development of the joint approach. In this, professional educators would be serving strategic, operational and, indirectly, even tactical purposes. Richmond's aim was to help develop what we would now call 'jointery', specifically by encouraging naval officers to think about their interrelationship with their Army and RAF colleagues. Naval strategy needed to be thought of as an essential but contributory part of general strategy:

> We all, of all three services, worked in the most complete harmony at the college. We were too busy seeking to understand each other's needs, to find ways by which we could combine our efforts, to descend to petty squabbles about the greater or lesser importance of our respective services.[101]

These early indications of a developing interest in 'joint' rather than simply naval thinking were of course built on foundations laid by Corbett and Callwell before the war.

But all three service chiefs were still wary of the IDC and everything it stood for, partly because they thought it might well encourage the creation of institutions, procedures and personnel that could in due course undermine their own service authority. In this, they were, of course, quite right.

There were also some misgivings amongst the thinkers about how far this could safely go. Aston, one of the first, as we have seen, to fold airpower within a joint strategy, very much approved of the fact that the services were now much more familiar with each other's work: 'Army officers are constantly to be met with in his Majesty's ships all over the world ... and naval officers see a good deal of the field training of troops. All this is very much to the good'.[102] But he was concerned by the increasingly common usage of the word 'military' to encompass all the services: 'This practice is objectionable, as it leads constantly to serious misunderstandings. As naval conditions transcend all others in importance to those interested in our security, it is desirable that this wide use of the term "military", swallowing the word "naval" into its maw, should be noticed by a public accustomed to use the word in its narrower sense in conversation'.[103] In effect, the worry was that 'joint' could all too easily become 'insufficiently naval'.

Aston was, for example, very concerned about what he called the 'air problem'. By this he meant the distressingly widespread view that the development of modern aviation meant that strategically speaking Britain was 'no longer an island', that many of the Royal Navy's traditional functions at home and abroad could be taken over by the Royal Air Force and that, in consequence the Royal Navy would in the future be less central to Britain's security concerns than it had been in the past. But as far as Aston was concerned, Britain's continued reliance on sea communications meant that 'air-power can be described as an aid to sea-power, never likely to be a substitute for it'.[104] Of course, in this he was speaking for the entire community of naval thinkers.

But despite such reservations, cooperation between the services advanced significantly in the interwar period. The Committee of Imperial Defence system was developed, and the Chiefs of Staff Committee and its advisory body, the Joint Planning Committee, were set up in 1922. The Navy contributed to the creation of tactical and administrative doctrine in the shape of the *Manual of Combined Operations* and took the lead in considering the amphibious side of combined operations. Thought was given to the development of prototype landing craft, headquarter-ships, floating tanks, means of suppressing chemical defences and so on. At the end of 1937 the Interservice Training and Development Centre was also set up. Nonetheless, what was clearly envisaged was a set of ideas and plans that could be put into effect *should the need arise* – a basis for mobilisation, in effect, rather than a fully formed specialised amphibious force. Even so, in this as in many other ways, the Navy that went to war in 1939 had, despite all the financial stringency of the period, come a long way since 1918 and the naval thinkers of the time had both influenced and reflected the process.[105]

Notes

1 Hurd (1915) p. 9.
2 Aston was in fact considered for the prestigious Chichele Chair at Oxford in 1919. Hunt (1982) p. 149.
3 Hunt (1982) pp. 237, 1.
4 Liddell Hart (1932) p. 7.
5 Cited in Bond (1977) p. 69.
6 Howard (1974) is a good example of both. See also French (1990) esp. pp. xi–xviii.
7 Creswell (1944) p. ix.
8 Ibid. p. 11.
9 Grenfell (1937) p. 11.
10 Hurd (1918) p. 1.
11 For a discussion of this see Hunt (1982) pp. 126–7.
12 Letter to A.H. Pollen cited in Hunt (1982) p. 225.
13 Grenfell (1937) p. 19.
14 Till (1979) deals with these issues in much greater detail, esp. pp. 111–36.
15 Schurman (1965) p. 145.
16 Hunt (1982) p. 214.
17 Hurd (1915) p. 14.
18 Corbett (1920) pp. 64–5, 105–6.
19 Cited in Hunt (1982) p. 50.
20 Cited in Baugh (1993) p. 22.
21 Corbett (1921) pp. 129–30. For further discussion of this campaign see Till (1996) and (2003).
22 Corbett (1921) emphasis added.
23 Callwell (1924) pp. 2–3, 105.

24 Creswell (1936) pp. 189–90.
25 Ibid. pp. 192–3.
26 Ibid. p. 196.
27 Ibid. (1936) p. 200.
28 Ibid. p. 216.
29 Callwell (1924) p. 335.
30 Liddell Hart (1939) p. 131.
31 Corbett (1921) p. 241.
32 See Wiest (1995), Massam (1995) and Till (1997).
33 This was inserted into Vol. III of Corbett (1920–31). For background see Ranft (1993).
34 Anon (1931) and also 'Some notes on the early days of the Royal Naval War College', in the same edition of the *Naval Review*.
35 Hurd (1918) p. 126.
36 See also Breemer (1993).
37 Aston (1927) pp. 20, 47, 64.
38 Richmond testimony to the Capital Ship Enquiry, 5 Jan 1921, Cab 16/37 PRO.
39 Schurman (1965) p. 142.
40 For an elegant exploration of this view see Baugh (1993).
41 Creswell (1936) p. 116.
42 Ibid. pp. 72–3 and the particularly thoughtful discussion on victory in battle at pp. 54–61.
43 Grenfell (1937) p. 137.
44 Ibid. pp. 149–50.
45 Cited in Hurd (1918) p. 51.
46 Creswell (1936) p. 34.
47 Acworth (1935) p. 116.
48 Acworth (1930) p. 12.
49 Creswell (1936) pp. 124, 136–7.
50 Grenfell (1937) pp. 164–91.
51 Creswell (1936) p. 139.
52 Grenfell (1937) p. 54.
53 Grenfell (1937) p. 91.
54 T124 (1940) p. 96.
55 Hurd (1915) p. 11.
56 Lewis (1959) p. 224.
57 Acworth (1930) p. 56.
58 Grenfell (1937) p. 45.
59 Bowles (1910) p. v.
60 Bowles (1926) p. 72.
61 Bowles (1910) p. 135.
62 Richmond (1934) cited in Baugh (1993) p. 28.
63 Creswell (1936) p. 182.
64 Ibid. p. 183.
65 Aston (1927) p. 9. See also ibid. pp. 16–21.
66 Aston (1927) p. v.
67 Hall in testimony to the Capital Ship Enquiry, 3 Jan 1921 Cab 16/37 PRO and for a convenient summary of Scott's views, which were regularly featured in *The Times* at this time. See also Hurd (1918) pp. 103–4. For the immediate background to the Enquiry see Till (1979) pp. 121–2, Hunt (1982) pp. 119–24 and Roskill (1968) pp. 221–5.
68 Letter 27 Mar 1923 in Brett (1938) p. 287.
69 Richmond, written submission to the Enquiry, NSC of 9 Feb 1921 in Cab 16/37 PRO.

70 Richmond, testimony to the Capital Ship Enquiry of 5th January 1921, Cab 16/37 PRO.
71 Grenfell (1937) pp. 92–3.
72 Hunt (1982) p. 126; Richmond to Henderson, 34 Mar 1929, RIC/7/1, NMM cited in Hunt (1982) p. 191. Ibid. p. 198.
73 Richmond, Diary, 19 Oct 1912, RIC/1/8, NMM.
74 Creswell (1936) p. vii.
75 Acworth (1935) p. 116.
76 See contemporary reviews in the *Naval Review*.
77 Hurd (1918) p. 145.
78 Grove (1993) p. 232.
79 Hunt (1982) p. 221.
80 Grenfell (1937) p. 232.
81 For more recent works tending to argue this point see Ranft (1977), Till (1979), Bell (2000), Moretz (2002) and Franklin (2003).
82 T124 (1940) p. 59.
83 Callender, 'An Educational Century' p. 23.
84 See the discussion in Goldrick and Hattendorf (1993) pp. 104–7.
85 Callender (1924) pp. v, 237.
86 Richmond to Dewar, 26 July 1923, DEW, 6. Cited in Hunt (1982) p. 128.
87 Callender, memorandum to Richmond of 22 Dec 1924, reproduced in Goldrick and Hattendorf (1982) pp. 107–8.
88 Lewis (1960) but see also Lewis (1959).
89 Lloyd (1954); see also Lloyd (1949) and Lloyd (1957).
90 I am grateful to several of my colleagues for this review, particularly Professor Nicholas Rodger and Commander Duncan Ellin.
91 Tunstall (1936b) p. 5.
92 Ibid. p. 9.
93 See Schurman's comment in Goldrick and Hattendorf (1982) p. 106.
94 The First World War, for example, hardly features even amongst Tunstall's major works, although it is briefly reviewed in Callender (1924).
95 Richmond, 'Naval Training: The Training of Officers', *The Fortnightly Review*, 132, August 1932, pp. 190–1, cited in Hunt (1992) pp. 65–81.
96 Richmond (1939).
97 Aston (1927) p. 20.
98 Creswell (1936) p. 9.
99 Adm 116/3060, Organization of War Courses and Training of Naval Officers for War. PRO. Discussed in Hunt, op. cit. p. 72.
100 Cited in Hunt (1992) p. 74.
101 Letter of 14 Oct 1942, cited in Hunt (1992) p. 78.
102 Aston (1927) p. 11.
103 Ibid. p. 70.
104 This huge issue is analysed at length in Till (1979) esp. pp. 187–201.
105 See Massam (1995). For a general survey of the interwar period see Roskill (1968), Till (1995) and Bell (2000).

7 All sorts of wars
British naval thinking and technology in the Second World War

Jock Gardner

In the beginning

It is a truism that nations rarely, if ever, go to war in quite the way in which they have contemplated fighting it. The German Navy in 1939, for instance, fell a long way short, in hulls alone, of that needed – and indeed promised – by the national leadership for a conflict against the British Empire. But neither was the latter ready in all respects for any conflict, far less the one that ensued.

To be sure, the worst case had been anticipated, that of a three-enemy war against France, Italy and Japan. This was a true nightmare as the combination of the size and quality of enemy forces together with the global extent of the opposition posited a very demanding scenario, probably incapable of being resisted should it have all come together simultaneously and in anything approaching a coordinated manner. Providentially for Britain and its empire, this did not happen in either case, the initiation of the European and later Asian conflicts being separated by over two years. Just as fortuitous was the lack of cooperation and even communication among the so-called Axis powers. To British advantage, too, was the acquisition of allies. The first year of the war saw a decline in this respect with the successive loss of Scandinavian countries followed by the Low Countries and most of Scandinavia.[1] But worst of all was the loss of France, bringing German forces to within a few miles of the United Kingdom, reducing the available trained land forces and much of their equipment and vastly improving the basing position of German air and naval forces. This was particularly marked in the access it afforded to U-boats, their position being immeasurably improved from north-German basing. The British position worsened further with Italy's entry into the war on the German side, opening up a new theatre of war in the Mediterranean both at sea and in North Africa. Perhaps more importantly it also jeopardised the British route to India and further east, making communication with the eastern Empire much lengthier and more hazardous. This was in many ways the lowest point as future developments were to result in net advantage rather than the opposite, no matter how black they may have appeared at the time. Roughly a year after the fall of France, Hitler's ambition took him to the East with the invasion of the USSR. Ultimately this action was to seal the fate of Germany at least as far as the land war was concerned. A further half year brought the Axis its greatest strategic coup and guaranteed its greatest grand strategic failure: Pearl Harbor. Despite the damage done to the naval forces of the USA it brought the world's greatest scientific, technological and economic power into the war on the Allied side and effectively determined the outcome, although that was to lie some four years in the future following the expenditure of much treasure and life. The subject of how British naval thinking progressed during the conflict is addressed in terms of the actions carried out. It could easily be argued that this is a faulty measure not least because of the presence of an enemy, but fighting the war that ensued can give a very clear idea of what lay behind. Thinking is, after all, of little use if it is not grounded in the strategic situation, one's own capabilities and those of the enemy. In the ensuing sections which start with a chronological theme, certain topics which clearly belong outside of that frame are introduced but there is always a linkage into the relevant time period. Thus, Dunkirk in the next section is used as a hook to describe all of amphibious warfare.

One-theatre war

British naval capability covered a wide spectrum of potential operations, especially when this was compared to German forces. There was certainly quantitative superiority in most fields, even submarines, but the qualitative situation was more ambiguous. Although there were some aged German units, many were relatively new and, at the heavy surface ship end of the array, often competent, if not superior in either speed, protection or striking power. They included novel types such as the *Panzerschiffe* whose combination of endurance, reasonable speed and, most of all, hitting power posed a potent threat to shipping if not to main fleet units.[2] Both these and disguised surface radars spawned no significant technical riposte but doctrinally they generated the need for many units to scout for them, then allowing concentration to deal with them. This was the dramatic outcome of the sortie of the *Graf Spee*, which was scuttled in 1939. Other disguised surface raiders were dealt with less dramatically but no less certainly.

The larger ships such as *Bismarck* and *Tirpitz* were more difficult to deal with than any single *Panzershiff* or disguised raider, and their disposal took much longer. In a sense the pursuit and sinking of the former was rather like the *Graf Spee* writ large, albeit in northern waters. It did involve greater forces, including most of the Home Fleet's heavy units and aircraft carriers. The latter's attacks included influence-fuzed torpedoes, although these proved a failure. Intelligence played a part in the pursuit, although the much-lauded Ultra had but a minor part and more significance is attributable to such techniques as air reconnaissance, high-frequency direction-finding and radio

136 *Jock Gardner*

fingerprinting.[3] Perhaps the most significant use of new technology was the British use of radar by cruisers tracking the *Bismarck* group from the Denmark Strait. Using radar enabled contact to be held, at least for a while, without the lesser gunned and armoured ships suffering significant harassment.

The timeframe of the German war was to extend until mid-1945 and so many of the events and developments considered under this heading do not truly belong in the period implied by the title, but it is convenient to consider them here. Staying with capital ships the next important event of interest is the disposal of the other large battleship *Tirpitz*. Her career is chronologically later than her sister and she was not to repeat her operational pattern of one significant and fatal sortie. In most ways she was more of a problem as a potential threat than anything she achieved directly in reality. In truth her greatest contribution to the German war effort lay in her very existence – a one ship fleet-in-being or in later language a 'virtual threat'. The event which highlighted this was probably the great damage wrought on convoy PQ17 on its way to Russia when its scattering was brought about not by the presence of *Tirpitz* but by the perception that she *might* be at sea.

The ultimate fate of *Tirpitz* was to be capsized by vast bombs dropped from land-based aircraft but it is probable that she was ineffective as a significant fighting unit some time before this. She was subjected to a number of different types of attack, mostly from the air.[4] However, the most innovative method was that of using midget submarines to penetrate net defences, then leave large timed charges under her hull. This drew for inspiration to some extent on the experience of the Japanese and the Italians, although both attempted their operations in a more benign natural environment. Although the difficulties of carrying out such a form of warfare at relatively long range and against such a well-protected target led to very significant attrition, *Tirpitz* suffered major damage.

The most important part of the sea war against Germany was the six-year long so-called Battle of the Atlantic. This was conducted almost entirely by submarines and it was to this problem that some of the greatest doctrinal and technological efforts were applied. It is a little difficult to do justice to this in such a small space but an attempt should be made. Doctrinally and organisationally the submarine problem produced many important innovations but its basic tenet was centuries old: convoy. Unlike the First World War where this had been introduced late and against some entrenched opposition, there was little question of its introduction early, albeit not as extensively as desired, but that was to happen. Further and contrary to some belief, suitable ships had been designed and were being built. This was particularly true of that workhorse, the corvette. Tactics against submarines were devised and perfected during the war.[5] It is worth mentioning tactical and training development as distinct achievements.[6]

Next it is probably appropriate to mention the soft or non-direct warfare fields of intelligence and operational research. Intelligence was not new in the sense of a discipline or practice but it is fair to say that British naval intelligence in the Second World War reached one of its greatest peaks. About 30 years ago it was fashionable to see this almost entirely in terms of one product only – Ultra – the decoding of German operational signals. But subsequent research has made it clear that this major achievement formed only part of a richer and more complex tapestry of information, the processing applied to it and its subsequent exploitation.[7]

Operational research (OR) was a way of doing things better without recourse to finding solutions entirely through new equipment. By taking a different view of sensors, weapons, procedures and tactics, it proposed methods of working which maximised performance. Examples of this were the debate about convoy size and the selection of depth setting for air-dropped depth charges.[8]

But the success of OR in making the best use of equipment in service should not obscure the enormous amount of development in technology that took place over the period of the war. There was significant progress in surface ship platforms. Certainly some of these were evolutionary such as the development of what would now be called frigates but there were more radical solutions, notably the small, or escort, aircraft carrier. These became available from about the midwar period, deploying a relatively small number of aircraft such as the Swordfish for anti-submarine warfare (ASW). One of the most important aspects of these ships was that their hulls were largely of merchant ship design, cutting cost and building time. Further, these were built on greenfield sites on the US west coast.

But it was in the area of land-based aircraft that perhaps the greatest strides were made. At the beginning of the conflict most maritime aircraft were little more than the castoffs of the RAF, little suited to oceanic warfare in general and badly equipped with sensors and weapons. A typical 1939 aircraft could spend a shortish time on task only a low number of hundreds of miles from its UK airfield equipped with visual observation and a couple of depth charges which at that time would be set to a depth likely to do little damage to a submarine. By 1943 there were many much more capable, much longer-legged aircraft equipped with good quality radar, a night illumination light and several more suitable depth charges. A few American aircraft had even advanced to carrying rudimentary sonobuoys and homing torpedoes, prefiguring the direction that airborne ASW was to take after the Second World War.

The equipment of surface ships improved immensely to fit them for ASW. In order to understand this fully and in context, it is necessary to realise that the submarines deployed by the Germans were critically and heavily dependent on the use of the surface for their operations. Further, their style of operations made a great deal of use of radio for information and group coordination. This made them particularly susceptible to two developments: radar and ship-fitted high-frequency direction-finding (HF DF). Both of these were fitted ever more widely during the war and underwent constant improvement. Radar, for example, changed from being a temperamental item of poor performance, especially against such a relatively small target such as a surfaced U-boat, to a much more accurate and reliable piece of equipment. HF DF enabled detection of the all-important contact-keeper submarine and allowed the despatch of forces to attack or at the very least submerge it, the latter resulting in its loss of contact with a convoy which had previously been liable to attack by the group which the U-boat had been attracting.

Underwater, too, Asdic or Sonar, was refined to improve its likelihood of detecting submarines and to provide better data on which weapons launch could be based. The Allied problems of detecting deeper submarines and of determining their depth were also addressed at least to some extent. As well as this, better methods of creating a coherent submarine track were developed.

Underwater weapons were also a priority in development. Apart from the ubiquitous depth charge, improved in detail in the course of the Battle of the Atlantic, ahead-thrown weapons were invented. Although the main impetus for them came about from the problem in a depth charge attack in which a single ship would have to overrun its submarine target, thus losing sonar contact, there was an additional factor present in one of the more ingenious of these weapons, Hedgehog. The other problem that this intended to solve was that of lack of depth determination and thus the quandary of what explosion depths to set on depth charges. This was normally a matter of experience and guesswork. Hedgehog attempted to solve the problem by not solving it. Each of its 24 projectiles had no depth initiation, instead relying purely on contact to detonate its relatively small charge. The weapons were fired so that the bombs formed a circle. This may have lacked the satisfying explosive thump on reaching depth but accounted for a fair number of submarines.

An important event in the summer of 1940 was the improvised amphibious withdrawal of the British Expeditionary Force from Dunkirk. Although this operation could never be described as a victory, it was important in salvaging a large part of British ground forces and making a subsequent German invasion of the United Kingdom less likely.[9] Future amphibious operations took place later in the war and were conducted worldwide and with varying degrees of competence. Largely these were meticulously planned and involved the construction of large fleets of specialised amphibious shipping. A whole naval, it might be said joint, subculture of doctrine, tactics and practice was built up involving integral and attached fire support, beach clearance and other arcane skills. Perhaps most importantly, this was manned almost entirely by officers and ratings who had not belonged to the prewar Royal Navy.

This raises the matter of recruitment and training. The Royal Navy, like most others, had to expand several-fold in wartime. It is fair to say that it did so with a minimum of strain and produced both officers and ratings who were able to fulfil the many demands made on them. This speaks well of the two important factors: organisation and training.[10]

Into the Mediterranean

The fall of France had several adverse consequences for the conduct of the war. The enemy was brought closer to the United Kingdom, German submarine operations were immeasurably eased by the acquisition of the Biscay bases, the French no longer operated on Allied behalf in the western Mediterranean and, perhaps worst of all, Italy now joined Germany in opposing a Britain all but alone. The Mediterranean was transformed from an uneasy neutrality to a hostile zone with important consequences. Direct communication to Egypt and thus further to the eastern empire could no longer be taken for granted. A land campaign started in North Africa which although initially successful against poor Italian opposition, then became a hard struggle against German troops, not finally resolved on that continent until some two years later, and Malta was threatened.

The continuing requirement to keep heavy units in home waters gave the relatively small Italian battlefleet an undue degree of leverage, but this was to a large extent countered by the innovative attack on the Italian fleet in harbour at Taranto in November 1940 by Swordfish aircraft. This was the first raid of such a nature and prefigured the larger scale effort by the Japanese against the US fleet in Pearl Harbor just over a year later. Probably a greater threat to British command of the Mediterranean came from the air, especially as Italian and then German forces began to move into Greece and the Balkans in 1941. The constrained nature of the Mediterranean made British naval forces very vulnerable to attack from the many aircraft based ashore and threatened both forces at sea and ships in bases as well, thus allowing little respite. From time to time, for example, Malta became untenable for surface ships and even submarines only survived by daytime submergence alongside in harbour.

Malta has become rightly known for its tenacity under ferocious attack from the air. It served as a base for offensive forces, air, surface and subsurface, which took the war to the Axis both on and *en route* to the North African littoral. However, Britain's tenuous hold on what has been described as the Verdun of the Second World War could not have been exercised without the difficult and costly operations of running supply convoys from either Alexandria in the east or Gibraltar in the west. The former had a (slightly) easier run but involved an enormous logistic tail starting in the UK and leading to Egypt via the Cape of Good Hope, a very long journey. The western Mediterranean convoys obviated this problem but were more likely to meet more intense opposition. Neither were easy and involved transits with opposition from, potentially, submarines, mines, surface ships and – most dangerous – aircraft.

Every operation to Malta was on a major scale and each saw determined Axis efforts to force them back or at least cause major attrition. It was in such an intense air environment that warning radar together with sets for gun direction and fire control came to maturity. Here too, the Allied discipline of fighter direction was born.[11] It was these innovative methods of exploiting existing sensors that allowed these operations to proceed with loss that was at least manageable.

Another aspect of the Mediterranean war was submarine operations, whether conducted from Malta or elsewhere. These were sometimes the only effective way of taking the war to the enemy. Whether it was intelligence gathering, minelaying or attacks on Axis shipping, the finest hour of the British submarine service was almost certainly during that campaign. Such an aggressive series of operations was not without cost and the losses suffered by the submarine flotilla were high.

The further object of many of these operations was the support of land operations, a theme that runs through many of the naval events of the Second World War. Sometimes this was less obvious, such as in the defence of shipping, sometimes more so, such as in the Mediterranean, but this concept, then as in the past and probably in the future, remains a constant theme.

Global war 1941

It is commonly assumed that the Japanese war started in December 1941 with the attack on the US fleet at Pearl Harbor. But such are the vagaries of international time zones and date lines that the Japanese attack on various British Empire territories came first. It really mattered little because Japanese gains were fast and extensive in area. British forces were generally outnumbered and outfought, largely as a consequence of being committed elsewhere. The naval low point was almost certainly the loss of *Prince of Wales* and *Repulse* in early 1942. Although barely a formality thereafter, Singapore, Malaya and Hong Kong fell, and the USA and the Netherlands also lost significant territories in what was the near high-water mark of the Japanese Empire.

The British naval war that ensued is probably best considered in three ways: holding actions, submarine warfare and the British Pacific Fleet. Initially there was no question that all the principal cards were held by the Japanese: air power, littoral bases and preponderant force. This dictated a policy of holding on to the Indian Ocean area as could best be done. Keeping the Japanese from Ceylon, then India was the key priority and the limited British naval forces largely had to fight by appearing to be stronger than they actually were – by advancing by night and withdrawing by day, and making maximum use of the bases in India, Ceylon and East Africa that were still held. The Japanese made incursions into this area, especially by air, but they too were approaching the limits of their power and were unable to build much on their initial surge which had peaked in 1942. The British campaign was skilfully conducted but was not without losses. It also proved difficult to reinforce the East Indies fleet whilst there were still large demands being made both in Atlantic and Mediterranean areas. Some temporary reallocation proved possible from the eastern Mediterranean to the

Indian Ocean but the overall tenor was of spreading a weak and old force very thinly, generally done with much skill by James Somerville.

At the same time the Royal Navy was exposed for the first proper time to the most advanced naval aviation nation when, in a period of severe need, the aircraft carrier *Victorious* was loaned to the Americans in the Pacific in late 1942. Here two strong themes of the Second World War came together: aviation and inter-Allied working. To be sure, limited Anglo-US cooperation had been practised in the Atlantic even before the formal entry of the latter into the war but this was never quite so integrated as with *Victorious* or with later exchanges of an American carrier into the Mediterranean, or with US ships on the Russian convoys. Despite a few initial cultural hitches this worked well and prefigured the heavy reliance of the Royal Navy later in the war on American equipment, especially aircraft, escort carriers and some escort ships such as the Captains class.

Submarines played a part in the eastern war rather different from either the Atlantic or Mediterranean. Instead of having secure bases, as in UK-based squadron, or a tenuous one in the case of Malta, there were virtually none reasonably close to the enemy. Instead it was necessary to operate either from Ceylon or the more secure but far distant Australia. Long passage times and narrow straits imposed further limits to time on task. Further, the Japanese did not have large numbers of medium merchant ships and were in any case very well spread, attempting to maintain their empire over many thousands of miles. There was also a significant difference in submarine operating characteristics, tending to result in American submarines operating in deeper water and British ones closer inshore in such areas as around the Malay peninsula. This meant that there was an emphasis on small targets, often attacked by surface gunfire, and attack on small ports. There was also a strong theme of transporting special forces to beaches by night. These built up expertise which was to continue in the postwar period. At the same time the east also saw the successful sinking of the cruiser *Ashigara* in June 1945 by *Trenchant*. Midget submarines were also used to attack targets in Singapore towards the end of the war.

The development that was to have one of the most important consequences for postwar developments occurred in the closing stages of the war with the establishment of the British Pacific Fleet. Although this contained some of the more modern elements of the Royal Navy of the period its dual significances lay elsewhere. Despite the best technical efforts it was clear that these ships lagged behind those of the USA that they fought the war alongside. It might be argued, for example, that the difference in aircraft carriers was merely one of style in which British armoured protection was preferred to American maximisation of aircraft capacity. But there were other important differences too in intensive utilisation of air groups. Perhaps, as importantly, British ships measured up poorly in terms of endurance and fuel efficiency.[12] This came as a revelation and encouraged postwar trends. Other systems, too, were not as good, such as anti-aircraft gunnery.

However, one of the biggest changes and culture shocks which came the way of the British Pacific Fleet was the necessity to cast off the shackles of immediate base support and instead rely on the services of a fleet train. This was nothing very new – Nelson's ships had been supported in a very similar manner but this was a new development for the twentieth-century Royal Navy. This requirement was brought about by having to conform to the American fleets' method of operations. It involved both a large demand for freighting and other specialist ships, even to the point of one which specialised in the brewing of beer.[13] But it was most of all in the skills of underway replenishment that the greatest advances had to be, and were, made. This was to be one of the greatest lasting legacies of the Second World War.

It would be wrong to suggest that in the eastern theatre or, to be more accurate and representative, theatres, there was little in the way of amphibious effort. Certainly this would appear from a British perspective at least, to be true, but the American campaigns in the Pacific were largely driven by amphibious operations and warfare. But there were, albeit minuscule, British efforts against Madagascar and in the eastern Indian Ocean.

The test of war

There were many familiar elements to the Royal Navy at the end of the Second World War which would have been recognised by an observer of the scene from 1939. There were similarities as well as contrasts. There were still battleships but their premier position had been usurped by the aircraft carrier. Perhaps the even more telling illustration than the large number of modern carriers was their aircraft which in a few years (and with a good deal of assistance from the USA) had gone from the biplane to the threshold of the jet age.

There were elements of equipment which had grown immeasurably such as radar – from a limited, often unreliable tool in 1939 to a very versatile sensor which transformed such fields as anti-aircraft gunnery, played a significant part in the defeat of the U-boat and enabled the whole subject of air defence. Perhaps, too, some stress should be laid on the 'soft' disciplines such as intelligence and operational research, not to mention the immense significance of underway replenishment.

There were two other important developments of note, one organisational and the other with technical and grand strategic implications. The Royal Navy had been well used over successive centuries to working with allies, often quite closely, but this was rarely as pronounced and developed as it was during the Second World War, specifically the cooperation with the USA which reached new heights. Not only were there large staffs in both capitals but operations such as the invasion of France in 1944 was truly allied involving British, American and Canadian forces (as well as representatives of others). The same was true of the later operations in the Mediterranean and, perhaps most marked and integrated of all, in the Pacific, as previously described.

This was to serve as a very good lead-in to the succeeding decades in which one of the important threads was that of alliances, and one in particular, NATO. For the Royal Navy the relationship that lay at the heart of this, and despite the tensions brought about by the end of Empire, was that with the United States Navy.

The other development, in which the Royal Navy had not been involved, was the development of the atomic bomb. To be sure, this had an important impact on postwar naval tactics and strategy, inducing a considerable amount of concern and uncertainty about the role of naval forces in the future. The greater effects brought about by the new intimate knowledge of the atom were not to be seen fully for another two decades or so.

Another way of looking at the Royal Navy in the Second World War would be to ask that somewhat old-fashioned question, 'Did the Royal Navy have a good war?' In the sense that the United Kingdom was part of an alliance system which won the war, the answer obviously has to be 'yes'. But this high-level response conceals almost as much as it reveals. The Grand Alliance was a magnificent monster of great complexity. Is it really possible to equate even in a rough order of significance the Red Army with American naval forces in the Pacific, far less the efforts of the various air forces engaged? The correct answer is, of course, that it cannot be done. In the words of a well known arithmetic trick practised sometimes on very young children, 'What do you get if you add three apples and two oranges?' The answer is either the return of the original question or else a fruit bowl. Similarly with large-scale wars involving all sorts of parallel activities: it can be very difficult to tease out critical dependencies or very precise orders of significance. Two things can be said with certainty: the Royal Navy played a full part in winning the war and it was also fully receptive to new technologies in a way which facilitated its part in the war.

* * *

Processing the experience

Overall, the Royal Navy had a better war in 1939–45 than it did in 1914–18. Perhaps because of that, there were far fewer major postwar controversies over matters of principle in maritime strategy that there had been in the 1920s and 1930s. There were arguments, of course, over particular issues, such as the overestimation of surface ships' capacity to defend themselves against air attack, the threat posed by U-boats operating on the surface at night or in packs in the mid-Atlantic, the confusions and errors of the Norwegian and Dakar campaigns, the despatch of the unsupported *Prince of Wales* and the *Repulse* and their fate upon arrival at Singapore, and the disastrous dispersal and subsequent destruction of Convoy PQ17. But these were more often disputes over implementation than over claimed errors of principle.

Nonetheless, there was clearly a need to review that experience, not least because, with the advent of a new and unfamiliar strategic environment dominated by the Cold War and the end of Empire on the one hand and the arrival of missiles and atomic weapons on the other, the Royal Navy was clearly about to sail in some quite uncharted and very challenging waters. One of the first naval thinkers to take this matter up was Vice Admiral Sir Peter Gretton.

Born in 1912, Admiral Gretton served throughout the Second World War, taking command of convoy escort groups from the end of 1942. After the war, he had a brief period as Senior Directing Staff at the IDC, ending his career as Deputy Chief of the Naval Staff and Fifth Sea Lord. Upon leaving the Navy, he became Senior Research Fellow at University College Oxford. Making use of his wartime experience, he wrote a number of books on convoy operations during the Atlantic campaign, a biography of Winston Churchill and, in 1965, *Maritime Strategy: A Study of British Defence Problems*. He died on Armistice day, 11 November 1992.

Gretton defined his task as 'to decide whether the principles of maritime strategy are still relevant'.[14] Most of his book was less about the lessons of the Second World War in themselves than it was about their continued applicability in the radically new conditions then obtaining. His conclusion, perhaps unsurprisingly, was that such lessons would indeed be found to apply to the novel and unsettling conditions of the nuclear age. It followed, therefore, that the study of naval history would retain its value. Climbing onto his admitted hobby horse, he complained that 'there seems to be something in the make-up of sea-faring men which discourages the study of the past, and especially the application of the lessons of the past to current events'. This failing, he added, 'has been the direct cause of many very expensive blunders in the fields of tactics, materials and strategy.'[15]

In the first part of his book, and wanting to get on to the challenge of dealing with the new security implications, he was content with a quick summary of what he took to be the broad principles of maritime strategy up to the advent of the nuclear age – principles which he considered had been validated by the experience of the Second World War. He interpreted the word 'maritime' in the Corbettian sense, namely that naval strategy was but one component of a maritime approach alongside elements of an air and land strategy:

> Its main weapons are the attack on the economic life of the enemy while preserving the essential trade of this country, and the use of the sea to conduct outflanking and diversionary movements of military forces with the object of obtaining a decisive result on land – a result which must be attained by the armies. A maritime strategy assists and supports a continental strategy . . . a maritime strategy is the method of employing all arms of all services. It should not be looked upon in any way as a purely 'naval' venture; the inter-dependence of armies, navies and air forces is

total and each should integrate its efforts with complete precision if success is to be achieved.[16]

The remembered wartime disputes over the allocation of aircraft to, and their use in, campaigns as diverse as the battle of the Atlantic and the Normandy landings reinforced this aspiration in the immediate postwar years. Sadly, the advent of nuclear weapons and the turf wars they produced both in Britain and the United States nonetheless bedevilled inter-service relations at least at the grand strategic level, for the better part of 20 years.

Gretton defined what he meant by maritime strategy as 'that which enables a nation to send its armies and commerce across those stretches of sea and ocean which lie between its country and the countries of its allies and those territories to which it needs access in war, and to prevent its enemy from doing the same'.[17] In fact this was a conscious appropriation of Richmond's definition of seapower. Gretton's doing this illustrated both the debt of his generation of naval thinkers to those who had gone before and the continuing lack of consensus on the meanings of the words used in maritime discourse.

Gretton's summary of the principles of maritime strategy largely followed the ideas and assumptions of Captain Stephen Roskill, the main naval thinker of the immediate postwar period, to whom had fallen the task of officially processing the experience of the Second World War for the Admiralty. Its allocation of this task to Roskill was a further indication that the Navy was taking its history more seriously than before.

Born in 1903, Roskill entered the Royal Naval College at Osborne 13 years later. From the start he developed an interest in naval history, winning the Navy's Naval History Prize for his account of the battle of Jutland. In connection with this he met and talked with Richmond for the first time.[18] Early in his career he became a gunnery specialist, and at the beginning of the Second World War served in the Gunnery Division of the Naval Staff where his task was to help repair the deficiencies caused by the policy errors and financial stringency of the interwar period. In this capacity he crossed swords with Churchill's scientific adviser Professor Lindemann (later Lord Cherwell) and with Admiral Sir Frederic Dreyer, the officer charged with, among other things, the supervision of Merchant Navy gunnery. Perhaps in partial consequence of this, Roskill soon found himself, like other undeferential subordinates before him, posted to a cruiser on a distant station.

In this case, it was HMS *Leander*, then serving in the Pacific. However, Japan's subsequent entry into the war changed this backwater into one of the main areas of conflict and Roskill was soon engaged in the operations of war. He was wounded and decorated with the DSC for his part in *Leander*'s conduct during the battle of Kolombangara in the Solomons on the night of 12/13 July 1943. In 1944, however, Roskill was posted to the British Admiralty Delegation in Washington, a position of responsibility and importance. His associations with the United States survived the ending of the war and he was the Senior British Observer at the atomic test on Bikini

Atoll in 1946. Suffering from deafness, that occupational hazard of his generation of gunnery officers, he knew himself to be effectively precluded from further positions of seagoing command. Recognising this, he asked for, and was granted, a premature retirement from the Navy on medical grounds in March 1949.

However, in his case, this disappointment led to a career change in which Roskill's prospects and his reputation were soon to flourish. Largely on the strength of the excellence of his report on the Bikini Atoll test, he was charged with the writing of the official history of the naval operations of the Second World War, as we have seen. On the face of it, this was an extraordinary gamble but one that paid off triumphantly. Originally conceived as a narrow operational history of the Atlantic War, Roskill's work blossomed into the mighty *The War at Sea* series. The appearance of the first volume of this in 1954 made his name as a historian and proved highly popular with the book-reading public. Two more volumes appeared, the last in two parts, with Volume III, Part II being finally published in 1961.

Roskill's success as a historian owed much to the tremendous efforts he made to get at all the facts relevant to the explanation of a particular situation. He insisted on seeing all the papers he needed. His determination to discover and print all the facets of the issue he was analysing, with a meticulous attention to the finest detail, demonstrated the true historian's concern to represent the unique and complex nature of his subject matter as fully and as fairly as he possibly could. In his case the findings of deep historical research were supplemented with the invaluable insights of one often actually involved in the events he studied and personally acquainted with many of their leading figures. The combination of these two advantages led to his work having an authority that verged on the magisterial. He was, moreover, able to present his narrative and his conclusions in a dignified yet readable fashion which appealed to the general public.

Accustomed to controversy, and as official historian (and one, moreover, who consciously had the example of his illustrious but unfortunate predecessor of the First World War, Sir Julian Corbett, before him), he was prepared to withstand the mightiest in the land if he thought their explanations for what had happened differed substantially from what he believed to be the truth. The strength of his feelings on this issue can best be gauged by looking at his remarks about the lamentable consequences of censorship and interference from those on high when it came to analysis of the conduct of the Gallipoli campaign, for example.[19]

Paradoxically enough, it was Mr Churchill himself who in Roskill's case proved difficult over the publication of uncomfortable conclusions about such matters as the Dudley North affair or the despatch of the *Prince of Wales* and *Repulse* to the Far East in 1941. Roskill insisted on having access to ULTRA intelligence but was careful to conceal it as basis for his conclusions. In other ways too, he was determined, as a true historian, to protect his sources. He was at his most acid when confronted by those who sought to deny him access to records he knew existed or by the consequences of those modern Visigoths of the Admiralty who had wantonly destroyed so much of the record on which he and other historians must depend. He should, incidentally, take considerable credit for the fact that the official record retention and weeding process of the period improved a great deal in his time.

In the spring of 1961, Roskill gave the Lees-Knowles lectures, accepted a Senior Research Fellowship at Churchill College, Cambridge, and embarked on a career as a general naval historian. His intensely industrious research programme eventually yielded a veritable library of meticulous and source-based books on British naval policy and operations in the twentieth century. He died in Cambridge on 4 November 1982.

The Strategy of Sea Power, an expanded version of his first lectures, appeared in February 1962; it was well received by reviewers and the general public alike. Inevitably there were some criticisms. In the *Daily Telegraph* C. Northcote Parkinson pointed out that Roskill relied almost exclusively on the experience of the Royal Navy, to the exclusion of other navies; other academics argued that Roskill had artificially polarised the 'continental' and 'maritime' schools of strategy – the relationship between the two being in fact more complex than mere competition. Some senior naval officers still in uniform were concerned that Roskill's enthusiastic espousal of the submarine as the capital ship of the future would make it more difficult for them to get the new carriers they thought they needed. But generally *The Strategy of Sea Power* was recognised as a 'masterly feat of compression' as rich in its analysis of the past as it was stimulating in its guidance to the future. The book sold steadily, was reprinted, appeared in the United States and was translated into German. It has continued to maintain a steady readership ever since.

Although in *The Strategy of Sea Power* Roskill's theoretical analysis of such components of maritime strategy as sea control, the nature of blockade and so on are scattered throughout his narrative, he in fact came closest to defining his philosophy explicitly in the first chapter of the first volume of *The War at Sea*. In the first paragraph of that work Roskill made the, by now familiar, basic maritime case:

> During the three centuries or so of our history as a world power it has several times happened that a far stronger continental coalition has pitted its might against Britain and her allies, has won a series of resounding victories on land only to find itself brought up against a method of waging war with which its leaders could not grapple and of which they had no clear understanding. Yet, ultimately, our maritime strategy, founded on centuries of experience of the sea, brought our enemies to utter defeat.
>
> When Britain and France took up the new German challenge in 1939 they took it up on the Continent. But when the enemy's land victories

of 1939 and 1940 had deprived us of all our continental allies, a change of emphasis in our strategy became inevitable – if for no other reason, because only two methods of continuing the war against Germany remained open to us. One was the offensive use of our initially small bomber force against German military and industrial targets; the other was to exploit to the utmost our traditional capacity to employ a maritime strategy as the means of bringing overwhelming forces to bear against the enemy in theatres of our own choice.[20]

In common with other strategists of seapower, Roskill considered it important to explore what he thought were the basic constituents of seapower. In his view, there were three:

The first comprises all the varied instruments of war which work on or beneath the surface of the sea or in the air above it. It can be called the Strength Element, for it is on their strength and numbers that maritime control greatly depends. Second comes the possession and safety of the bases from which all the instruments of maritime power must work. If bases are lacking, or are inadequately defended, the ships and aircraft cannot fulfil their functions. This can be called the Security Element. The third element of maritime power comprises the Merchant Navy, which must be adequate to feed our home population, to bring in the raw materials needed by our industries, to carry our exports overseas and to transport our armies and their multifarious supplies to the theatres where they are required to fight. Nor is the Merchant Navy by itself enough. It must be supported by an adequate shipbuilding and ship repairing industry to enable losses to be replaced and damaged ships to be returned rapidly to service. This can, perhaps, best be called the Transport Element. If it is inevitable that, in maritime war, the actions fought by the warships and aircraft gain most attention, it must never be forgotten that the purpose of those actions is, nearly always, the protection of the merchantmen; and without the steady devotion of the men who man those ships the whole structure of maritime power must crumble.

Such, then, appear to be the elements comprising maritime power in a modern context; and each of them must be present in adequate form if the nation's maritime strategy is to be fulfilled.[21]

He was alert to the possibility that the precise form of these elements might vary over time. In the Second World War, for instance, aircraft of both the land – and sea-based variety had come to exert a very great influence indeed over events at sea. Technology meant that the capacity to control the surface of the sea depended in large measure on control of the water beneath and the air above. The arrival of the aircraft and its impact on maritime operations made it necessary to redefine the elements of maritime power which used until then to bear considerable similarity to the ancient

All sorts of wars 149

order of things when it was accepted that the fleet which controlled the sea routes and fought off all challengers must comprise three classes of warship. They were called the ships of the line or battleships, the cruisers and the flotilla vessels: 'The cruisers actually exercised control of our sea communications – supported by the battle fleets to prevent interference with our cruisers by more powerful enemy units – and the flotilla vessels acted as scouts for the battle fleet and carried out multifarious functions as escorts and in local defence'.[22]

In the Second World War however, aircraft showed themselves capable of performing part or indeed sometimes the whole of the duties hitherto borne exclusively by all three types of surface warship. They attacked the enemy's principal naval units (the function of battleships), carried out increasingly effective reconnaissance and shadowing work (the function of cruisers), and supplemented the flotilla vessels in their multifarious duties in convoy escort, anti-submarine and fleet defence work. Very evidently the material may change, but the principles remained.

Turning to the conduct of general war, Roskill believed that the experience of the Second World War showed that the prosecution of a maritime strategy tends to follow a common pattern:

> The experiences of the last war appear to reinforce those of earlier struggles which had shown that the prosecution of maritime strategy passes through several phases. In the first it is probable that our strategy will be defensive, particularly if a new continental coalition has to be constructed. During this phase our maritime power is used to defend these islands from invasion, to cut the enemy off from the rest of the world and weaken his economy by enforcing a blockade, to hold and reinforce certain key points and areas overseas and to bring to this country the supplies which are essential to its survival. But while it may be necessary to accept that our strategy must, during this phase, remain defensive it is of cardinal importance that no opportunity should be lost to assume the tactical and local offensive against such forces as may present themselves. If such opportunities are lost the period of the strategic defensive may bring about a decline of morale and of the will to fight. Assuming however that war remains such as it has been hitherto, and that our commanders seize every opportunity for local and tactical offensives, the period of the strategic defensive possesses certain inherent compensations. Chief among these is that, while our war economy develops, while our resources are mustered and our military strength expands, the enemy is forced, if he wishes to attack us, to do so across seas which he does not control. Such ventures, if made, expose his forces to drastic counter-measures and may result in expensive failures. The unwillingness of the Germans to accept such risks during the recent war is underlined by the immunity from attack of such key points as Iceland and the Azores. During the second phase our maritime forces

continue to carry out the functions which occupied their whole capacity during the first, but in addition the nation's offensive power is being developed. Forces of all armies are being built up, assembled and trained; and plans for their offensive employment are being prepared. This phase, which ends with the first major offensive operation, may well be entitled 'The Period of Balance' since the success or failure of the first offensive has yet to be decided. In the third phase the full advantages of the patient pursuit of a maritime strategy are reaped and our forces are transported overseas to assume the offensive.[23]

The immediate aim of maritime strategy is, Roskill thought, to establish command of the sea, or sea control, but this need not necessarily be an absolute control:

The aim of maritime strategy is therefore not so much to establish complete control of all sea communications, which would be an ideal hardly attainable until final victory was almost won, as to develop the ability to establish zones of maritime control wherever and whenever they may be necessary for the prosecution of the war in accordance with the directions of the Government. And a zone of maritime control means no more than an ability to pass ships safely across an area of water which may be quite small in extent or may cover many thousands of square miles of ocean. Thus the enemy, mainly by the use of aircraft, established for some time a zone of maritime control in the central Mediterranean which, while it lasted, virtually denied to us the use of the communications through that sea. And the crisis of the whole struggle in the west developed, after the Battle of Britain had been won, from our need to establish a zone of maritime control over the entire length of the Atlantic shipping lanes and the enemy's sustained attempts to defeat that control. It must, however, be emphasised that complete control of even a restricted zone is rarely established, and that it is far more common for control to be in dispute than undisputed. Moreover, if control over a particular zone is lost by one belligerent, it is by no means certain that it will pass to the other. In this stage it is more likely that control will remain in dispute and such, for example, was the condition in the English Channel in the summer of 1940. Furthermore, throughout the period when control of sea communications is in dispute, and even after the establishment of a reasonably firm zone of maritime control, sporadic attacks will remain a possibility. Such attacks on our sea communications persisted almost to the end of the recent war.

Wherever, therefore, a zone of maritime control is established, our own commercial and military seaborne traffic will be able to pass in reasonable safety. But there is a further effect of the establishment of such a zone. It will automatically bring about the denial to the enemy of the use of the same sea communications. In other words, the creation of such a zone produces a positive result to ourselves and a negative result to the enemy; and the latter can be as important as the former. Thus by creating a zone of maritime control in the focal area for shipping off the River Plate we protected our own South American trade and prevented the enemy from using the same routes; and when the zone of maritime control essential for the North African landings of 1942–43 had been completely established, we denied the enemy the use of sea communications adequately to succour and support his own armies in that continent.[24]

This capacity to control the sea plainly demands flexibility in the application of maritime power and in the concentration of its instruments. This concentration is more than the simple massing of numbers of warships. It calls for an intelligent distribution of force so that on the one hand it can cope with possibly widespread and simultaneous calls on its services but can, on the other, still be wielded as a cohesive unit. The proper balance between the concentration and division of force is difficult to achieve. Roskill was, like Sir Julian Corbett (whom he much admired and frequently quoted), suspicious of the tradition of massing forces as a prerequisite to seeking decision with the enemy by battle at sea:

This has long been a fundamental precept in our maritime services, and it is a tradition of immense power and value. Nonetheless it is a precept which can be carried too far, and our history contains examples where it has only led to indecisive battles. It must, in truth, be constantly tempered by the judgment and experience of those responsible for the conduct of operations, since it is well established that, if enthusiasm for battle outruns judgment, the blow will fall upon air; whereas by waiting with forces correctly disposed we shall compel the enemy ultimately to offer an opportunity for action. It happened many times in the war that the commanders of our maritime forces assumed the tactical offensive, often against superior strength, with great gallantry and most favourable results; and it now seems that our adversaries sometimes sacrificed a potential advantage through reluctance (often imposed on them by higher direction) to do likewise. Nonetheless the well-known capacity of a defensive strategy in certain conditions to inflict grievous injury on the enemy and to stultify his purpose still holds good. Perhaps the outstanding example from the last war relates to the defeat of the enemy's attack on our merchant shipping. Though it was not at once accepted there now seems no doubt at all that it was the defensive strategy of sailing ships in convoy and of providing the convoys with powerful surface and air escorts which did most to accomplish that decisive victory. Yet it was the desire at once to assume the offensive against the U-boats which led to the persistent employment, during the first year and more of the war, of flotilla vessels to hunt enemy submarines in the vast ocean spaces instead of using them to escort our convoys. Not only did the early hunting groups achieve negligible success, but the dispersal of our slender resources in that manner led to our convoys being inadequately escorted, and so suffering heavy losses, and to many good opportunities to destroy the submarines which attacked them being missed. Equally the view that bomber aircraft could contribute most to the defeat of the U-boat by taking the offensive against the enemy's bases and his building and repair yards rather than by escorting and protecting the convoys far out at sea, is not substantiated by post-war analysis of their achievements. It is today impossible to avoid the conclusion that the most effective way of defeating the U-boat was by waiting for it in the vicinity of the prey which it was seeking.

The chief difficulty in implementing this policy of waiting is the reluctance of public opinion to believe that it can be a deliberate strategical move and not an example of timidity or pusillanimity on the part of our commanders. Yet the truth is that nearly all of the really effective blows struck at our enemies' maritime power have come about through a deliberate tempering of the desire to seek and destroy the enemy by judgment and experience, which had taught that the object would be more assuredly achieved by offering the enemy a bait and then waiting for him to present himself. The sinking of the *Bismarck* and of the *Scharnhorst* provide examples of this, though in the case of the latter ship it was necessary to wait many months before she came to her destruction. All the major warships of the Japanese Navy which could be made fit for sea also came, ultimately, of their own accord to meet their end.[25]

Roskill and Corbett both attributed the fatal tendency to concentrate too much on the exciting business of preparing for a decisive battle to a failure properly to appreciate that command of the sea and the control of sea communications was not an end in itself but simply a means to an end. The point of maritime power was to be able to use the sea for one's own use and to prevent the enemy from using it for his. Roskill believed that the Royal Navy sometimes suffered from devoting too many of its assets to winning command and not enough to the tasks of exploiting it.

Roskill recognised that the sea is vital as a means of transportation of men and material essential for the conduct of war. It followed that one corollary of having the necessary command to use the sea in this way could be to stop the enemy from doing the same:

> The denial to the enemy of the use of sea communications is accomplished by the application of all the various instruments comprising maritime power, but the sum total of their effects can be described as being the establishment of a blockade. This is one of the chief means whereby a nation which is stronger at sea may be able to impose its will

on one which, though stronger on land, is not self-supporting in food and raw materials. In spite of German arguments to the contrary, which read strangely from a nation well versed in the exaction of all sorts of rights, penalties and requisitions from nations subjugated by continental campaigns, it is a relatively humane form of war. In common, however, with other aspects of the exercise of maritime power it is slow and cumulative in its effects; on the other hand, it starts to function from the day on which hostilities open.[26]

Control of the sea is also a prerequisite to operations against the shore. By denying it to the enemy, the navy can prevent him from launching a successful invasion:

Maritime strategy in face of a threat to invade our shores also requires some special consideration. There is a tendency, in such circumstances, for the public to demand the massing of our forces around our coasts. Such a policy, if adopted, would be a false concentration; the attitude adopted would be wholly defensive, and the initiative would rest with the enemy who might thereby be given the very opportunity he seeks. The traditional British policy, and it has been successfully applied many times in our history, is quite different. In the first place the enemy transports which are assembling to carry, or are actually carrying his army, displace his warships as the primary object of our maritime forces. A firm grip over the assembly of the transports is established by blockade. Today this includes bombing, bombardment and minelaying as well as constant watch and patrol off his assembly ports. The blockade is enforced by flotilla vessels and aircraft, but they must be supported by greater strength and covered by the battle force in the background. The threat of invasion is clearly visible to the layman; the countermeasures are probably concealed from him. But they are none the less effective for their invisibility from the land, and there should be no uneasiness in British homes as long as the old methods are applied and the strength and vigour of our maritime forces remain unimpaired.

Assuming, however, that the old policy is adopted, the enemy must try either to force his invasion army through in one large mass, or slip through whilst evading our blockading forces. The second choice can hardly be applicable to a modern expedition attempting to cross narrow seas. The first choice is extremely favourable to the defence; it produces exactly the conditions for which we have always hoped and has, again and again in our history, led to decisive sea battles. It appears that Hitler intended to adopt this course in 1940, thereby following in the path of many earlier continental strategists, and that the British policy which frustrated and defeated the intentions of his forerunners also destroyed his plans. Indeed, study of contemporary German documents leaves little doubt that the quarrelsome vacillations of the German leaders were chiefly caused by the uneasiness which always seems to be produced among our enemies when it becomes apparent that an invasion is to be launched across seas which they do not adequately control. The lessons of 1940 appear to reinforce our knowledge that, although continental enemies have repeatedly tried to find a way to invade these islands without first defeating our maritime forces, no such short cut exists.[27]

By the same token, with the necessary control of the sea the Navy can make possible those operations against the enemy's shore which are at once the final aim and crowning glory of a successfully conducted maritime war:

> Finally – and this point is placed last in this discussion because it is not reached until the application of our maritime strategy has begun to bear fruit and the early strategic defensive can be exchanged for the offensive – we must consider the employment of maritime power to transport our armies overseas, to place them on shore in the chosen theatres, to support and supply them as may be necessary and to shift their bases forward as their land campaigns advance. It is plain that the establishment of an adequate and effective zone of maritime control in the approaches to, and the coastal waters off, the disembarkation area is an absolute prerequisite for success in this type of operation. The functions of our maritime forces in an amphibious expedition of this nature differ considerably from those of the forces employed on mercantile convoy work. In the latter case their duties end with the safe arrival of the convoy in port; but in the former case they must continue to support and assist the army after it has landed, and continue to maintain the maritime control on which success on land hinges. Their function, in fact, ceases to be purely maritime; they become a part of one vast and integrated organisation comprising all arms of all services, and all working towards the common end of defeating the enemy's land forces.
>
> The great merits of amphibious expeditions of this nature are their mobility and secrecy. By making good use of strategic and tactical feints and defeating the enemy's reconnaissance it is possible to achieve surprise in both spheres, as, contrary to all expectations, occurred in the case of all three major enterprises (North Africa, Sicily and Normandy) launched by us and our Allies against our European enemies during the late war.[28]

The Strategy of Sea Power can be looked at in two ways. Firstly, as a traditional naval history of Britain, it describes the evolution of British seapower from its earliest days and shows its importance in British history. As such it might be thought vulnerable to various sorts of criticism. In the first place, Roskill's use of the first person plural throughout his book would seem old-fashioned when set against the stern objectivity of modern historians. More substantially, a generalised *tour d'horizon* of the whole of Britain's maritime history was bound to be challengeable in the light of later, more detailed work on finer points. Yet despite this, the broad thrust of his treatment of the conduct of this and other conflicts remains as valid now as it was when it first appeared. Indeed, later scholarship has often demonstrated the succinct perceptiveness of Roskill's earlier commentary. His analysis of the despatch of the *Prince of Wales* and *Repulse* to the Far East in 1941, for instance, is a miracle of accurate compression.[29]

The thrust of *The Strategy of Sea Power* has also been challenged, less for its treatment of specific events than for the general assumptions on which it is founded. For instance, Paul Kennedy's seminal and much admired book, *The Rise and Fall of British Naval Mastery*, took the usual navalist hypothesis, which plainly underlies Roskill's work, and turned it back to front: British seapower, by his account, was made possible by and determined by British economic power rather than the other way about.[30] This challenge to the importance of maritime power relative to other forms of power was perhaps inevitably attacked in its turn by other writers basically sympathetic to the Roskill/Gretton line and the debate once again became a major theme for the rest of the century.[31]

Roskill and Gretton were both aware of a sea power's limitations in dealing with a land power. 'Seapower' said Gretton, 'is not a universal panacea. The wielders of sea power have in the past obtained great advantage from its use, yet they have found themselves vulnerable to its exercise and thus in a position of potential weakness'.[32] They both accepted that British seapower could not on its own have defeated Hitler any more than it defeated Napoleon. Because, as Roskill put it, 'the defeat of the renewed invasion threat, the close blockade of French ports, and the protection of our trade could not by themselves bring victory, it became essential to build up another continental coalition'.[33] The same applied in 1939–45. Paradoxicaly, he thought, it was Germany's victories in 1940 that forced the British to revert to a maritime strategy after a period in which the long preoccupation with the Continental alternative had sapped the armed forces' capacity to fight what he thought was the normal kind of 'British' war. Equally, Roskill and Gretton accepted the point made earlier in the century by Charles Callwell and demonstrated all too graphically by the Germans in the Norway campaign in 1940 or the Scheldt operation in 1944 that the control of the land may often facilitate the control of the sea.[34] Generally geo-strategic conditions in the European theatre were rather less suited to the application of decisive maritime power in the shape of blockade or amphibious operations than they were in the Far East where Japan and the Allies were truly engaged in a Homeric maritime struggle of the sort rarely seen since the Anglo-Dutch wars of the seventeenth century. In the Far East 'once command of the sea had been won in the Indian Ocean and Pacific, victory over Japan was achieved with amazing speed and economy'.[35] This campaign was seen as a triumphant vindication of the offensive potential of seapower; the Royal Navy's participation in this final phase of the maritime war through the action of the British Pacific Fleet boosted its confidence in tackling the future challenge of the atomic era.

But, Roskill concluded, even in Europe and although seapower did not act in isolation and needed to be 'employed in skilful conjunction with the other arms', it was decisive: his closing conclusion on the Second World War was that 'the strategy which brought about first the downfall of Italy, then the surrender of Germany, and finally that of Japan, was always predominantly maritime'.[36] Roskill accepted that the Russian army was due much of the credit for the final defeat of Germany, but his argument was still rejected by them and indeed seriously questioned by many historians since. Thus the Soviet Navy's Admiral Gorshkov: 'The war in the European theatre assumed an explicitly continental character and the operations of the fleets in the Atlantic theatre including the Mediterranean, Baltic and Black Seas were increasingly aimed at meeting the requirements of the land forces emphasizing the land nature of the greatest battle in history'.[37]

It is certainly true that what Richmond had argued was one of the major weapons of seapower – the commercial blockade – was much less effective in the Second World War than it had been in 1914–18 because of Germany's ability to build up stocks and substitutes before the war and to exploit the resources of occupied Europe after the opening campaigns. Before the summer of 1941, moreover, Germany derived much essential material from neutrals.[38] This tended to support Gorshkov's proposition that what really mattered was the situation on land.

Finally, both Roskill and Gretton maintained that seapower was less immediately successful than it would otherwise have been because mistakes were made. Roskill attributed many of these, especially what he considered the neglect of Britain's amphibious capacity, to the country's Continental preoccupations and financial stringency in the interwar period. But the Navy made mistakes too. Both Roskill and Gretton were critical of certain parts of the Navy's war in defence of Allied shipping against German submarine, surface and air attack. Partly this was held to be a matter of ASDIC-induced complacency[39] but less forgivably, perhaps, it was attributed to faulty doctrine. Gretton put it like this:

> When I read on the naval recruiting posters 'Join the Navy and help to protect Britain's Sea Lanes', my heart sinks for another ignorant officer has been allowed to perpetuate the old aimless catchwords. It is not possible to protect a lane in the sea unless it is short and narrow, like the approach to a harbour which can be kept clear of mines. In the first world war millions, and in the last war, thousands of miles were patrolled uselessly both by cruisers and destroyers before this simple fact became clearly understood. It is *ships* which must be protected, not lines drawn across charts. The core of the problem of sailing a ship or ships from one port to another in war is to control the slice of water in which the ships float, as well as the air above and the depths below. Any wider degree of control is welcome but not essential . . .[40]

Gretton thought that the analogies such as sea lanes, or sea lines of communication encouraged the unwary to think in terms of notional 'roads' across the sea which needed to be patrolled as the highway patrol does motorways. In fact, this activity was almost pointless, certainly when compared to the tactic of convoy-and-escort which, by concentrating defensive assets where the commerce raiders could potentially do them most harm, in fact provided the best means of destroying them. Moreover, if the raiders failed to locate their targets, they could safely be ignored, since the safe and timely arrival of the convoys in itself would meet the strategic purposes of the whole operation. Roskill, for his part, attacked the Admiralty's perverse inclination towards offensive hunting groups in the early stages of war, its reluctance to drop the 'all the eggs in one basket' proposition against large convoys,[41] and the continuing temptation to release faster ships of moderate speed from the constraints of convoy, and attributed some of these mistakes to the Navy's fixation on securing a decisive engagement against the adversary in terms which consciously echoed the earlier strictures of Sir Julian Corbett. Gretton was less severe: 'Whatever the composition of the menacing force', he wrote, 'it must be either destroyed or else prevented by other means from becoming effective, before sea power can be fully exercised'.[42]

Roskill accordingly maintained that there had been a tendency in the interwar period and in the early stages of the war to pay too much attention to the requirements of a major battlefleet encounter at the expense of other less exciting but more useful naval activities, such as defending merchant shipping. The balance struck between securing command of the sea and exploiting it, in other words, had been wrong. There is certainly no doubt that offensive action against the enemy's navy was at the very centre of the amended *Naval War Manual* of 1925: 'In every maritime war, the control of sea communications and tradeways has hitherto been exercised by that power which, in addition to possessing sufficient vessels to exercise this control, has been able to concentrate a battlefleet sufficient to destroy or neutralize similar enemy forces'.[43]

The difficulty for the Royal Navy was that its European adversaries were unprepared or unable to engage in a decisive battle of the familiar sort. The campaign of destruction and neutralisation therefore took longer to achieve, and seemed to demand more resources than prewar planners had anticipated. In this situation it proved easier to get the balance wrong between securing and exploiting command of the sea, if that is indeed what happened.

The style of the decisive battle the Navy pursued so ardently was misperceived as well: in Roskill's view, old-fashioned admirals were inclined to conceive of battle primarily in terms of a prolonged duel between parallel lines of heavy gunships and paid too little attention to new naval developments in aircraft and submarines.[44] This was a point made much less judiciously by Lewis:

In this war our battleships escorted convoys, fought raiders, bombarded coasts, and did innumerable other things. But they did not, in a compact and formal fleet, fight a pitched gun-battle with the enemy. Concentrations of vastly expensive heavy ships were becoming altogether too vulnerable to the new undersea and aerial weapons. Both submarines and aircraft could strike them long before they came within range to use their guns on other battleships. In the West, where Germany had no battlefleet, there was little chance to discover this; but in the East it became clear.[45]

The key point here was that neither of the Royal Navy's adversaries in Europe was inclined and/or had the resources for a main fleet engagement. Nonetheless there were numerous small-scale engagements (such as the pursuit of the *Bismarck*, and the battles of Matapan and the North Cape) which were 'decisive battles' in miniature. What did become clear, however, was that the *nature* of the battlefleet changed during the course of the war. It became more diverse, more dispersed and involved a balance of many different sorts of fighting units which saw aircraft carriers taking over some of the major roles of battleships. All this was exemplified by the Royal Navy's last battlefleet of the Second World War – the British Pacific Fleet. This was a radically different force, not least in its reliance on a fleet train, that indeed comprised a concentration of large and expensive ships, that held its own against enemy air and submarine attack and, by now enjoying command of the sea, projected power against the shore.

Despite their criticisms, both Roskill and Gretton concluded that for all its mistakes, the Royal Navy had performed well and 'for that reason . . . at the conclusion of the struggle, there was none of that disappointment at the service's performance, nor any repetition of the controversies regarding the causes of failure, which had been so marked a feature of the early 1920s'.[46] Moreover, they both concluded that the impact of new technology had not in the end required major departures from the traditional principles of maritime strategy. The war had also provided a triumphant vindication of the potentiality of maritime power and of the wisdom of the Britain's continued adherence to a maritime strategy. It showed that a maritime strategy's potentialities were undiminished. Having established sea control, the Royal Navy had been able to prosecute the war through its operations in the defence and attack of trade and in the mounting of overseas expeditions which had a decisive impact on its outcome. The experience of the Second World War, in short, had both confirmed the continuing importance of seapower and offered a confident guide for an uncertain nuclear future.

Notes

1 Some of these were technically neutral but were helpful generally towards the Allied war effort, especially in the provision of merchant shipping.

2 Known generally in English as pocket battleships.
 3 Hinsley *et al.* (1979), Chapter 5.
 4 A problem in determining the effort to be made against *Tirpitz* was the difficulty in understanding what damage had been done by previous attacks and then determining the progress of repairs. This was never satisfactorily addressed until the battleship rolled over. See Sweetman (2000).
 5 A canard has persisted that anti-submarine warfare was almost entirely neglected in the interwar years. This has been authoritatively refuted in Franklin (2003).
 6 Williams (1972), Baker (1972).
 7 Gardner (1999).
 8 Llewellyn-Jones (2003), Waddington (1973).
 9 Gardner (2000).
10 Lavery (2004).
11 Pout (1995).
12 Le Bailly (1991).
13 Kennedy (2004), Chapter 7.
14 Gretton (1965) p. 1.
15 Gretton (1965) pp. 193–4.
16 Ibid. p. 3.
17 Richmond's original definition is in Richmond (1946) p. ix.
18 Roskill (1963) p. 26.
19 Roskill (1962) pp. 241–2.
20 Roskill (1954–61) p. 1.
21 Ibid. pp. 6–7.
22 Ibid. p. 5.
23 Ibid. pp. 1–2.
24 Ibid. pp. 3–4.
25 Ibid. pp. 10–11.
26 Ibid. p. 4.
27 Ibid. pp. 9–10.
28 Ibid. pp. 11–12.
29 Roskill (1962) pp. 174–5.
30 Kennedy (1976).
31 Gray (1992) is a particularly good exposition of the maritime case. See also Till (2004).
32 Gretton (1965) p. 23.
33 Roskill (1962) p. 77.
34 Ibid. pp. 162–3, 221.
35 Ibid. p. 241.
36 Roskill op. cit. p. 234.
37 Gorshkov (1979) p. 110.
38 Roskill (1962) p. 245; for a recent account of the effectiveness, or otherwise of the commercial blockade, see Ellerman (2005).
39 This point of view is strongly contested in Franklin (2003).
40 Gretton (1965) p. 23.
41 The classic exposure of this error may be found in Waters (1957).
42 Gretton (1965) p. 26.
43 *Naval War Manual* 1925, amended in 1940. Adm 186/66 PRO. I am am indebted to my colleague Jon Robb-Webb for this reference.
44 However, see Till (1979), Bell (2000) and Moretz (2002).
45 Lewis (1959) p. 238.
46 Roskill (1962) p. 248.

8 British naval thinking in the nuclear age

Richard Hill

British naval thinking

For the British, practice often tends to precede, and sometimes to supplant, theory. Even in the sunny afternoon of British maritime power, it took an American[1] to distil the essence of its strategy just as it had taken a Frenchman[2] to analyse its tactical principles 200 years before. British theorists did exist of course, but the limelight was not theirs. And in the period covered by this chapter (say 1945–95), American, Russian and French writers – to say nothing of Indian and Australian theorists in the later decades – produced a body of substantial and often highly publicised work.

But without doubt a significant mainstream of British published material, with countercurrents, does exist; so while the influence of other nationals' views will be acknowledged where appropriate, overwhelmingly this chapter (like the rest of the book) will be concerned with *British* work. That this work was often introspective, in the sense that it was trying to find a specific place for *British* seapower, is implicit in the circumstances of the period; much of it had a general application nonetheless.

Then the title tells us that we are concerned with *naval* thinking. Just how far, in the last half-century, does 'naval' extend? Surely subject matter must comprehend the business of sea communication and all its instruments; Ranft as a disciple of Corbett would have shunned any narrowing there. Nor would it be right or even possible to exclude the air or amphibious elements of the sea affair. And the ancient and modern uses of the sea and its resources, which have so affected the economic aspects of the last half of the century, must be addressed at least in so far as they affect naval thinking. So 'naval' will be interpreted as 'maritime' here.

'Naval' must also, perforce, include the nuclear element, certainly so far as delivery by sea of nuclear weapons is concerned. There will be more detailed treatment of this topic further on, but it is necessary to give a warning at this point: it is hard to identify even one British naval thinker who produced a coherent, published concept of nuclear war at sea. Partly this was due to the naval view, akin to the Army's, that nuclear weapons interfered with good fighting; partly it was a naval belief that conflict would have to go a very long way before nuclear use was contemplated; and partly it was the assumption that if things did get that far, the situation from there on would need more improvisation than forethought. Immediate tactical measures and material provision could be planned, and were; subsequent activity was not so predictable.

As to authorship, it would clearly be absurd to define 'naval' in any narrow way. Naval officers, academics, civil servants and even politicians and journalists have all contributed to the mainstream and countercurrents, and all must be acknowledged in this survey.

Finally, what about *thinking*? Here we have the most obscure word of the three. No doubt all published material is the product of thought of some kind. But the kinds of thought vary greatly. Government documents (much more numerous in this than any previous era) almost always represent corporate thought, usually a distillation of compromises though they may sometimes put forward important ideas or lines of policy. Over the last two decades, there has been a tendency for officialdom to allow publication of documents at naval staff level; these too are corporate thought but put forward an, albeit 'cleared', naval line; and even before that occasional sallies of this sort, under individual names, saw publication. More individual still, and often under the protection of pseudonyms, were contributions to that privileged publication the *Naval Review*; while some retired officers wrote books of considerable significance.

All these were the work of naval officers and/or civil servants with input from their political masters, sometimes in relative harmony, sometimes in uneasy negotiation, sometimes in isolation. But there was also, importantly, the work of academics, not least Bryan Ranft himself. Some, like him, had deep background in the naval educational establishments; others came relatively fresh to the maritime scene. While only a few had much knowledge of classified material, all brought insight and individuality to naval thinking, and some (not all) a relative freedom from assumptions.

Almost throughout the period, naval thinking did include – to the writer's certain knowledge – a great deal of unstated or unarticulated thought. Partly this came from people who, in official positions, followed a particular line of thinking and knew it simply would not 'run' in the context of current policy, but nevertheless sought to produce its effects by other means. A prime example was the retention of considerable capacity for worldwide naval reach during the NATO-dominated 1970s and 1980s. The limits of the NATO sea area did not justify such capacity, but the naval staff used every device of argument, surreptitious planning and official allies – notably the Foreign Office – to achieve it. Partly, also, it came from practitioners who were not accustomed to expressing themselves on paper but knew very well what they reckoned ought to be done. This approach was particularly to be found in the work of fleet commanders and staffs, who assessed, and moved ships towards, potential trouble spots as they had always done; the disposition of forces to support Kuwait in 1961 was an example. It is, of all things, difficult to unravel such influences, but they were often powerful and an attempt will be made to identify them in what follows.

Finally, gut or emotional drives cannot be discounted. Rigorous critics may not class them as thinking at all, but those who have had to do with (for example) threatened cap-badge units of the Army know how influential they can be.

The questions before the court

In the environment of the second half of the twentieth century, when so much was changing so fast, British naval thinking had to answer a linked and often overlapping series of questions. *What* did seapower consist of in the nuclear age: were the classical constituents still valid, and what elements if any had to be added? *Why* was seapower (and naval power in particular) important, desirable or necessary? For Britain? If so, *how* was it to be exercised? And, in a Britain whose relative economic position was declining, was the *wherewithal* achievable?

It is fair to say that all too often that sequence was entered halfway through, and the nearer one got to Whitehall the more dominant the later questions became, the more fundamental being replaced by assumptions shown later to have been flawed, partial or irrelevant. The analysis and commentary in the rest of this chapter will seek to point out such shortcuts, particularly in official thought, while itself following the *what/why/how/with what* sequence.

What? The elements of seapower

Mahan famously adumbrated six elements that made up the potential for mastery at sea.[3] Three were geographical: position, harbours and adequate territory. Three were social: adequate population, seafaring character and appropriate government. He argued that in the eighteenth and nineteenth centuries, Britain had peerlessly made the most of these characteristics to make her pre-eminent. Writing in 1976, Paul Kennedy developed the theme in describing the three-sided equation of *Pax Britannica*:[4]

> An adequate, not to say overwhelming, naval force which utilized a whole host of bases and protected an ever-growing global trade; an expanding formal empire which offered harbour facilities for the Navy and focal centres of power, together with a far larger informal empire, both of which provided essential raw materials and markets for the British economy; and an industrial revolution which poured out its products into the rest of the world, drew large overseas territories into its commercial and financial orbit, encouraged an enormous merchant marine, and provided the material strength to support its great fleets. It was an outstandingly strong framework for national and world power,

and one which would remain effective, provided that no one side of it was so weakened that the whole edifice collapsed.

This passage represents an important trend in the approach to the elements of seapower. It was, to an extent not previously attempted, holistic; it owed much to previous work by Correlli Barnett where topics as diverse as education, the banking system and industrial technology were brought into discussion of defence. The business of fighting for supremacy or survival was acknowledged as one of the elements, but not always as a dominant factor and sometimes, indeed, as a source of weakness or bankruptcy. All this was founded upon quantitative analysis – one of Barnett's books was called *The Audit of War* – and it led to judgements such as the memorable ending of Kennedy's *Rise and Fall of British Naval Mastery*: 'questions . . . anxiously debated today, shrink into proper perspective when compared with the larger movement we have traced of the rise and fall of Britain as an independent world naval power. Since she is no longer the latter, this story can safely be brought to its conclusion'.[5] The passage smacks of smug pessimism. It would be cheap to say that six years after it was published, Britain regained the Falkland Islands through the exercise of seapower, but it is more valid to point out that Kennedy's words 'independent' and 'world' both beg central questions that will recur throughout this chapter.

Questions of judgement aside, the holistic approach was surely correct for the ever more complex world of 1945–95. However, the weight given to the various elements might be, and indeed was, endlessly disputed.

If one factor stands out as consistently weightier than the rest, it is that of sea communications. Indeed, in the writings of many in the two decades after the Second World War, it figured so prominently as almost to exclude other considerations. The great Second World War convoy battles in the Atlantic, Arctic and Mediterranean were held to contain enduring lessons, and Britain's vulnerability to interruptions of sea traffic was emphasised.[6] Bryan Ranft himself often pointed out that the other side of this coin of 'seapower' was 'sea vulnerability'. The positive use of sea communications, the ability to convey force or influence to more or less remote parts of the globe, was less emphasised in those early decades, though some writers quoted it generally in the context of protection of British interests in the Empire or, later, Commonwealth. It gained steadily in credence from the late 1950s, with the repeated demonstration of the utility of amphibious forces.

Nuclear considerations figured prominently in most naval writing after 1945. Chronologically, they followed the sequence in the thinking of the general public and the Army: at first simply as a means of causing devastatingly powerful explosions, then as an overwhelming menace that made other forms of warfare irrelevant (except for 'broken-backed' war, a concept that never really caught on in the Service), then as a self-cancelling structure of deterrence that would allow lesser forms of conflict to proceed in its shadow (this increasingly became the consensus view, so far as its effects on naval planning were concerned), and finally, with some reluctance, accepted (in the case of the strategic deterrent) as a custodial charge on the Navy itself. At least up to 1975 the consensus among naval officers appears to have been that strategic nuclear deterrence was not an element of seapower as such, but a politico-military capability that happened to be most conveniently placed at sea.[7] It was a point of view quite different from that of the Royal Air Force when that service had custody of the deterrent. It may be that in the last quarter century naval attitudes have changed, but the process is slow and uncertain.

Well before the Second World War, the military ingredients of seapower had extended into the air and underwater dimensions. The war had shown their potency, often in fields that had not been fully foreseen, and after the war the pace of their development continued to outstrip that of the surface ship. Here, clearly, was a challenge to simple Mahanian concepts, yet in the minds of many it was largely a matter of *how* these elements were to be provided, organised and used rather than *what* kind of seapower they represented. In general, to British writers and analysts, phrases like 'the submarine is the capital ship of the future' or 'command of the sea is no more than command of the air over the sea' rang somewhat emptily; for every would-be visionary statement of the sort, there were several voices suggesting that life never had been that simple and certainly was not now.[8] That was not to say that these relatively novel elements were in any way discounted; on the contrary, millions of words were devoted to their impact.

These were accretions to the elements of seapower, but at the same time one of the classical ingredients was steadily withering away. The possession of overseas bases, so essential in the days of coal and highly desirable even before that, became politically unpopular in the post-1945 burgeoning of newly independent states, and less critical as the means of replenishment at sea developed. Many writers of the old school were well behind the game in their failure to understand how quickly new techniques were coming into operation;[9] in the western navies at least, practicalities really did tend to lead theory.

But probably it was the non-military elements of seapower that, in the last quarter of the century, came relatively into greater prominence than previously. Several factors were at work. The technology of sea-resource exploration and exploitation had gathered pace, most remarkably in the extraction of oil and other minerals, but also in fishing methods. It had been matched, often led, by oceanographic research of quality and originality; knowledge was, indeed, power.[10] The International Law of the Sea was in constant development, a milestone being the United Nations Convention of 1982. Merchant marines changed not only in their technology – container ships, supertankers – but in their ownership and nationality; flags of convenience proliferated, the older nations' fleets dwindled, standards of both maintenance and operation varied widely with the worst dire indeed. Pollution of the sea was seen as a menace; so was the depletion of resources.[11]

British students of the sea affair were not, in hindsight, slow to acknowledge that these were all manifestations of seapower in the modern age. The fact that nearly all affected British interests directed attention to them; senior officers and publicists alike took them up as topics for discussion and coordination; and powerful impetus was given to viewing them as a whole by the gathering of a high-level conference at Greenwich in September 1973. This led to the foundation of The Greenwich Forum, a pressure group whose slogan is 'Britain and the Sea' and which, since then, has consistently promoted discussion of these wider aspects of maritime power.[12]

Why? The benefits and vulnerabilities of seapower

The alleged benefits of seapower were succinctly stated by Geoffrey Till as 'prosperity and security'.[13] A thread of quoted authorities stretched from Themistocles, through Raleigh, Haversham and Mahan, to support those in the post-1945 world who stated these benefits as self-evident facts, or were prepared to accept them as (often unstated) assumptions.

But they found themselves under challenge. The 'prosperity' argument focused upon the cost-effectiveness of the traditional maritime industries. What was the purpose of a large merchant fleet under the national flag, or of a shipbuilding industry, or of an extensive national fishery, if none was efficient, let alone profitable? The British case, where all these industries wilted under competition to an extent unparalleled even on the continent of Europe, and sucked in huge subsidies particularly for shipbuilding, was seen as extreme (sometimes, wrongly, as unique). When in the 1980s government support was virtually abandoned, decline was very rapid.[14]

True, there were other maritime businesses that continued to be assets. In Britain, insurance markets, the Baltic Exchange, classification societies and legal services maintained their expertise and tended to prosper, and a number of new ventures, most notably the exploitation of offshore oil and other mineral resources, became prominent, reflecting developments in the world economy. But their very diversity militated against any view of them as an overall maritime polity.

Thus the 'security' side of the benefits of seapower, which previously had owed so much to the protection of maritime assets and above all trade, increasingly required subtler arguments to support it. In this, from the western and particularly the British standpoint, those arguments were overlaid by the phenomenon of the Cold War.

The perceived menace of the Soviet Union led to the formation of NATO in the early 1950s, with (critically) the engagement of the United States in the security of western Europe. In this situation, the security benefits of seapower were in for reappraisal. First, safeguard against invasion – one of the classical benefits – was more likely to be achieved by strategic deterrence than by direct defence. Second, the protection of trade was largely overshadowed by the protection of transatlantic reinforcement and flank support shipping. Third, the American predilection for the offensive favoured forward deployment at sea as strongly as German imperatives demanded it on land. Finally, the NATO sea area terminated in the Atlantic at the Tropic of Cancer and this could not but inhibit any European nation that wished to be loyal to the alliance but saw its national security interest as extending further afield.

The capacity and intended use of the Soviet Navy was a burning topic. The facts were apparent: it had always been numerically large, but from the middle 1950s steadily increased in quality and diversity until, by the mid-1970s, some serious commentators judged it to match the United States Navy, although its make-up was radically different. But views on its likely employment ranged, indeed raged, widely. At one end of the spectrum McGwire and Herrick[15] argued that its purpose was primarily defence of the homeland, its major preoccupation first the carrier threat and then Polaris; at the other, Onslow, Jungius, LeBailly and others conjured the nightmare of a planned Soviet fleet stranglehold on western sea communication.[16] In 1970 a voice from the Royal College of Defence Studies suggested some middle ground,[17] and was commended by Bryan Ranft; following the testament of Fleet Admiral Gorshkov in *The Sea Power of the State* (1978), Ranft and Till published a balanced assessment in *The Sea in Soviet Strategy* (1983) with the navy cast as a 'general-purpose instrument of state policy'.[18]

But it was said, with some justification, that the naval staffs of the West should get down on their knees nightly to thank their Maker for the Soviet Navy. Its very existence and size was enough to convince the media and ministers that some counter, in kind, was needed; its improvement in technical capacity was enough to supply arguments that comparable improvements in the quality of western naval forces were necessary; its widening deployments were sufficient to dismay foreign offices and put further pressure on governments to respond. Quite often the alarms were raised with a fair degree of cynicism, and played on the gut feelings of politicians and public; this was nothing new, and land and air services did the same. But if the Soviet Navy had not existed, it would have been hard to invent it.

There were counter-arguments, of course. Most potent, in the inner counsels of governments, was the notion that a war in Europe – the governing scenario of NATO strategy – would last so short a time that seapower in any meaningful sense would have no impact.[19] Even the change in NATO doctrine from massive retaliation to flexible response,[20] which occurred in the late 1960s, did not silence those who argued that warning time would be minimal and recourse to nuclear weaponry rapid. Here, surprisingly, the protagonists of maritime power seem to have missed a trick. For hardly any argument is shown to have been advanced on the lines that if the West was planning for a war that short, it was planning to lose; no outcome satisfactory to NATO could be conceived. Had that debate been carried in those terms into the public arena, it is hard to believe it could have ended without the acknowledgement that use of the Atlantic Ocean for reinforcement was a precondition of success.[21]

The period when NATO topics dominated British naval thinking stretched, roughly, between 1965 and 1990. Before the earlier date, a more traditionalist and certainly more national view had prevailed. Up to the Suez debacle of 1956 Britain had taken a largely great-power attitude aspiring to the worldwide application of maritime strength, and after Suez it had quite rapidly adopted a more realistic policy aimed at containing 'brush fires', with high success in Kuwait (1961), Indonesia's confrontation with Malaysia (1964–5) and Tanzania (1964).[22] That 'East-of-Suez' phase was terminated by the Healey Defence Review of 1966 and the even more radical decisions of January 1968;[23] after that it was virtually NATO or nothing, until the collapse of the Soviet Union in 1990.

Nevertheless, even during what may be called the NATO quarter-century, work was going on which suggested that there was a world elsewhere, and that maritime power could operate in it to the benefit of the operator. In 1967 Laurence Martin published *The Sea in Modern Strategy*, the first attempt since the Second World War to produce a coherent survey that was not derivative from earlier publicists, or overmuch from 'the lessons of history'. It is indicative that well over half the book is devoted to limited conflict and non-belligerent action. While Martin was perhaps over-eager to draw modern instances, for example from Vietnam, he was not short of wise saws either: '... effectiveness short of war ... may well comprise the most significant benefit a nation derives from its naval investment';[24] and his later conclusions that deterrence is an all-level affair, and that mobility, flexibility and the ability to 'hover' are advantages of naval power, have, in 2005, a modern ring.

Four years later another book from the same stable – the International Institute for Strategic Studies – made an even greater impact. This was James Cable's *Gunboat Diplomacy*, a study of 'the use or threat of limited naval force, otherwise than as an act of war, in order to secure advantage, or avert loss, either in the furtherance of an international dispute or else against foreign nationals within the territory or the jurisdiction of their own state'.[25] Cable then formulated, through study of over 100 incidents worldwide between 1919 and 1969, four categories of force – definitive, purposeful, catalytic and expressive – which defined the broad nature of such incidents and governed their conduct. In each case 'assailants' and 'victims' were identified and success, or otherwise, assessed. The book turned out to be seminal. It sharpened to a point the theory and experience of 'effectiveness short of war' and reminded navies of what they had so often been *doing* rather than what they had been *training for*. It went through three editions.

Discussion of the utility of maritime forces in furtherance of international disputes was carried on by Ken Booth in two important books, *Navies and Foreign Policy* and *Law, Force and Diplomacy at Sea*. In the latter, Booth put stress on the implications of the International Law of the Sea, as it was emerging from the 1982 United Nations convention. His vision of the almost inevitable success of states in increasing their jurisdiction over coastal zones may not have been to the taste of proponents of distant seapower, but his construct of a triumvirate of roles for maritime forces – diplomatic, constabulary and military – was useful ammunition for those who argued that navies were by no means simply instruments for fighting wars that were never going to happen.[26]

Indeed, from the late 1970s onwards, the versatility of navies at all levels of conflict, and their relative freedom from the constraints of territory and other states' sovereignty, became an increasingly important factor in the case for their utility as both deterrent and operational forces. Nor, even in the most rigidly NATO-orientated times, were these arguments regarded as valid for the superpowers alone. Hill, in *Maritime Strategy for Medium Powers*, published some four years after the Falklands conflict, developed themes he had first put forward ten years earlier in a *Naval Review* series,[27] and held that a medium power with naval forces of sufficient autonomy and reach could often exert decisive influence when its own vital interests were at stake. The book was better received in Australia, India and Canada than in Britain, where perhaps the naval staff were reluctant to accept the medium-power tag.

Indeed, the 1980s saw two distinct trends, which could in other circumstances have diverged in a way quite unsettling for British seapower. One emphasised the general utility of such power, as described above. The other adopted the American 'maritime strategy', a forward concept aimed at penning the Soviet fleets in their own bastions by threatening in particular their strategic nuclear missile submarines, and by operating carriers as far north as the Vestfjord in Norway. This strategy was foreshadowed as 'offensive defence' by Sir James Eberle, possibly the most NATO-orientated of all UK fleet Commanders-in-Chief, in 1981.[28] It firmly allotted to the Royal Navy a contributory role as anti-submarine support for the US strike fleet.

Whether, as some believed, the US maritime strategy contained large elements of bluff, or whether it was a confident expression of the benefits of overwhelming fighting power at sea, will probably never be known; it clearly was not put to the test. What is certain is that some British officials, both civil and naval, professed adherence to it in the mid-1980s and at least one academic was much impressed by the 'Teamwork' exercise based upon it in 1988.[29] There is a good deal of anecdotal evidence that some of the support was rhetorical, in the sense that the strategy would generate the kind of quantified case which would appeal to the Treasury, and justify in particular high-quality forces. Moreover, it did not by itself preclude cashing in on the other, lower-intensity benefits of seapower, though it might produce somewhat different force requirements.

That was without doubt the view of the academic present at Teamwork 88, Eric Grove, and he should have the last word in this survey of the benefits of seapower as seen by the British in the nuclear age. The final chapter of his book *The Future of Sea Power* suggests three theoretical frameworks for considering seapower: the Mahanian, the Booth 'use of the sea' triangle, and a typology of navies ranging from superpower to token, first adumbrated by Michael Morris.[30] All are modified by Grove in a constructive way, but all point out the all-level effect of naval power and deterrence, its mobility, flexibility and versatile nature; and it is noteworthy that virtually all the pronouncements of Royal Navy and Royal Marines officers in the 1990s were at pains to emphasise the benefits conferred by these aspects of maritime power.

How? The application of seapower

What I have called elsewhere[31] the Historians' Joke ('I can teach you nothing: the pace of change is so rapid that history – even quite recent history – is irrelevant when considering current and future problems') was widespread in the nuclear age, and not only among historians. The tenets of classical seapower theory – command of the sea, the decisive battle, the ineffectiveness of the *guerre de course* – were all under challenge as never before, and there were many to argue that there were in fact no 'eternal verities' of seapower, and that its application required a radical appraisal starting from the current position – material, social and political – and predicted future developments.

The more realistic and constructive view, and one that Bryan Ranft among others was instrumental in putting forward,[32] was that the dogma had never been entirely dogmatic and that the classicists, Corbett in particular, had qualified it in such a way that it could readily be adapted to fit modern conditions. Thus 'command of the sea' was modified into theories of 'control' or 'dominance' of those parts of the sea that were necessary for the fulfilment of any particular objective; 'battle' was not something that necessarily needed to be sought, but must be prepared for with the prospect of success; the *guerre de course*, conducted primarily by submarines, was to be regarded as a critical threat against which provision must be made.

Two concepts were to be added to those already existing. The first was that of deterrence. It had been implicit in the theory of seapower, and even more in its practice in the nineteenth century and the first half of the twentieth (what else, after all, had underlain *Pax Britannica?*), but the term only became fashionable in the nuclear age, and then often in its narrow nuclear-strategic context. It was the business of naval thinkers to emphasise that deterrence operated throughout the spectrum of military power, and this they did with varying degrees of success.[33] The second concept, power projection, had some connection with strategic nuclear deterrence – that was, after all, the top end of its range – but was of wide scope, its conventional elements extending from peacemaking deployments from the sea at one end to full-scale amphibious assault at the other.

It is fair to say that these concepts, and that of sea control, were not products of British naval thinking *per se*. Rather, they were taken up by a kind of osmosis from the generality of naval thinking worldwide; both sea control and power projection were put forward, in terms, by the Stansfield Turner/Zumwalt school of thoughtful US admirals, and Gorshkov's 'sea versus shore' formulation mirrored in particular the power projection theory.[34] Deterrence had been a watchword of Royal Air Force thinking since it was put forward by Slessor on the outbreak of peace in 1945; its necessary extension and adaptation by naval theory came later.

Apart from deterrence, these were all war-fighting concepts, and as such jelled well with NATO scenarios. Britain, as a contributor – even though a major contributor – to NATO's maritime effort, had perforce to follow NATO strategic patterns and tactical procedures. In fact, since many of these drew on British experience and some indeed were drafted by British staff officers, they were unlikely to cause too much difficulty.

Sea control, for example, continued to emphasise the concept of protected shipping, with at least the principles of convoy widely accepted and provided for, even if they did not follow in full the precepts and 'laws' evolved by Waters[35] from his research into the experience of the Second World War. A major challenge to the principle came, indeed, from the British establishment itself in 1981, when the then Defence Scientific Adviser influenced the Nott defence review away from convoy and towards anti-submarine defence based mainly upon the combination – untried in war – of maritime patrol aircraft and submarines.[36] It is likely that this was modified in the mid-1980s towards a more all-arms approach. So far as the protection of major naval forces was concerned, this within NATO was mainly in the province of the US Navy with ASW help from the British; while in the purely national field the provision for it was vindicated, just and with more than a little luck, by the performance of the Royal Navy's 'balanced fleet' against Argentina in South Atlantic in 1982. Later in the century, sea control was exercised in a variety of environments, mostly against light or no opposition, but demonstrating its versatility and effectiveness.

Similarly, power projection as practised by the British had a distinctive flavour. The ever-resourceful Royal Marines re-roled themselves several times during the half-century while preserving their elite Commando quality. Suez in 1956, East of Suez in 1957–70, a largely Arctic-warfare force in the NATO era, the excursion to the Falklands in 1982 and a variety of roles post-1990 demonstrated their adaptability.[37] British naval thinking was quick to capitalise on this quality, and the application of amphibious capacity was one of the major pluspoints of the whole half-century.

In classical thinking, command of the sea had always had an obverse quality: denial of its use to the enemy. In the new 'control and projection' formulations, denial still had a place. Indeed, during the height of the NATO era, that place was prominent; barriers across the Greenland-Iceland-UK gaps, plans for extensive minefields to deny passage, and later under the American maritime strategy the preoccupation of Soviet forces with protection of their own bastions, all were elements of sea-denial.[38] It is fair to say that British thought generally was a good deal more sceptical of such concepts than was American. Where denial came more centrally into British calculations was in a different context.

For British thinking made its most distinctive contribution in the field of limited warfare and non-belligerent naval activity. This stemmed partly from British experience, which over the years had been probably more extensive in this area than that of any other nation, and partly from the fact that both the US and Soviet Navies were more specifically war-fighting instruments, supplemented as they were by the US Coast Guard and Border Guard respectively. French thought tended towards nuclear matters and geostrategy; South American to geostrategy alone; the Chinese remained inscrutable; India and Pakistan were preoccupied with perceived warlike threats from each other. Australia, perhaps, most closely matched the British approach to operations short of high-level conflict.[39]

The contributions of Martin, Cable, Booth and Grove have already been mentioned, and it is as well to recall that Corbett in particular among earlier writers had emphasised that sea warfare was not confined to titanic struggles between the battle fleets of major powers.[40] But from the early 1970s a good deal of the thinking of naval officers (serving and retired) as well as academics concentrated on limited conflict and constabulary work. As editor of *Brassey's*, for example, Major General J.L. Moulton RM not only argued that 'Convulsive War' had given way to 'Prolonged Confrontation', but sponsored articles by other authors on similar topics.[41]

Even here some American influence could be detected; Herman Kahn's *On Escalation* featured in several British articles soon after its publication. In general the detailed and somewhat mechanistic ladders set out by Kahn were simplified and blurred by British commentators; on the other hand, the NATO categories of peace, tension and war were regarded as too imprecise to be useful in formulating concepts. Captain (later Vice Admiral Sir) Peter Stanford, under his well-blown pseudonym 'Splitcane', contributed a particularly thoughtful and well-constructed series to the *Naval Review*,[42] in which he sought to bridge the gap, and this work was carried on by other naval writers, both within and outside the Ministry of Defence, in the early 1970s. It culminated in a paper by the Naval Staff in 1975 where four 'levels of conflict' – normal conditions, low intensity operations, higher level operations and general war – were identified.[43]

That paper, which had been intended for wide unclassified distribution, was suppressed at ministerial level, probably because it accepted that there would be occasions where British naval forces might have to undertake operations – possibly, indeed, up to the higher level, which implied systematic warlike acts – independently of NATO. Even its identification of the Soviet Union as the most likely progenitor of confrontation – a feature, which later experience suggested was naïve, of most of the writing of this period – did not, it appeared, sufficiently reduce its political sensitivity.

It was here that the unarticulated side of British naval thinking stepped in. As Vice Chief of the Naval Staff in the early 1970s, Sir Terence Lewin had initiated, and persuaded the Foreign Office to support, plans to deploy groups of Royal Navy ships outside the NATO area for substantial periods of time, for the purposes of training, visits to friendly or potentially friendly countries, national and international exercises and the support of defence sales.[44] Group deployments, which have continued at roughly 18-month intervals ever since, were never justified as such by a mass of paper reasoning, rather by a steady fostering of the assumption that this was what ships of the Royal Navy did, that it was good for Britain that they did it and that NATO did not mind so long as earmarkings remained secure.

There were times when such itinerant deployments were supplemented or overlaid by the perceived need for a permanent presence in seas beyond the NATO area. One such was the Armilla Patrol, instituted in the early stages of the Gulf War between Iraq and Iran to give support to British shipping;[45] another was a permanent presence in the Falkland Islands area after the South Atlantic campaign. Both deployments were looked upon as an operational necessity rather than a demonstration of the rightness of British naval thinking; indeed, in their garrison-like posture they ran counter to British theory, which emphasised mobility and versatility. 'Presence' in the British vocabulary was a fluid, not a static, thing.

But both group deployments and standing patrols were exemplars of a concept that acquired increasing importance as NATO and Eurocentric pressures were felt in the 1970 and 1980s: that of reach.[46] Defined as the distance from the home base at which operations could be sustained, it was not clear-cut (what level of operation, sustained for how long?) but did give some basis for planning. It was not, of course, risk-free; faced with a Treasury given to imposing stringent tests based upon a restricted role for British forces, and particularly naval forces, too much emphasis on extended reach could be self-defeating. It was often safer to justify the attributes associated with reach on the grounds of giving a lead within NATO to European partners.

On one further element in limited conflict, British thinking can be held to have played a distinctive part. This was in the business of Rules of Engagement (RoE).[47] It was a phrase hardly heard before the Second World War – in those simpler times, it was more usual to talk of the Laws of War – but from the earliest days after 1945, such rules became part of daily operational life. Illegal Jewish immigration to Palestine; the Corfu Channel incident of 1946; the Malayan insurgency: these initiated the British very early into a new and complex world. The corpus of experience grew in succeeding decades into a unique basis for highly sophisticated sets of rules, tailored to the perceived requirements of each operation, culminating in the arrangements for the South Atlantic campaign of 1982 when, according to one informant, a team headed by a Flag Officer was occupied almost exclusively in writing and rewriting RoE as the situation changed.[48]

Naval thinking in the nuclear age   173

If British experience was uniquely deep, its outcomes were not always accepted. There is ample evidence that the United States took from the start a more robust stance on the right to initiate violent action, particularly on the vexed and crucial question of the distinction between 'hostile intent' and 'hostile act' on the part of a potential enemy. British publicists, in particular Professor Daniel O'Connell (New Zealand born and a Commander in the Royal Australian Naval Reserve, but at that time Professor of International Law at Oxford University), stressed that the diplomatic premium on not firing the first shot was considerable, and that in view of the difficulty of identifying hostile intent it might be necessary to accept the possibility of the first casualty being sustained by one's own side.[49] The differences of view probably came to a head in discussions on NATO-wide RoE, with the result that a series of rules was evolved that tried to be all things to all men, with the option to pick and mix.

At the lowest level of all on the conflict ladder, that of constabulary duties in home waters, Britain again had a depth of experience and a spread of interests that made her a distinctive contributor to naval thinking. Activities which, in some cases for hundreds of years, had occupied the Royal Navy assumed increasing emphasis as the century went on. Partly this was due to technology: the oil drilling rig, the purse seine fishing vessel, the supertanker and the container ship all imposed new requirements for regulation, constabulary and hydrographic duties. Partly it was due to the evolving law of the sea; extended territorial sea and fishing zones, traffic separation schemes, jurisdiction over pollution incidents and safety zones round rigs on the continental shelf, all widened the area in which regulation was needed. Finally, the dimension of policy imposed by Britain's accession to the European Economic Community, later the European Union, assumed steadily increasing proportions.

British thinking on all these matters began to focus in the early 1970s. Commander Michael Ranken was early in the field and has occupied a prominent place in it ever since.[50] Members of Parliament pressed for regulation of 'the offshore estate'.[51] Lewin, as VCNS, initiated studies into what became known as 'The Offshore Tapestry' masterminded by Captain David Macey.[52] The 1973 Greenwich Conference and its successor the Greenwich Forum, already mentioned, took the whole matter under its wing; the writer Elizabeth Young (Lady Kennet) played a leading part.[53]

But the institutional obstacles to radical change were formidable. There were already well-entrenched agencies in many of the areas that might be thought candidates for overall control: not only the Royal Navy but HM Coastguard, the Royal National Lifeboat Institution, the Scottish fisheries service, Trinity House, the Royal Air Force, to say nothing of numerous port and local authorities. The consensus – not without dissenting voices – was that coordination, rather than a merger of all the necessary services into a single body on the lines of the United States Coast Guard, was the answer in the British case.[54] In this, progress has been made, though major pollution incidents seldom pass without the machinery being criticised in the press and subject to subsequent public inquiry.

Non-belligerent activity is not confined to constabulary work round the British Isles. The readiness of naval forces, and their deterrent effect, has been constantly emphasised by naval publicists ever since the 'presentation of the naval case' to the public seriously began in the early 1970s.[55] In this, British practice tended to precede publicity; rigorous working-up of ships under the Flag Officer Sea Training began in 1958, and its reputation became widespread throughout European members of NATO, many of whose navies participated. Such training was not, from the earliest days, confined to warlike activities; realistic disaster control exercises prepared ships' companies for the real thing, which they came across quite frequently both in and outside the NATO area.

In summary, on the central matter of how seapower was to be applied in the nuclear age, British thinking took on the new factors and looked comprehensively at the way in which they affected classical tenets. The result was neither cataclysm nor chaos. The old precepts did need modifying and extending, and they were so modified and extended. So far as Britain and her interests were concerned, some skewing was imposed by politics and finance in the NATO quarter-century, but that (as Chapter 9 shows) was to be straightened out in the 1990s as the Cold War receded. In that meantime between 1968 and 1990, enough writers and thinkers, and above all naval staff officers, kept the faith to ensure that there was a sound conceptual basis for the future.

The wherewithal: force size and shape

Overshadowing all discussion of the wherewithal to put into practice British seapower theory was the economic state of the country. Britain had ended the Second World War pitifully weak – effectively bankrupt, according to Barnett's analysis[56] – and her relative (though not her absolute) position worsened for the next quarter century. At the same time she sought to preserve effective fighting forces, responding for example to the demands of the Korean War, the Suez crisis, the Indonesian confrontation, to a degree unmatched by any European competitor except France and Portugal, who had their own post-colonial problems. The result was a defence burden that was consistently higher than that of any comparable power.

Yet the Navy (not alone among the fighting services) was always asking for more. In 1946, a contributor to the *Naval Review* argued with perfect seriousness for a peacetime Navy including ten fleet carriers, 17 light fleet carriers and 18 escort carriers;[57] and as is well known, the proposals of the Harwood Committee in 1949 for a Navy of under 100,000 men were rejected by the board as too sweeping.[58] Even in 1954, the future Navy proposed by the naval staff included 14 aircraft carriers and 160 fleet and convoy escorts.[59]

In retrospect it is surprising that the axes did not fall more rapidly and brutally than they did. Possibly gut and emotional drives were operating, in spite of remonstrances from the Treasury and the would-be clinical approach of politicians such as Sandys. All the greater was the shock in the mid-1960s when Denis Healey demolished the carefully constructed case for a new generation of fixed-wing aircraft carriers and, later, committed the United Kingdom to an 'irreducible' defence policy based upon NATO and, by implication, confined for the purposes of material provision to that role.

It might be fair to say that up to that time the size and shape of the planned Navy had been predicated on experience during and after the Second World War. The large number of anti-submarine escorts, both for combatant forces and convoys, and the emphasis on aircraft carriers owed much to the Battle of the Atlantic, the British Pacific Fleet in 1945–6, the Korean War and the numerous brush-fire, predominantly east-of-Suez, operations of the 1950s and early 1960s. Nuclear-powered submarines were in the programme, but though their potency was acknowledged their roles were not yet clarified, and as a result of the Nassau agreement of 1962, priority had been given to the ballistic missile version. A new generation of specialised amphibious units was entering service, but in a circumscribed area of operations their utility became more questionable.

This then was an outright and radical challenge to naval staff thinking about size and shape. It was made no easier by the fact that the shift in British defence policy occurred in two stages: the decisions of the Healey Defence Review in February 1966 suggested an east-of-Suez role that tapered off fairly slowly, while those of January 1968 vastly accelerated and indeed gave a terminal date to the process.[60]

To a considerable degree the naval staff was wrong-footed by the two-year gap. The Future Fleet Working Party, set up after the 1966 decisions, worked from assumptions that were quickly proved out of date. Only some remarkable prescience by Captain David Williams, the Director of Naval Plans, ensured that a sufficient NATO role for the fleet, as plans for it were beginning to evolve, was in place by the time the fateful January 1968 decisions were made. From then on it was a matter of justifying, on a NATO ticket, every new project.

Of these the most critical was the so-called 'command cruiser'. It was often said that the name was coined deliberately to downplay the size and importance of the ship that eventually became the 'Invincible' class. That is partly correct, but the genesis of the design was really a cruiser concept that had been around for years – not indeed as the principal force ship of the fleet, but an 'escort cruiser' which could give anti-submarine support (mainly by helicopters) to the aircraft carrier, and be capable of independent operations within a traditional cruiser role.[61] Over the seven years from 1967, aided by very careful and deliberate staff work, a great deal of tact *vis-à-vis* the other two services, and some engineering luck in the evolution of the Harrier aircraft from an underpowered toy into a fighting machine, the Navy got a ship capable of exercising sea control – not, indeed, against the advertised threat posed by the Soviet Navy and Naval Air Force, but against lesser threats that it was much more likely to face, and of course eventually did.

One striking fact about naval thought on the peripheries of Whitehall in this period is the amount of scepticism concerning the 'Invincible' class. Several writers condemned it as a white elephant, toothless and vulnerable; others suggested alternatives that, if accepted, would undoubtedly have killed the project.[62] This was not due only to the residual big-carrier lobby, though that remained powerful, with emotion understandably playing a large part; it owed something to thinkers claiming panaceas in radically reconstructed fleets, emphasising generally smaller, more agile, more numerous craft, usually without sufficient attention paid to qualities such as sea-keeping and endurance. While these might have been suitable for constabulary roles, they would scarcely have made an appropriate 'contribution to NATO', given sea conditions in the NATO area.

A more dangerous challenge came from beneath the surface. The war-fighting potential of the nuclear-powered submarine was self-evident, even though in its early days it was ill-supplied with weaponry to match its speed, concealment and agility. Britain was committed to a programme of construction that, industry-led to a marked degree, turned out one boat every 15 months or so. Submariners understandably emphasised their vessels' capabilities, their intelligence-gathering and war-fighting skills. Some journalists and politicians, and naval officers too, were so struck that they concluded that 'the fleet must go under water'.[63] Theory should have taught them that the submarine's mission is sea denial and this is no substitute for sea control, but people who have hold of what they believe to be a new idea are not always interested in theory; and if anyone had referred them to Richmond's gentle but masterly stressing of the point in 1914[64] they probably would have replied with the Historians' Joke.

In any event, during the 1970s the naval staff held its nerve, and though the Royal Navy was by 1980 more submarine-orientated than any other in the West, it was close to commissioning HMS *Invincible* and bringing into service a generation of surface ships – including a 30-ship auxiliary for afloat support – that were capable of keeping the sea and of controlling the use of selected areas, not confined to the NATO zone, in limited operations. It had not been achieved without careful planning, sound staff work and a bit of subterfuge.

Aberrations and distortions there undoubtedly were. Two sins of commission, and one of omission, stand out. The first was the modification of the eight Batch 2 'Leander' class frigates to mount the Ikara stand-off anti-submarine system. This entailed the removal of the 4.5-inch gun mounting, leaving the ship with a single NATO role (untried in war) and virtually no means of looking after itself against air attack. It was undeployable on its own, and probably the most unbalanced ship of its size in any navy. It had a ship's company of over 200.

Naval thinking in the nuclear age 177

The second was the new generation of conventionally-powered submarines. These, the 'Upholder' class, evolved into a sophisticated design destined for the single role of operating in the Greenland-Iceland-Faeroes gap to inhibit the passage of Soviet submarines. As they came into service, late and plagued by teething problems because of the complication of their systems,[65] the Cold War ended. Arguably, there had been and still was a need for cheap, simple conventionally-powered submarines for training and offshore work, and had that been foreseen a billion-pound programme could have been avoided and a useful force provided. Perhaps the lessons of history could have been used: the previous 'U' class had been built for just such purposes, yet had been outstandingly successful operationally in the Second World War.

The sin of omission was Airborne Early Warning (AEW). It was apparent when the fixed-wing carriers went that this capability, essential to surface forces under air threat, would be difficult to provide from a ship's deck. Moreover, if operating under such a threat was to be confined to the NATO sea area, it was hard to justify because it could be argued that within that area shore-based aircraft could do the job. Thus the naval staff did not feel themselves able to argue for organic AEW during the 1970s; it was one request too many. The omission was glaringly and painfully obvious in the South Atlantic campaign,[66] and was quickly rectified by mounting an existing radar in a modified Sea King helicopter.

Chagrin might have been compounded by the unhappy story of the Nimrod 3 shorebased AEW aircraft planned to succeed the venerable Shackleton. This project, employing a British radar and computer system, cost a billion pounds and achieved precisely nothing, cancelled as it was in the early 1980s and replaced by a system bought from the USA.[67]

The story of the Nimrod 3 highlights a problem that bedevilled British procurement in the nuclear age and has not yet been resolved. Many factors conspired to ensure that in the vast majority of cases national research, development and manufacture were preferred to acquisition offshore. The perceived need to support British jobs; the highly influential leaders of the British armament industries; the very large government-funded research and development base for most of the period; the powerful Royal Corps of Naval Constructors; and some bad experience of collaborative projects that either foundered early, or appeared to have cost more than national ones would have done: all these supported a procurement policy that was strongly nationalistic, in marked contrast to a strategy that was 'contributory'.[68]

One even more fundamental debate pervaded the whole business of material provision in the period under review. This was, in an often-used nutshell, quality versus quantity. Examples of it have been apparent in the preceding paragraphs, but it went deeper than that. The 'quantity' argument ran thus: commitments, in peace, neither-peace-nor-war and war, will always outstrip availability of units, therefore numbers are needed; this is particularly important in modern conditions where constabulary work is emphasised; in distant waters weaker units up front, if sufficiently backed by stronger cover, will not be at undue risk because of deterrence; savings in money and manpower are achievable. The 'quality' counter-arguments were: the Royal Navy must be able to take on a high-quality threat in the Soviet Navy; it must in any case operate, as befits the naval force of a developed power, near the leading edge of technology; all major units must be able to look after themselves in independent operation; and Whitehall experience suggests that if you ask for low-quality units you will get them – but only in the same numbers as the high-quality units you might have asked for.[69]

It is a fair assessment that the 'quality' school nearly always won. Very occasionally a stopgap system inched through, such as the Type 21 frigates – commercially designed and bitterly opposed by the Constructors. Their performance in the Falklands conflict was criticised subsequently, often through ignorance (aluminium does not burn), but in crude terms their survival rate was rather higher than that of the Type 42s. In general, however, the Royal Navy insisted on units – above, on and below the surface – it believed to have operational integrity within their role. Probably historians will continue the debate long into the future, for although the South Atlantic conflict was a better test than most navies have had in the past half-century, it was by no means conclusive. In the meantime, the reader can be referred to Philip Pugh's instructive book *The Cost of Sea Power*, where the evidence is reviewed in detail.[70] It is tempting to say that had this book been published 10 or 20 years earlier, it might have saved a few of the more glaring errors. But one wonders.

In any case, British naval material development got more right than it got wrong in the nuclear age. Above all, it maintained the fleet – in all its three dimensions – as a balanced instrument of state power for a nation of medium rank. The greatest threat to this balance came, as a result of preconceived thinking and false assumptions, in 1981; the situation might have been retrievable even had the Falklands conflict not occurred in 1982, but that question remains moot. As it was, balance, based around the carriers, nuclear-powered submarines and amphibious shipping, has been preserved.

Conclusion

With the Cold War ended also some distortions of the classical manifestation of seapower, as it affected Britain. A single scenario for conflict; force provision based upon a single threat; a 'contributory' strategy, if it could be called a strategy; dubious assumptions on the likely duration of conflict; a constricted and strategically unrealistic sea area: all these were, or should have been, swept away with the debris of the Berlin Wall. And indeed, when analysed, the language of British Defence White Papers since about 1992 has dramatically changed in both tone and content, emphasising national interests and flexible, versatile forces in which the sea must inevitably have a leading role.

It will be for the next chapter to interpret how the 'eternal verities' of seapower are being implemented in the post-Cold War world. It need only be added that the new generation of naval thinkers are entirely worthy of the legacy left by Bryan Ranft and all those others who worked in the previous half-century. Among the historians and analysts Rodger, Till, Grove, Lambert, Gordon and Benbow; among the officers Band, Blackham, Fry and Haines, and many unnamed, and others to come, will, it is certain, maintain the level and quality of discussion necessary for this island.

Notes

1 Mahan (1890).
2 Père Paul Hoste, *L'art des armeés navales*, NMM, TUN/82.
3 Till (1984) p. 31.
4 Kennedy (1976) p. 157.
5 Ibid. p. 346.
6 Among numerous examples see 'Dad', 'The Future of British Sea Power', 38 the *Naval Review* (subsequently *NR*) (1950) p. 313; 'Scimitarian', 'More Forethought', 40 *NR* (1952) p. 286 ff.; and speeches by Naval Peers in the Debate on the Address, House of Lords, 2 December 1954 (42 *NR* (1954) p. 84 ff.).
7 Leach (1993) p. 203. For argument by a naval officer against Britain's continued possession of a seaborne nuclear deterrent, see 'Willow' and 'Moryak' in 50 and 51 *NR* (1962 and 1963) at pp. 26 and 150 respectively.
8 See, among examples too many to count, J.L. Moulton, 'Maritime Strategy in the 1970s', 57 *NR* (1969) p. 5; J.R. Hill, 'The Role of Navies' in *Brassey's Annual* (Clowes, London, Beccles and Colchester, 1970) pp. 97–8.
9 Roskill (1962) p. 257. Although in most areas Roskill's final chapter was prescient, his anxiety about bases was ill-founded.
10 Captain G.A. French, 'Oceanography – the Ten Years Ahead', 53 *NR* (1965) p. 204 ff.; Commander M.B.F. Ranken, 'Oceanology – The World's Lifeline for the Future', 56 *NR* (1968) p. 223 ff.
11 Clark (1987); Brown (1994) for a comprehensive survey.
12 See e.g. Watt (1980) and Ranken (1981). The Forum held no less than six fishing conferences in the late 1990s.
13 Till (1984) n. 3, p. 3.
14 Jamieson (2001) p. 51 ff.; Johnman (2001) p. 77; British Maritime Charitable Foundation, *Why the Ships Went* (London, 1987).
15 Herrick (1968); McGwire (1968) and numerous subsequent publications.
16 R.G.O., 'Defence of the Realm', 59 *NR* (1971) p. 12 ff.; 'Lampray', 'Soviet Maritime Strategy Minus Rose Tinted Spectacles', 60 *NR* (1972) p. 205.
17 Captain C.E. Price, 'The Soviet Concept of Sea Power', Seaford House Papers, Royal College of Defence Studies, London, 1970.
18 Ranft and Till (1989) p. 205. See also Fairhall (1981).
19 Hill (1986) p. 220.
20 MC 14/2 was succeeded by MC 14/3 in 1967.
21 Watt (2001) p. 328. See also Hill (1984) p. 94.
22 Grove (1987) Chapter 7.
23 Hill (1995) p. 387.
24 Martin (1967) p. 133.
25 Cable (1971) p. 21.
26 Booth (1977) pp. 15–16.

27 'Marlowe', 'The Medium Maritime Power', 64 *NR* (1976) p. 106, and three subsequent articles.
28 'Mariner', 'Strategy and Maritime Capabilities', 70 *NR* (1982) pp. 22–4.
29 Grove and Thompson (1991) p. 124.
30 Morris (1987).
31 Hill (1995) p. 434.
32 Bryan Ranft, in Till (1982) pp. 39–43.
33 Martin (1967) p. 134; Hill (1986) pp. 79–81; Cable (1983) *passim*.
34 Grove (1990) p. 12.
35 D.W. Waters, 'Some Reflections upon the Battle of the Atlantic, 1939–45, and Historical Maritime Operational Research', 83 *NR* (1995) p. 349, and subsequent articles.
36 Sir Ronald Mason, 'Problems of Fleet Balance' in Till (1984) p. 213 ff., expands the statement made in Cmnd 8288, *The UK Defence Programme: The Way Forward*, para. 23.
37 Grove (1987) p. 323.
38 See Gray and Barnett (1989) particularly Chapter 13 at p. 324 ff.
39 Dibb (1986) pp. 31–7; and Australian Department of Defence, *The Defence of Australia* (AGPS, Canberra, 1987) Chapter 3.
40 Corbett (1988).
41 Moulton (1970) p. 130 ff.
42 'Splitcane', 'The Mechanics of Deterrence', 61 *NR* (1973) p. 205, and subsequent articles.
43 The Navy Department, *The Role of the Royal Navy in a Changing World*, January 1975.
44 Hill (2000) pp. 248–51.
45 Cmd 101–1, *Statement on the Defence Estimates 1987*, p. 23. The apologetic cough that accompanies all such statements of 'out-of-area' activities in the 1980s is indicative.
46 Hill (1986) p. 149.
47 Ibid. pp. 127–9, 133.
48 Rear Admiral D.M. Eckersley-Maslin, in conversation with the author.
49 O'Connell (1975) pp. 82–3.
50 M.B.F.R., 'Ocean Industry in the UK', 62 *NR* (1974) p. 119.
51 Laurence Reed MP, 'The Conservation and Management of our Offshore Estate', 60 *NR* (1973) p. 9.
52 Hill (1995) p. 252; 'Weaver', 'The Offshore Tapestry', 62 *NR* (1974) p. 119.
53 Young (1974) p. 262.
54 'Weaver', see n. 52.
55 R.E.C., 'The Royal Navy Presentation', 61 *NR* (1973) p. 45.
56 Correlli Barnett, 'The Verdict of Peace', 146 RUSI *Journal* (2001, December) p. 54.
57 'Nico', 'The Navy of the Future', 34 *NR* (1946) p. 150.
58 Hill (1995) p. 382.
59 Grove (1987) p. 109.
60 Jackson and Bramall (1992) p. 374.
61 Paper, 'The Navy Without Carriers': CNS to SofS, 17 September 1965, in PRO DEFE 13/589.
62 F.P.U. Croker, 'The Conservation of the Eagle', 59 *NR* (1971) p. 24; 'Cecil', 'The Board Bulletin', 59 *NR* (1971) p. 36.
63 Typically Owen; see his (1991) p. 147.
64 'The Submarine and the Surface Vessel', unsigned but known to be by Captain H.W. Richmond, 2 *NR* (1914) p. 171.
65 The change from confident prediction to bald announcement of disposal was striking: cf Royal Navy *Broadsheet 1992*, p. 55, and *Broadsheet 1993*, p. 21.

66 Cmnd 8758, *The Falklands Campaign: the Lessons* (HMSO, 1982) para. 228.
67 Cm 101–1, *Statement on the Defence Estimates 1987*, para. 508.
68 Hill (1986) p. 210.
69 Even specific works on this topic are too numerous to mention, while implicit references are legion. In general, the 'quantity' lobby appeared as *demandeurs* with 'quality' firmly in the establishment seat.
70 Pugh (1986). See particularly pp. 269 on balanced fleets, 273 on real cost escalation and 343 on operational degradation.

9 The discovery of doctrine
British naval thinking at the close of the twentieth century

Eric Grove

At the end of 1995 at the Royal United Services Institute in Whitehall the launch took place of *The Fundamentals of British Maritime Doctrine*, numbered BR 1806 in the official naval publications series.[1] The Royal Navy had been late in climbing on the 'doctrinal' bandwagon. The Army had led the way with *British Military Doctrine*, first published in 1989. The Royal Air Force had followed with the first edition of AP3000, *Air Power Doctrine* in 1991. The Royal Navy, however was a little reluctant to go down the 'doctrinal' route. The Assistant Director Data and Doctrine on the Naval Staff, the late and much lamented David Brown, was a staunch opponent and some senior admirals were also dubious. The reason was an understandable reluctance for the Royal Navy to become too dogmatic in its professional approach. The essence of the naval profession was deemed to be flexibility of mind and a willingness to think 'out of the box'. The contrast between the perception of Nelson as a (good and successful) tactical innovator compared to the apparently sclerotic and over-centralised Grand Fleet of Sir John Jellicoe (that failed to achieve another Trafalgar at Jutland) was a potent one. The Grand Fleet had too much doctrine in Grand Fleet Battle Orders; Nelson had just told his commanders to 'do their duty'.[2]

The weakness in such arguments was that, firstly, there had always been doctrine in the Royal Navy at various levels from the tactical to the strategic. As the First Sea Lord Admiral Sir Jock Slater put it in his foreword to BR 1806: 'There has always been a doctrine, an evolving set of principles, practices and procedures that has provided the basis for our actions. This doctrine has been laid out somewhat piecemeal in various publications and there has never been a single unclassified book describing how and why we do our business. This publication seeks to fill that gap by drawing together the fundamentals of maritime doctrine'.[3]

The numbering of the book BR1806 was a deliberate attempt to confirm the point of continuity. This was the number of the old *Naval War Manual* last issued in the 1960s. The *War Manual* was an attempt to set out an agreed operational and strategic framework for the Service, primarily with an educational purpose in mind. Unfortunately it failed as a doctrinal manual

The discovery of doctrine 183

in the fullest sense as its contents were little, if ever, taught. During my time as a lecturer in strategic studies at the Britannia Royal Naval College, Dartmouth (1971 to 1984), there was no attempt to bring the old 1806 to my attention, let alone any expectation that its contents were to be inculcated in the officers under training. There were copies of the *Naval War Manual* in the confidential bookstore and eventually they were used by myself and at least one colleague as a source, but this lack of attention seems to be all too typical of prevailing attitudes towards the earlier incarnation of 1806.

The lack of a coherent and authoritative statement of naval doctrine in the fullest sense had negative effects. As I have argued elsewhere it 'acted as an undesirable brake on the development of a proper professional culture in the service'.[4] During the 1970s in the bleak period after the withdrawal from east of Suez and before the articulation of the forward maritime strategy in the 1980s, teaching the role and functions of the Royal Navy was a somewhat haphazard and unsystematic business. Worse still, important studies of operational doctrine, notably on the defence of shipping, were carried out in a deeply flawed manner with the lessons of experience ignored or misunderstood.[5]

As remarked earlier, the opposition to doctrine within the Service remained strong but the backing of successive Assistant Chiefs of Naval Staff and Directors of Naval Staff Duties saw the project through nonetheless. As well as the inherent merits of the exercise it was clear that the other services were gaining considerable advantages from their doctrinal development in the coherence of the single service 'cases' they could present both within and without Whitehall. There was also 'the key consideration that the development of joint doctrine was only a matter of time and it was crucial that the Navy have a document 'on the table' when such a development began'.[6]

The two main authors of the first edition of BR1806 were the writer of this chapter and Commander Mike Codner RN, an officer of remarkable intellectual depth with whom I had been associated previously when he had been working in the Ministry's Concepts department. This pairing brought two important strands together. Commander Codner had spent much time at the US Naval War College where he had been imbued with the rigour of that institution's work on the higher dimension of the profession of naval command. I represented what might be called the 'English School' of maritime strategy handed down from Corbett to his successors.

Professor Ranft, to whom this volume is dedicated, played a central role in the dissemination of that tradition, especially in his twin roles as a long-standing member of the teaching staff at the Royal Naval College Greenwich and also Visiting Professor of Naval Studies in the Department of War Studies at Kings College, London. As a former Army officer Professor Ranft was instinctively as well as intellectually attracted by Corbett's emphasis on the 'maritime' rather than the purely 'naval'. The key paragraph in Corbett's *Some Principles of Maritime Strategy* bears repeating:

> By maritime strategy we mean the principles which govern a war in which the sea is a substantial factor. Naval strategy is but that part of it which determines the movements of the fleet when maritime strategy has determined what part the fleet must play in relation to the action of the land forces; for it scarcely needs saying that it is almost impossible that a war can be decided by naval action alone... Since men live upon the land and not upon the sea, great issues between nations at war have always been decided – except in the rarest cases – either by what your army can do to the enemy's territory and national life or else by the fear of what the fleet makes it possible for your army to do.[7]

One of the greatest achievements of Greenwich was to inculcate this 'maritime' emphasis in the Royal Navy's thinking. It became customary for the Service – particularly in the second half of the twentieth century – to use the term 'maritime' instead of 'naval'. The only drawback to this is that 'maritime' has consequently become a 'dark blue' word, almost a synonym for 'naval'. Such was not Sir Julian's intention. This elision has forced the use of other terms, notably 'expeditionary', in more recent 'joint' articulations of strategic policy.

If the self-conscious adoption of 'maritime' as the epithet for the Royal Navy's business was one success for Corbett and his successors, the adoption of a commonly accepted 'theory' was a more uphill task. Clearly Corbett's 'theory' is much like the conception of 'doctrine' that BR1806 would later promulgate. Corbett even rehearses the arguments that would reappear almost a century later:

> The truth is that the mistrust of theory arises from a misconception of what it is that theory claims to do. It does not pretend to give the power of conduct in the field; it claims no more than to increase the effective power of conduct... It is not enough that a leader should have the ability to decide rightly; his subordinates must seize at once the full meaning of his decision and be able to express it with certainty in well adjusted action. For every man must have been trained to think in the same plane; the chief's order must awake in every brain the same process of thought; his words must have the same meaning for all.[8]

It is quite clear from contemporary sources that Corbett's 'theory' was what we should now call 'doctrine'. French officers visiting the Grand Fleet in the First World War were referred to *Some Principles* when they enquired about British naval doctrine. It seemed obvious to say in the box on page 13 of the first edition of BR1806 that Corbett 'provided the Royal Navy of the early twentieth century with its strategic doctrine. He set out clearly what doctrine was and what it was not. Corbett always warned against slavishly following simple maxims and using them as substitutes for judgement. As he put it in his lectures, "You might as well try to plan a campaign by singing Rule Britannia"'.[9]

In BR1806 we began by defining what doctrine was: 'a framework of principles, practices and procedures, understanding of which provides a basis for action'. This action might be taken either in conflict (a term we preferred to 'war') or in peacetime applications of military power. BR1806 was to set out 'the principles that govern the translation of national security and defence policy into maritime strategy, campaigns and operations', to 'establish a core understanding of the nature of maritime power both within and outside the naval Service'.[10]

We followed Corbett in stressing the importance of the careful study of experience. At first we were a little reluctant to use the word 'history', but at a seminar held at the Royal Naval College, Greenwich, during the production of the drafting of the book we were encouraged[11] not to be so reticent. Thus there appeared under the heading 'The Currency of Doctrine' the bald statement: 'Doctrine has its foundation in history; the study, analysis and interpretation of history. It provides a shared interpretation of that experience which can be taught, in order to provide a common starting point for thinking about future action'.[12] In drafting this we had in mind Corbett's wise words in *Some Principles*:

> Having determined the normal, we are at once in a stronger position. Any proposal can be compared with it, and we can proceed to discuss clearly the weight of the factors that prompt us to depart from the normal. Every case must be judged on its merits, but without a normal to work from, we cannot form any real judgement at all; we can only guess. Every case will assuredly depart from the normal to a greater or less extent, and it is equally certain that the greatest successes in war have been the boldest departures from the normal. But for the most part they have been departures made with open eyes by geniuses who could perceive in the accidents of the case a just reason for the departure.[13]

We decided to approach the subject from the general to the particular, starting off with a consideration of combat, hostilities and war and a definition of the ways in which military forces can be used which we defined as military, constabulary and benign. This classification seemed particularly appropriate for maritime forces whose actions can vary from a nuclear strike to a cocktail party. Military use is when force is used or threatened, constabulary use is when forces are used to enforce law or other regime established by international mandate and benign use is when 'violence has no part to play in their execution'.[14] The chapter then went on to define the various levels of command and planning for armed conflict, the grand strategic, military strategic, operational and tactical.

The next three chapters formed the heart of BR1806 and covered 'The Maritime Environment and the Nature of Maritime Power' 'Concepts

Governing the Use of Maritime Power' and 'The Application of Maritime Power'. The first stressed the nature of the planet, its coverage by the sea and the high proportion of the world's population that live close to the sea. In its consideration of the balance between the offensive and defensive at sea my Clausewitzian and Corbettian principles were clearly seen in the balance between the offensive and the defensive:

> In open waters attacking forces will usually have wide options for a direction of approach and may pose an all round threat, placing large demands on defending forces. This factor will tend to favour the offensive, though defending forces can concentrate strength around units at risk. The possibility of drawing the attacker to his destruction in certain circumstances can redress the balance in favour of the defensive. Indeed an engagement might be positively welcome in providing an opportunity to inflict attrition on the enemy.

There we had in mind the use made of convoys in 1943 and the carrier battles carried out in the Pacific in 1944 and planned for the Norwegian Sea in the 1980s.

The chapter concluded with an important section of the 'attributes' of maritime power. The principal ones were defined as: mobility, versatility, sustained reach, resilience, lift capacity, poise and leverage. Our summary tried to draw together the themes:

> Maritime forces operate in an environment that allows them access to most potential crisis areas of concern to the United Kingdom and our Allies. Maritime forces are mobile, versatile and resilient, and can contribute sustained reach and lift capacity to a joint campaign or operation. Their ability to poise makes them powerful tools of diplomacy, and a capacity for leverage particularly in the context of expeditionary operations is of greater importance than ever in today's world of risks and uncertainties.[15]

The chapter on 'Concepts Governing the Use of Maritime Power' differentiated command of the sea from sea control, the concept developed by Stansfield Turner and his staff at the War College at Newport in the 1970s: 'the condition in which one has freedom of action to use the seas for one's own purposes in specified areas and for specified periods of time and, where necessary, to deny its use to an enemy'.[16] The chapter also explored the wider American concept of battlespace dominance as well as the more traditional concepts of sea denial, fleet in being (a particular favourite of Corbett's) and maritime power projection. Given the contemporary debate on 'manoeuvre' and its adoption as a doctrinal concept by the US Navy we had to consider the question of its applicability in the maritime concept, giving particular emphasis to the idea of manoeuvre from the sea.

This section also returned to the 'offensive/defensive' debate. In earlier work on the 'Forward Maritime Strategy' of the 1980s, I had emphasised the necessity to separate the 'initiative' from the 'offensive'. We explored the argument (in my opinion erroneous) that the offensive is the stronger form of warfare at sea because of the lack of a clearly defined defence perimeter and the possibility of attack from any direction. It might 'therefore take large resources to construct a robust defence while a single offensive unit, for example a submarine operating in waters close to an enemy shore, can generate disproportionate defensive effort'.[17]

Our compromise on this issue appeared in the following paragraph:

> However a slavish adherence to 'the offensive' can lead to important strategic and operational errors, such as British failure to convoy in favour of 'hunting groups' during the First World War. A more useful analysis of modern maritime combat is the division into proactive and reactive elements. To be successful in maritime combat a commander must seize the initiative to force a response to his actions, thereby ensuring that engagements take place on his own terms.[18]

This led on to the chapter on the 'Application of Maritime Power'. First of all, in reflection of the 1990s setting, this addressed 'maritime power from the sea' in the forms of nuclear deterrence, the various conventional forms of combat operations against the land, operations in defence of forces ashore, evacuation operations and the various aspects of naval force in support of diplomacy. We were not completely satisfied with Sir James Cable's taxonomy of 'gunboat diplomacy' for the purposes of doctrine and instead adopted 'presence', 'symbolic use', 'coercion' and 'preventive, precautionary and pre-emptive naval diplomacy'.[19] In the context of the times we paid particular attention to peace support operations, making the vital distinction between 'peace enforcement' – a military task – and 'peace keeping' – a constabulary task.

We then moved on to the application of maritime power at sea, listing the various forms of operation against enemy forces: interdiction, blockade, containment by distraction (e.g. using the threat of NATO SSNs to tie down the Soviet Navy defending its own SSBNs), area sea control operations, establishment and maintenance of exclusion zones, barrier operations, defended areas (that *might* be more practical with modern sensors, precursor operations and layered defence).

This led on to discussion of the means of protecting merchant shipping. On this issue Corbett had been at his weakest. As Professor Ranft had correctly argued in the introduction to his 1972 edition of *Some Principles* two 'valid charges' can be brought against Corbett:

> By playing down the threat of commerce war he encouraged an already dangerous tendency in the Navy not to give its problems adequate

consideration. By not following Mahan's example in emphasising the permanent tactical advantages of the convoy system, he made himself a party to the most costly mistake in British naval thinking ever made.[20]

We were determined not to repeat this error and worked hard to put into BR1806 as strong a vote of confidence in convoy as possible. This was toned down a little in the final version; our wording 'no lesson of history is clearer' was deleted but we were generally content with the final result.

There was much emphasis in BR1806 on the joint and combined attributes of maritime power and it gave its authors, and the Navy in general, disproportionate leverage in the production of the first 1996 edition of *British Defence Doctrine* (*BDD*). As I have reported elsewhere:

> The dynamics of the creation of this document vindicated the architects of 1806. Not only were the authors of 1806 fully involved in its drafting (and the naval perspectives fully inputted) but Chapter 2 of 1806, 'General Concepts of Armed Conflict', proved a useful starting point for the authors of the new joint document – even if it did not prove possible to transpose all of its ideas directly into joint doctrine.[21]

The main problem here was the use of the term 'constabulary' as a way of employing armed forces. It is an important constitutional point that the Army operates in aid of the civil constabulary, not as a constabulary force in its own right. *BDD* therefore did not take this approach but when the new edition of BR1806 appeared in 1999 'The Constabulary Application of Maritime Power' remained as a heading and this question was specifically addressed in the introduction.[22]

This second edition of BR1806, renamed *British Maritime Doctrine* was prepared within the Naval Staff by Commander Steve Haines, as he then was, an extremely able officer of unusually extensive academic experience who later went on to serve in the Joint Doctrine and Concepts Centre set up at Shrivenham. He developed various aspects of the original volume in the context of the overall doctrinal and policy developments of the late 1990s. Much emphasis was placed on the position of BR1806 in the 'Hierarchy of Doctrine' above the classified *Fighting Instructions* and alongside the other single Service doctrine publications. There was rather more stress on 'The Principles of War' than in our volume, a reflection of the emphasis in *BDD* that had revised them a little.

The basics of the analysis of 'The Maritime Environment and the Nature of Maritime Power' and 'Concepts Governing the Use of Maritime Power' remained similar to the earlier iteration with the important addition of 'Cover' to the latter chapter. Rear Admiral Richard Hill had pointed out the lack of a section on this important point in the first edition and I was able to assist the author in developing this new section with a useful 1954 quotation comparing the NATO Striking Fleet of the Cold War with the Grand Fleet of the First World War and the Home Fleet of the Second as a 'covering force ... the umbrella under which we exercise command of sea communications'.[23]

The section on convoy was less happy since it contained the quite serious error that it was a 'popular myth' that convoy had been useful because of its making shipping difficult to find. At times, for example during the First World War and in 1941, when the main impact of code-breaking was diversionary routing, convoys had indeed reduced encounter probabilities.[24] At other times, as in 1943, convoy provided the context for decisive action against enemy forces. The two are not mutually exclusive; it depends on such factors as the extent of the threat and the strength of defending forces. It is good to see that this section has been much improved in the third (2004) edition of BR1806, which makes the point that in the Second World War only about one convoy in ten was actually located by U-boats.[25]

An important addition to the list of 'applications' of maritime power was 'defence diplomacy'. It was satisfying to see the RUKUS confidence-building and cooperation talks between the British American and Soviet Navies, which I initiated in 1988, being quoted as a good example.

Even more important was an additional chapter summarising the key concept of 'The Maritime Contribution to Joint Operations'. This had been first drawn up in 1997 as 'The Contribution of Maritime Forces to Joint Operations and their Wider Utility'. NAVB/P97(9) MCJO soon emerged as the Navy's core 'operational doctrine'.[26] MCJO was intended 'to improve the meshing of the attributes of maritime forces with other elements of UK capability, both military and non military'.[27] The chapter in BR1806 stressed the changed international environment and the move to the littoral: 'the area from the open ocean which must be controlled to support operations ashore and the area inland from shore that can be supported directly from the sea'. It stressed the attributes of maritime forces that made them uniquely valuable for manoeuvre warfare in this context and the utility of task groups variously configured to engage in such operations. Its approach had a decidedly Corbettian ring:

> Maritime force has to be regarded in a joint context in which naval assets provided are to a large degree the servants of purposes which will frequently and ultimately be executed on shore and by land forces. By maritime manoeuvre, the maritime contribution to this venture, offers a sensitive application of force or influence, enabling intervention at a time and place of political choice and an opportunity to exploit joint assets. Maritime power allows the projection of force to be carried out at minimum risk, reducing financial and diplomatic cost and concentrating and easing the protection problem.[28]

MCJO was an outgrowth of the Royal Navy's doctrinal revolution of the previous decade. It allowed the Service to produce a 'theory ... rooted in traditional virtues yet highly relevant to, and congruent with, modern needs, operational and tactical doctrine and providing as much strategic choice and operational flexibility as is likely to be possible'.[29]

It led directly to important papers drawn up in 2000–1, 'The Future Navy' and 'Future Navy Operational Concept'. These developed the idea of 'The Versatile Maritime Force', one optimised for joint power projection, assured access, joint rapid effect and information superiority, able to play its part in all levels of conflict, with global reach sustainability and endurance, and fully interoperable on both a joint and combined basis. The 'Enabling Concept' of the Versatile Maritime Force was defined in a new doctrinal term, 'Swing . . . the ability to configure a force, formation or unit to allow it to operate successfully and cost effectively, across a range of mission types and roles'.[30] The components of swing were defined as adaptability, configurability, standardisation, simplicity of operation and information superiority.[31]

This document in turn provided the context for the 'Future Navy Operational Concept' that first appeared in 2001. This mapped out four core capabilities for the future fleet on a 2015 timescale:

- *Power projection*, including Maritime strike and littoral manoeuvre.
- *Flexible global reach*, including maritime leverage to achieve rapid effect.
- *Optimised access* for the joint force via sea control and theatre entry.
- *C4ISR*, the sea-based contribution to joint C4ISR which will enable information superiority, greater situational awareness and a real-time common tactical picture.[32]

The rest of the paper provided more detail on these capabilities. The result is a remarkably clear road map for the future set out in self-consciously 'doctrinal' terms. BR1806 appears in the footnotes and the paper in turn develops new doctrinal points that will appear in the next edition. Within less than a decade, therefore, a revolution had taken place. The Royal Navy was developing and utilising doctrine in a highly effective way to provide itself with a plan for the future that had considerable appeal to its political masters not least for its intellectual coherence. It was no coincidence that the self same Service had a building programme that was in process of giving it a power projection capability, based around two new large deck carriers and a greatly enhanced amphibious squadron that would rival, if not surpass, that of the fleet at its post-1945 peak. The Royal Navy's discovery of the utility of doctrine was at the heart of this post Cold War naval revolution. It is most gratifying to have been allowed to play some part in this process.

Notes

1 BR1806, *The Fundamentals of British Maritime Doctrine* (London, HMSO, 1995).
2 It is interesting to see how Andrew Gordon's (1996) has at times been misused to draw a contrast between having doctrine and relying on some more intuitive style. What Dr Gordon was demonstrating was a *conflict* of doctrines.
3 BR1806, 1995 edition, p. 5.

4 Grove (1999).
5 Ibid. p. 58.
6 Ibid.
7 Corbett (1911) pp. 15–16.
8 Ibid.
9 BR1806, 1995 edition, p. 13.
10 Ibid. p. 12.
11 Notably by Professor Andrew Lambert.
12 1806, 1995 edition, pp. 12–13.
13 Corbett (1911), ibid. p. 9.
14 BR1806, 1995 edition, p. 34.
15 Ibid. p. 63.
16 Ibid. p. 66.
17 Ibid. p. 76.
18 Ibid. pp. 76–7.
19 Cable (1999) pp. 15–64.
20 Foreword to Ranft (1972) dated 14 August 1971, p. xvi.
21 Grove (1999) p. 59.
22 BR1806, 1999 edition.
23 BR1806, 1999 edition, pp. 37–8.
24 See the excellent Sims (1920) for a clear exposition of the First World War case. He goes as far as to argue that even unescorted convoys would have been useful because of their ability to avoid U-boats.
25 BR1806, 2004 edition, p. 64
26 *The Future Navy*, Admiralty Board Paper 2/00, paragraph 13.
27 Quoted in *The Future Navy Operational Concept* paper NAVB/P(01)13.
28 BR1806, 1999 edition, p. 170.
29 Ibid. p. 171.
30 *The Future Navy*, para. 8. The concept was developed in particular by Captain Steve Jermy when he was the Naval Staff's Head of Defence Studies.
31 Ibid. para. 9.
32 C4ISR is Command, Control, Communications, Computers, Intelligence, Surveillance and Reconnaissance.

Epilogue
Professor Bryan McLaren Ranft

Geoffrey Till

Born on 14 July 1917, Bryan Ranft dedicated his life to the education and study of the Royal Navy, its peers and its adversaries, in the past, the present and the future. Whilst never a sailor himself, he knew more about why the Navy was the way it was than did most professional naval officers of his generation.

Educated at Manchester Grammar School and Balliol College, Oxford, Bryan Ranft's wartime service was in the Royal Artillery, in which he ended as a Major. Despite, or perhaps because of, this, he joined the staff of the Royal Naval College Greenwich where he rose eventually to become Professor of History and International Affairs. These were tumultuous times at Greenwich and Bryan Ranft needed all his political savvy, negotiating skills and strength of character to steer his department and the Naval College generally through to success. The sudden closure of many of its academic departments in 1968 and the constant rumours of the imminent demise of the college itself demanded eternal vigilance. Changing fashions and the never-ending rotation of senior officers keen to make a mark meant that service education was in a state of permanent revolution.

Despite everything, Bryan Ranft did much to help turn Greenwich into the Navy's university. Throughout his time, standards and Greenwich's intellectual reputation steadily rose, although, perversely, its institutional vulnerability remained. The secret of his success was to stay alongside his naval colleagues, quietly influencing and steadying their deliberations, telling them things they did not always want to hear and playing it long – preparing for the time when his students would come back as Admirals, ensuring that they would remember him and his department with fondness and respect. He was equally well connected with the great political figures of his day from his time at Oxford.

The same challenging approach informed his teaching, especially of naval history, where his mischievous sense of humour was perhaps more evident. Many will also remember his lectures on Marxism-Leninism which were delivered with such power and conviction that the more gullible in his audience were quite convinced he believed in it himself – an unsettling thought in the darker days of the Cold War! According to one regular member of his audience, he broke every rule of the manual of instructional technique but still held them riveted because what he had to say was so interesting. He was liked and admired by all.

His main mission in life was to teach his naval students the realities, not the glossy images, of maritime power, its limitations as well as its manifold strengths. As Admiral Sir Julian Oswald says in the foreword, he wanted them, above all else, to be realistic in their future anticipations.

Bryan Ranft retired from Greenwich in 1977, by which time he had already revived the old linkages between that college and King's College London. At King's, Bryan Ranft was firstly a Visiting Professor in Naval History and from 1982 a Visiting Fellow. There, he taught naval history to generations of civilian postgraduate students and did much to steady the Department of War Studies. He was delighted when the Department assumed responsibility for the academic support of all British staff training and would have felt equally vindicated by the establishment of the Laughton chair in Naval History at King's.

In his time, it was not incumbent upon academics to fill libraries with their publications – indeed he only completed his Ph.D. (back at Balliol) in the 1960s, but he edited a reprint of *The Vernon Papers* and *Some Principles of Maritime Strategy* by Sir Julian Corbett (a writer he much admired), a further work on the Royal Navy's experience with technology and a joint study of the rise of the Soviet Navy. In later years, he rescued the project to produce the papers of Admiral Beatty for the Navy Records Society. Council members of the time will long remember the papers' triumphant arrival at one Publications Committee in a plastic shopping bag. Behind the scenes, he did much to rally the Navy Records Society itself. Bryan Ranft's abiding interest in naval history never flagged; indeed he completed the new *Dictionary of National Biography* entry on Beatty shortly before he died.

Bryan Ranft had many other interests too. He was a regular attender, and asker of perceptive and irreverent questions, at the International Institute for Strategic Studies. He did much quiet work for boys' homes (as usual behind the scenes), he loved gardening (one reason why he was reluctant to go away to conferences), he was a questioning but committed member of the Parish of St Michael and All Angels in Blackheath Park, and he enjoyed a fine glass of claret at his club – or indeed anywhere. He died on 14 April 2003, aged 83, being survived by his wife, Marjory.

Major Works

Bryan Ranft (Ed.) *The Vernon Papers* (London: Navy Records Society, 1958).

Bryan Ranft (Ed.) *Some Principles of Maritime Strategy* by Sir Julian Corbett (London: Conway Maritime Press, 1972).

Bryan Ranft (Contributing Ed.) *Technical Change and British Naval Policy, 1860–1939*. (London: Hodder & Stoughton, 1977).

Bryan Ranft (Ed.) *Ironclad to Trident: 100 years of Defence Commentary: Brassey's 1886–1986*. (London: Brassey's 1986).

Bryan Ranft and Geoffrey Till, *The Sea in Soviet Strategy.* (London: Macmillan, 1983, 1989).

Bryan Ranft, *The Beatty Papers. Selections from the Private and Official Correspondence and Papers of Admiral of the Fleet, Earl Beatty, 1902–1927.* (London: Navy Records Society, 1993).

Bryan Ranft, Consultant Editor to J.R. Hill (Ed.) *The Oxford Illustrated History of the Royal Navy* (Oxford: University Press, 1995).

Bibliography

Acworth, B. (1930) *Navies of Today and Tomorrow* (London: Eyre & Spottiswoode).
Acworth, B. (1935) *The Restoration of England's Seapower* (London: Eyre & Spottiswoode).
Adams, Thomas R. and Waters, David W. (Eds) (1995) *English Maritime Books Printed before 1801* (Providence, R.I.).
Anon (1931) 'Some Notes on the Early Days of the Royal Naval War College' in *Naval Review* (Feb).
Aston, Sir George (1911) *Letters on Amphibious Wars* (London: John Murray).
Aston, Sir George (1914) *Sea, Land and Air Strategy: A Companion* (London: John Murray).
Aston, Sir George (1919) *Memoires of a Marine* (London: John Murray).
Aston, Sir George (1927) *The Navy Today* (London: Methuen).
Baker, Richard (1972) *The Terror of Tobermory: Vice Admiral Sir Gilbert Stephenson KBE, CB, CMG* (London: W.H. Allen).
Ballard, Admiral (1976) 'Admiral Ballard's Memoirs' in *The Mariner's Mirror* Vol. 62, pp. 23–32; 249–52; 347–52.
Barfleur (1907) *Naval Policy – A Plea for the Study of War* (Edinburgh: Blackwood).
Bartlett, C.J. (1963) *Great Britain and Sea Power, 1815–1853* (Oxford: Oxford University Press).
Baudi di Vesme, Carlo (1953) 'Il potere marittimo e la guerra di successione d'Austria' in *Nuova Rivista Storica*, XXXVII, pp. 19–43.
Baugh, Daniel A. (1965) *British Naval Administration in the Age of Walpole* (Princeton, NJ: Princeton University Press).
Baugh, Daniel A. (1988a) 'Great Britain's Blue-Water Policy, *1689–1815*' in *International History Review* (Feb).
Baugh, Daniel A. (1988b) 'Why did Britain Lose Command of the Sea During the War for America?' in Black and Woodfine (1988) pp. 149–69.
Baugh, Daniel A. (1992) 'The Politics of British Naval Failure, 1775–1777' in *American Neptune* LII, pp. 221–46.
Baugh, Daniel A. (1993) 'Admiral Sir Herbert Richmond and the Objects of Sea Power' in Goldrick and Hattendorf (1993) pp. 13–37.
Baugh, Daniel A. (1994) 'Maritime Strength and Atlantic Commerce: The Uses of "A Grand Maritime Empire"' in *An Imperial State of War: Britain from 1689 to 1815*, Ed. Lawrence Stone (London: Routledge) pp. 185–223.
Beeler, John F. (1997) *British Naval Policy in the Gladstone-Disraeli Era, 1866–1880* (Stanford, CA: Stanford University Press).

Bibliography

Beesley, Patrick (2000) *Very Special Intelligence: The Story of the Admiralty's Operational Intelligence Centre 1939–1945* (London: Greenhill Books).
Bell, Christopher M. (2000) *The Royal Navy, Seapower and Strategy Between the Wars* (Basingstoke: Macmillan).
Bellairs, Carlyon (1919) *The Battle of Jutland: the Sowing and the Reaping* (London: Hodder & Stoughton).
Black, Jeremy (1986) *Natural and Necessary Enemies: Anglo-French Relations in the Eighteenth Century* (London: Duckworth).
Black, Jeremy (1988) 'Naval Power and British Foreign Policy in the Age of Pitt the Elder' in Black and Woodfine (1988) pp. 91–107.
Black, Jeremy (1989) 'The Crown, Hanover and the Shift in British Foreign Policy in the 1760s' in *Knights Errant and True Englishmen: British Foreign Policy, 1660–1800*, Ed. Black (Edinburgh: Edinburgh University Press) pp. 113–34.
Black, Jeremy (1991) 'Anglo-Spanish Naval Relations in the Eighteenth Century', *Mariner's Mirror* LXXVII, pp. 235–58.
Black, Jeremy (1992a) 'British Naval Power and International Commitments: Political and Strategic Problems, 1688–1770' in Duffy (1992a) pp. 39–59.
Black, Jeremy (1992b) 'Naval Power, Strategy and Foreign Policy 1775–1791' in Duffy (1992a) pp. 93–120.
Black, Jeremy (2004) *The British Seaborne Empire* (London: Yale University Press).
Black, Jeremy and Woodfine, Philip (1988) *The British Navy and the Use of Naval Power in the Eighteenth Century* (Leicester: Leicester University Press).
Bond, B. (1972) *The Victorian Army and the Staff College 1854–1914* (London: Eyre Methuen).
Bond, B. (1977) *Liddell Hart: A Study of His Military Thought* (London: Cassell).
Booth, Ken (1977) *Navies and Foreign Policy* (London: Croom Helm).
Bourdé de Villehuet, Jacques (1788) *The Manoeuverer, or Skilful Seaman*, trans from *Le manoeuvrier* (Paris 1765).
Bowles, George F.S. (1926) *The Strength of England* (London: Methuen).
Bowles, T. Gibson (1910) *Sea Law and Sea Power* (London: John Murray).
Breemer, Jan S. (1993) *The Burden of Trafalgar: Decisive Battle and Naval Strategic Expectations on the Eve of the First World War* (Newport, RI: Naval War College Press).
Brett, M.V. (Ed.) (1934) *Journals and Letters of Reginald Viscount Esher*, Vol. 2 (London: Ivor Nicholson & Watson).
Bridge, Admiral Sir Cyprian (1907) *The Art of Naval Warfare* (London: Smith, Elder).
Bridge, Admiral Sir Cyprian (1910) *Sea Power and Other Studies* (London: Smith, Elder).
BR1806 (2004) *British Maritime Doctrine*, 3rd edn (London: HMSO). (1st edn, *The Fundamentals of British Maritime Doctrine* (London: HMSO, 1995); 2nd edn (London: HMSO, 1999).)
Brown, E.D. (1994) *The International Law of the Sea*, Vol. I (Aldershot: Dartmouth Publishing).
Bruijn, R. *et al.* (Eds) (2001) *Strategy and Response in the 20th Century Maritime World* (The Hague: Batavian Lion International).
Burrows, M. (1869) *Memoir of Admiral Sir H.D. Chads* (Portsea: Griffin).
Cable, James (1983) *Britain's Naval Future* (Annapolis, MD: Naval Institute Press).

Cable, J. (1998) *The Political Influence of Naval Force in History* (Basingstoke: Macmillan).
Cable, James (1999) *Gunboat Diplomacy 1919–1979: Political Application of Limited Naval Force*, 3rd edn (Basingstoke: Macmillan).
Callender, Geoffrey (1924) *The Naval Side of British History* (London: Christopher).
Callender, Geoffrey (1939) 'An Educational Century: December 1838–1938' in *Mariner's Mirror*, Jan 1939, pp. 11–23.
Callwell, Charles, E. (1897) *The Effect of Maritime Command on Land Campaigns Since Waterloo* (London: Blackwood).
Callwell, Charles, E. (1924) *The Dardanelles* (London: Constable).
Callwell, Charles, E. (1996) *Military Operations and Maritime Preponderance: Their Relation and Interdependence* (Annapolis, MD: Naval Institute Press).
Cannadine, David (2005) *Admiral Lord Nelson: Context and Legacy* (London: Palgrave).
Churchill, W.S. (1927) *The World Crisis* (London: Butterworth).
Clark, R.B. (1987) *The Waters Around the British Isles: Their Conflicting Uses* (Oxford: Clarendon Press).
Clarke, Lt Col Sir George (Lord Sydenham of Coombe) (1931) 'Sea Heresies' in *Naval Review*, Feb 1931.
Clarke, Lt Col Sir George, and Thursfield, James R. (1897) *The Navy and the Nation* (London: John Murray).
Clerk, John (1790) *Essay on Naval Tactics* (London: Constable).
Clowes, Sir William Laird (1902) *Four Modern Naval Campaigns* (London: Unit Library).
Cobden, R. (1862) *The Three Panics* (London: publisher unknown).
Colomb, Sir John (1880) *The Defence of Great and Greater Britain* (London: Stanford).
Colomb, P.H. (1896) *Essays on Naval Defence* (London: Allen).
Colomb, P.H. (1898) *Memoirs of Sir Astley Cooper Key* (London: Methuen).
Colomb, P.H. (1899) *Naval Warfare* (London: Allen).
Corbett, Sir Julian (1900) *The Successors of Drake* (London: Longmans, reprinted 1990).
Corbett, Sir Julian (1904) *England in the Mediterranean* (London: Longmans).
Corbett, Sir Julian (1905) *Fighting Instructions 1530–1816* (London: Navy Records Society).
Corbett, Sir Julian (1907) *England in the Seven Years' War* (London: Longmans).
Corbett, Sir Julian (1911) *Some Principles of Maritime Strategy* (London: Longmans, reprinted 1988).
Corbett, J.S. (1914) *Maritime Operations in the Russo-Japanese War 1904–5* (London: Admiralty War Staff).
Corbett, J.S. (1916) 'The Teaching of Naval and Military History' in *History*, April 1916, pp. 12–19.
Corbett, Sir Julian (1917) *Drake and the Tudor Navy* (London: Longmans).
Corbett, Sir Julian (1920) *History of the Great War: Naval Operations* (London: Longmans).
Creswell, Cdr John ([1936] 1944, revised reprint) *Naval Warfare: An Introductory Study* (London: Sampson Low Marston & Co).
Cushner, Nicholas P. (1971) *Documents Illustrating the British Conquest of Manila, 1762–1763* (London: Camden Society).

Bibliography

Davies, David (1992) 'The Birth of the Imperial Navy? Aspects of Maritime Strategy, c.1650–90' in Duffy (1992a) pp. 14–38.

Dibb, Paul (1986) *Review of Australia's Defence Capabilities* (Canberra: Australian Government Publishing Service).

Dickinson, H.W. (1999) 'The Origins and Foundation of the Royal Naval College, Greenwich' in *Historical Research*, Vol. 72, no. 177, pp. 92–111.

Dorman, A. *et al.* (1999) *The Changing Face of Maritime Power* (London: Macmillan).

Duffy, Michael (1983) 'British Policy in the War against Revolutionary France' in *Britain and Revolutionary France: Conflict, Subversion and Propaganda*, Ed. Colin Jones (Exeter: Exeter University Press) pp. 11–26.

Duffy, Michael (1987) *Soldiers, Sugar and Seapower: The British Expeditions to the West Indies and the War against Revolutionary France* (Oxford: Oxford University Press).

Duffy, Michael (Ed.) (1992a) *Parameters of British Naval Power, 1650–1850* (Exeter: Exeter University Press).

Duffy, Michael (1992b) 'The Establishment of the Western Squadron as the Linchpin of British Naval Strategy' in Duffy (1992a) pp. 60–81.

Duffy, Michael (1992–4) 'Devon and the Naval Strategy of the French Wars 1689–1815' in *The New Maritime History of Devon*, Vol. 1, Ed. Michael Duffy *et al.* (London: Exeter Conway Maritime Press and Exeter University Press) pp. 182–91.

Duffy, Michael (1998) 'Worldwide War and British Expansion, 1793–1815' in *The Oxford History of the British Empire, Vol. II The Eighteenth Century*, Ed. P.J. Marshall (Oxford: Oxford University Press) pp. 189–207.

Egerton, F. (1896) *The Life of Admiral Sir Geoffrey Phipps Hornby* (Edinburgh: Wm Blackwood).

Elleman, Bruce (2005) *Naval Blockade Strategies and Counter-Strategies: An International Perspective* (London: Frank Cass).

Ellison, D. (1991) *Quarter Deck Cambridge: Francis Price Blackwood* (Cambridge: Cambridge University Press).

Fairhall, David (1971) *Russia Looks to the Sea* (London: Andre Deutsch).

Ferguson, Niall (2004) *Empire: How Britain made the Modern World* (London: Penguin).

Fisher (1919a) *Admiral of the Fleet Lord, Records* (London: Hodder & Stoughton).

Fisher (1919b) *Admiral of the Fleet Lord, Memories* (London: Hodder & Stoughton).

Franklin, G. (2003) *The Development of Britain's Anti-Submarine Capability* (London: Frank Cass).

French, David (1990) *The British Way in Warfare 1688–2000* (London: Unwin Hyams).

Furse, Col. G.A. (1897) *Military Expeditions Beyond the Seas* (London: William Clowes).

Gardner, W.J.R. (1999) *Decoding History: The Battle of the Atlantic and Ultra* (Basingstoke: Macmillan).

Gardner, W.J.R. (Ed.) (2000) *The Evacuation from Dunkirk: Operation Dynamo 26 May–04 June 1940* (London: Frank Cass).

Gat, Azar (1992) *The Development of Military Thought: The Nineteenth Century* (Oxford: Clarendon Press).

Gibson, R.H. and Prendergast, M. (1931) *The German Submarine War 1914–1918* (London: Constable).

Goldrick, J. (1984) *The King's Ships Were at Sea: The War in the North Sea August 1914–February 1915* (Annapolis, MD: Naval Institute Press).
Goldrick, J. (1993) 'The Irrisistible Force and Immovable Object: The *Naval Review*' in Goldrick and Hattendorf (1993) pp. 83–102.
Goldrick, J. and Hattendorf, J. (1993) *Mahan is Not Enough: The Proceedings of a Conference on the Works of Sir Julian Corbett and Admiral Sir Hubert Richmond* (Newport, RI: Naval War College Press).
Gooch, J. (1974) *The Plans of War: The General Staff and British Military Strategy 1900–1916* (London: Routledge & Kegan Paul).
Gordon, Andrew (1996) *The Rules of the Game: Jutland and British Naval Command* (London: John Murray).
Gordon, Andrew (2001) 'The Doctrine Pendulum' in Hore (2001) pp. 73–102.
Gorshkov, Sergei (1979) *The Seapower of the State* (London: Pergamon).
Granier, Hubert (1993) 'La pensee navale française au XVIIIe siècle' in *L'evolution de la pensée navale III*, Ed. Hervé Coutau-Bégarie (Paris: Foundation pour les Etudes de Defense Nationale).
Gray, Colin S. and Barnett, Roger W. (1989) *Sea Power and Strategy* (London: Tri-Service Press).
Gray, Colin (1992) *The Leverage of Sea Power: The Strategic Advantage of Navies in War* (New York: The Free Press).
Grenfell, R. (1937) *The Art of the Admiral* (London: Faber).
Grenier, Jacques Raymond de (1788) 'Vicomte de Grenier', *The Art of War at Sea* trans from *L'Art de la guerre sur mer* (Paris: Didot l'ainé fils).
Gretton, Admiral Sir Peter (1965) *Maritime Strategy* (London: Cassell).
Grove, Eric (1987) *Vanguard to Trident* (London: The Bodley Head).
Grove, Eric (1990) *The Future of Seapower* (London: Routledge).
Grove, Eric (1993) 'Richmond and Arms Control' in Goldrick and Hattendorf (1993) pp. 227–42.
Grove, Eric (1999) BR1806, 'Joint Doctrine and Beyond' in Dorman (1999) pp. 57–64.
Grove, Eric and Thompson, G. (1991) *Battle for the Fjords* (London: Ian Allan).
Hall, Christopher D. (1992) *British Strategy in the Napoleonic War, 1803–15* (Manchester: Manchester University Press).
Hamilton, C.I. (1993) *Anglo-French Naval Rivalry 1840–1870* (Oxford: Oxford University Press).
Hannay, D. (1913) *The Navy and Seapower* (London: Thornton Butterworth).
Hattendorf, John B. (1987a) *England in the War of the Spanish Succession: A Study of the English View and Conduct of Grand Strategy, 1702–1712* (New York: Garland).
Hattendorf, John B. (1987b) 'Admiral Sir George Byng and the Cape Passaro Incident, 1718. A Case Study in the Use of the Royal Navy as a Deterrent' in *Guerres et paix 1660–1815* (Vincennes: Service Historique de la Marine) pp. 19–40.
Hattendorf, John B. (1992) 'Sea Power as Control: Britain's Defensive Naval Strategy in the Mediterranean, 1793–1815' in *Français et Anglais en Méditerranée de la révolution française à l'indépendence de la Grèce (1789–1830)* (Vincennes: Service Historique de la Marine) pp. 203–220.
Hattendorf, John B. (Ed.) (1994) *Ubi Sumus? The State of Naval and Maritime History* (Newport, RI: Naval War College Press).

Bibliography

Hattendorf, John B. (Ed.) (1995) *Doing Naval History: Essays Toward Improvement* (Newport, RI: Naval War College Press).

Hattendorf, John B. (2005) 'Nelson Afloat: A Hero Among the World's Navies' in Cannadine (2005) pp. 166–92.

Hattendorf, John B. *et al.* (Eds) (1993) *British Naval Documents, 1204–1960* (London: Navy Records Society).

Hayes, J. and Hattendorf, J. (1975) *The Writings of Stephen B. Luce* (Newport, RI: Naval War College Press).

Herrick, R.W. (1968) *Soviet Naval Strategy* (Annapolis, MD: Naval Institute Press).

Hibbert, Christopher (1990) *Redcoats and Rebels: The War for America, 1770–1781* (London: Penguin).

Hill, J.R. (1984) *Anti-Submarine Warfare* (London: Ian Allan).

Hill, J.R. (1986) *Maritime Strategy for Medium Powers* (Annapolis, MD: Naval Institute Press).

Hill, J.R. (1995) *The Oxford Illustrated History of the Royal Navy* (Oxford: Oxford University Press).

Hill, J.R. (1996) 'British Naval Planning Post 1945' in Rodger (1996) pp. 215–26.

Hill, Richard (2000) *Lewin of Greenwich* (London: Cassell).

Hinsley, F.H., Thomas, E.E. *et al.* (1979) *British Intelligence in the Second World War: Its Influence on Strategy and Operations*, Vol. 1 (London: HMSO).

Hore, P. (2001) *The Hudson Papers*, Vol. 1 (London: MoD).

Hoste, Paul (1762) *Naval Evolutions: Or, A System of Sea-discipline* (London 1762) trans. C. O'Bryen from *L'Art des armies navales* (Lyons: Anisson & Posuel 1697).

Howard, Michael (1962) 'The Use and Abuse of Military History' in *RUSI Journal*, no. 107, February, pp. 9–14.

Howard, Michael (1972) *The Continental Commitment* (London: Temple Smith).

Howard, Michael (1974) 'The British Way in Warfare: A Reappraisal' (Lecture at University College London. Printed in *The Causes of War and Other Essays*) (London: Maurice Temple Smith, 1983).

Hunt, Barry D. (1982) *Sailor – Scholar: Admiral Sir Herbert Richmond 1871–1946* (Waterloo, Ontario: Wilfred Laurier Press).

Hunt, Barry D. (1993) 'Richmond and the Education of the Royal Navy', in Goldrick and Hattendorf (1993) pp. 65–81.

Huntington, S. (1957) *The Soldier and the State* (Cambridge, MA: Harvard University Press).

Hurd, Archibald (1915) *The Fleets at War* (London: *Daily Telegraph*).

Hurd, Archibald (1918) *The British Fleet in the Great War* (London: Constable).

Jackson, Bill and Bramall, David (1992) *The Chiefs* (London: Brassey's).

James, G.F. (1938–9) 'The Admiralty Establishment, 1759' in *Bulletin of the Institute of Historical Research, XVI (1938–9)* pp. 24–7.

James, W. (2002) *The Naval History of Great Britain* (6 vols), introduction by A. Lambert (London: Conway Press). (Originally printed in London, 1826).

Jamieson, A.G. (1986) 'The Channel Islands and British Maritime Strategy, 1689–1945' in his own *A People of the Sea: The Maritime History of the Channel Islands* (London: Methuen) pp. 220–44.

Jamieson, A.G. (2001) 'British Government Shipping Policy From 1945 to 1990' in Bruijn (2001) pp. 51–61.

Johnman, Lewis (2001) 'Strategy and Response in British Shipbuilding 1945–1972' in Bruijn (2001) pp. 77–99.

Jomini, A.H. (1838) *The Art of War Paris 1838* (London: Greenhill Books 1992).
Jordan, Gerald and Rogers, Nicholas (1989) 'Admirals as Heroes: Patriotism and Liberty in Hanoverian England' in *Journal of British Studies XXVIII (1989)* pp. 201–24.
Kemp, Lt Cdr P.K. (1964) *The Papers of Admiral Sir John Fisher*, Vol. II (London: Navy Records Society).
Kemp, Peter (1977) 'From Tryon to Fisher: The Regeneration of the Navy' in Gerald Jordan (Ed.) *Naval Warfare in the Twentieth Century, 1900–1945: Essays in Honour of Arthur Marder* (London: Croom Helm) pp. 16–31.
Kennedy, Greg (Ed.) (2004) *British Maritime Strategy East of Suez: Influence and Actions* (London: Frank Cass). Chapter 7.
Kennedy, P.M. (1976) *The Rise and Fall of British Naval Mastery* (London: Allen Lane).
Kennedy, P.M. (1983) *Strategy and Diplomacy 1870–1945* (London: Fontana).
Kennedy, P.M. (1989) 'The Relevance of the Prewar British and American Strategies of the First World War and its Aftermath' in J.B. Hattendorf and R.S. Jordan (Eds) *Maritime Strategy and the Balance of Power* (Basingstoke: Macmillan) pp. 165–88.
King-Hall, Stephen (1952) *My Naval Life: 1906–1929* (London: Faber & Faber).
Kipling, R. (1916) *The Seven Seas* (London: Methuen).
Lambert, A.D. (1987) *Warrior: The First Ironclad* (London: Conway Maritime Press).
Lambert, A.D. (1990) *The Crimean War: British Grand Strategy Against Russia* (Manchester: Manchester University Press).
Lambert, Andrew (1991) *The Last Sailing Battlefleet: Maintaining Naval Mastery 1815–1850* (London: Conway Maritime Press).
Lambert, Andrew (1996) 'Preparing for the Long Peace: The Reconstruction of the Royal Navy 1815–1830' in *Mariners Mirror LXXXII*, pp. 41–54.
Lambert, Andrew (1998a) *The Foundations of Naval History: John Knox Laughton, the Royal Navy and the Historical Profession* (London: Chatham Publishing).
Lambert, A.D. (1998b) 'Politics, Technology and Policy-Making: Palmerston, Gladstone and the Management of the Ironclad Naval Race, 1859–68' in *The Northern Mariner*, July.
Lambert, A.D. (2001) 'The Principal Source of Understanding Navies and the Educational Role of the Past' in Hore (2001) pp. 35–47.
Lambert, A.D. (2002) *Letters and Papers of Sir John Knox Laughton 1830–1915* (London: Navy Records Society).
Lambert, N. (1999) *Sir John Fisher's Naval Revolution* (Columbia, SC: University of South Carolina Press).
Laughton, J.K. (1872) *An Introduction to the Practical and Theoretical Study of Nautical Surveying* (London: Longmans, Green & Co).
Laughton, J.K. (1874) 'The Scientific Study of Naval History' in *Journal of the RUSI*, Vol. XVIII, pp. 508–27.
Laughton, J.K. (1875) 'Scientific Education in the Royal Navy' in *Journal of the RUSI 1875*, Vol. XIX.
Laughton, J.K. (1885) 'Naval Warfare' in *The Edinburgh Review*, July, pp. 234–64.
Laughton, J.K. (1886) *Letters and Despatches of Horatio, Viscount Nelson* (London: Longmans).
Laughton, J.K. (1887) *Studies in Naval History* (London: Longmans).
Laughton, J.K. (1899) *From Howard to Nelson* (London: Heinemann).

Lavery, Brian (2004) *Hostilities Only: Training the Wartime Royal Navy* (London: National Maritime Museum).
Le Bailly, Vice Admiral Sir Louis (1991) *From Fisher to the Falklands* (London: Marine Management (Holdings) for the Institute of Marine Engineers).
Le Goff, T.J.A. (1990) 'Problémes de recruitement de la marine française pendant la Guerre de Sept Ans', *Revue Historique*, CCLXXXIII, pp. 205–33.
Lehman, John F. (1988) *Command of the Seas: Building the 600 Ship Navy* (New York: Charles Scribner).
Leach, Henry (1993) *Endure No Makeshifts* (London: Leo Cooper).
Lewis, M.A. (1959) *The History of the British Navy* (London: Allen & Unwin).
Lewis, M.A. (1960) *A Social History of the Navy 1793–1815* (London: Allen & Unwin).
Liddell, Hart, B.H. (1932) *The British Way in Warfare* (London: Faber).
Liddell, Hart, B.H. (1939) *The Defence of Britain* (London: Faber).
Liddell, Hart, B.H. (1967) *Strategy: The Indirect Approach* (London: Faber).
Llewellyn-Jones, M. (2003) 'A Clash of Cultures: The Case for Large Convoys' in Hore, P. (Ed.) *Patrick Blackett: Sailor, Scientist, Socialist* (London: Frank Cass) pp. 138–66.
Lloyd, Christopher (1949) *The Navy and the Slave Trade: The Suppression of the Africa Slave Trade in the Nineteenth Century* (London: Longman).
Lloyd, Christopher (1954) *The Nation and the Navy – A History of Naval Life and Policy* (London: The Correct Press).
Lloyd, Christopher (1966) 'The Royal Naval Colleges at Portsmouth and Greenwich', *Mariner's Mirror*, May, pp. 145–56.
Lloyd, Christopher and Coulter, Jack L.S. (1957) *Medicine and the Navy 1200–1900* (Edinburgh: E & S Livingston).
Luttwak, E. (1975) *The Political Uses of Sea Power* (Baltimore, MA: Johns Hopkins University Press).
MacGregor, David (1992) 'The Use, Misuse and Non Use of History: The Royal Navy and the Operational Lessons of the First World War' in *Journal of Military History*, Oct.
Mackay, Ruddock F. (1973) *Fisher of Kilverstone* (Oxford: Clarendon Press).
Mackesy, Piers (1974) *Statesmen at War: The Strategy of Overthrow 1798–1799* (London: Longman).
Mackesy, Piers (1984) *War Without Victory: The Downfall of Pitt 1799–1802* (Oxford: Oxford University Press).
Mackinder, H.J. (1969) *Britain and the British Seas* (New York: Haskell House).
Mahan, A.T. (1890) *The Influence of Sea Power Upon History 1660–1783* (London: Sampson, Low, Marston & Co.).
Mahan, A.T. (1902) *Retrospect and Prospect* (London: Sampson, Low, Marston & Co.).
Marder, Arthur J. (1940) *The Anatomy of British Sea Power* (London: Frank Cass, reprinted 1972).
Marder, Arthur J. (1952) *Portrait of an Admiral – The Life and Papers of Sir Herbert Richmond* (London: Jonathan Cape).
Marder, Arthur J. (1961) *From the Dreadnought to Scapa Flow*, Vol. I, 1904–1914 (Oxford: Oxford University Press).
Martin, L.W. (1967) *The Sea in Modern Strategy* (London: Chatto & Windus).
Mason, Sir Ronald (1984) 'Problems of Fleet Balance' in Till (1984) pp. 213–17.

Massam, D. (1995) *British Maritime Strategy and Amphibious Capability 1900–1940* (Oxford University D.Phil. dissertation).
Mather, I.R. (1996) *The Royal Navy in America and the West Indies, 1660–1720* (Oxford University D.Phil. thesis).
McGwire, M.K. (1968) 'The Background to Russian Naval Policy' in *Brassey's Annual* (London: Clowes).
McKenzie, John M. (2005) 'Nelson Goes Global' in Carradine (2005) pp. 144–65.
Merino Navarro, José P. (1981) *La Armada Española en el Siglo XVIII* (Madrid: Fundacion Universitana Espanola).
Meyer, Jean (1986) 'Les problèmes de personnel de la marine de guerre française aux XVIIe et XVIIIe siècles' in *Les Hommes et la Mer dans l'Europe du Nord-Ouest de l'Antiquité à nos jours*, Eds Alain Lottin, Jean-Claude Hocquet and Stéphane Lebecq (Revue du Nord extra number) pp. 107–24.
Middleton, Richard (1985) *The Bells of Victory: The Pitt-Newcastle Ministry and the Conduct of the Seven Years' War, 1757–1762* (Cambridge: Cambridge University Press).
Middleton, Richard (1989) 'British Naval Strategy 1755–62: The Western Squadron' in *Mariner's Mirror LXXV*, pp. 349–67.
Mimler, Manfred (1983) *Der Einfluss kolonialer Interessen in Nordamerika auf die Strategie und Diplomatie Grossbritanniens während des Österreichischen Erbfolgekrieges, 1744–1748* (Hildesheim: Olms).
Molyneux, Thomas M. (1759) *Conjunct Expedition or Expeditions that Have been Carried on Jointly by the Fleet and Army, with a Commentary on a Littoral War* (London: R&J Dodsley).
Moreby, John (1909) *Two Admirals: Sir Fairfax Moresby: A Record of a Hundred Years* (London: Murray).
Moretz, Joseph (2002) *The Royal Navy and the Capital Ship in the Interwar Period* (London: Frank Cass).
Morris, Michael, A. (1987) *Expansion of Third World Navies* (London: Macmillan).
Moulton, J.L. (1970) *Brassey's Annual* (London: Clowes).
Mühlmann, Rolf (1975) *Die Reorganisation der Spanischen Kriegsmarine im 18: Jahrhundert* (Cologne: Bönlau).
Mullins, R.E. (2000) Sharpening the Trident: the Decisions of 1889 and the Creation of Modern Seapower, unpublished Ph.D. thesis, University of London.
Nailor, Peter (1988) *The Nassau Connection: The Organisation and Management of the British Polaris Project* (London: HMSO).
Nash, P. (2004) 'The Royal Navy in Korea – Replenishment and Sustainability' in Kennedy, Greg (Ed.) *British Maritime Strategy East of Suez: Influence and Actions* (London: Frank Cass) pp. 154–77.
Newbolt, Henry (1995) *The Island Race* (Oxford: Woodstock Books).
Newnham Collingwood, C.L. (1828) *A Selection from the Dairies and Private Correspondence of Vice Admiral Lord Collingwood, Interspersed with Memoirs of this Life*.
Nicolas, Sir H. (1844–6) *Dispatches and Letters of Lord Nelson* (7 vols) (London: Chatham Publishing, reprinted 1998).
Nicolson, Harold (1952) *King George V: His Life and Reign* (London: John Constable).
Niedhart, Gottfried (1979) *Handel und Krieg in der Britischen Weltpolitik, 1738–1763* (Munich: Fink).
Noel, G.H.U. (1873) *Gun, Ram and Torpedo* (Portsmouth: Gieves & Hawkes).

O'Connell, D.P. (1975) *The Influence of Law on Sea Power* (Manchester: Manchester University Press).
Offer, A. (1989) *The First World War: An Agrarian Interpretation* (Oxford: University Press).
Osgood, R.E. (1962) *NATO: The Entangling Alliance* (Chicago, IL: Chicago University Press).
Owen, Dr David (1991) *Time to Declare* (London: Penguin).
Padfield, Peter (1999) *Maritime Supremacy and the Opening of the Western Mind* (New York: The Overlook Press).
Padfield, Peter (2003) *Maritime Power and the Struggle for Freedom: Naval Campaigns that Shaped the Modern World 1788–1851* (London: John Murray).
Pares, Richard (1936a) 'American versus Continental Warfare, 1739–1763' in *English Historical Review LI*, pp. 429–65.
Pares, Richard (1936b) *War and Trade in the West Indies, 1739–1763* (Oxford: Oxford University Press).
Parkes, Oscar (1957) *British Battleships* (London: Seeley Service).
Partridge, M. (1989) *Military Planning for the Defense of the United Kingdom, 1814–1870* (Westport, CT: Greenwood).
Partridge, M. (1999) *The Royal Naval College, Osborne* (Stroud: Sutton Publishing).
Pitt, W. (1806) *The Speeches of the Right Honourable William Pitt in the House of Commons* (4 vols) (London).
Pollen, A.H. (1918) *The Navy in Battle* (London: Chatto & Windus).
Pout, H.W. (1995) 'Monograph 4 – Fighter-Direction Material and Technique' in *The Applications of Radar and other Electronic Systems in the Royal Navy and World War 2*, Ed. F.A. Kingsley (Basingstoke: Macmillan).
Pugh, Philip (1986) *The Cost of Sea Power* (London: Conway).
Ranft, B. McL. (1958) *The Vernon Papers* (London: Navy Records Society Vol. 99).
Ranft, B. McL. (Ed.) (1972) *Julian Corbett, Some Principles of Maritime Strategy* (London: Conway Maritime Press).
Ranft, Bryan (Ed.) (1977a) *Technical Change and British Naval Policy 1860–1939* (London: Hodder & Stoughton).
Ranft, Bryan (1977b) 'The Protection of British Seaborne Trade and the Development of Systematic Planning for War 1860–1906' in Ranft (1977).
Ranft, Bryan (1993) *The Beatty Papers* (London: Scolar Press, for Navy Records Society).
Ranft, Bryan, and Till, G. (1989) *The Sea in Soviet Strategy* (London: Macmillan).
Ranken, M.B.F. (Ed.) (1981) *Greenwich Forum VI: World Shipping in the 1990s* (London: Westbury).
Richmond, H.W. (1920) *The Navy in the War of 1739–48* (Cambridge: Cambridge University Press).
Richmond, H.W. (1930) *Naval Warfare* (London: Ernest Benn).
Richmond, H.W. (1931) *The Navy in India 1763–1783* (London: Ernest Benn).
Richmond, H.W. (1934) *Seapower in the Modern World* (London: Bell).
Richmond, H.W. (1939) 'The Importance of the Study of Naval History' in *Naval Review* May, reprinted in *Naval Review* April 1980, pp. 139–50.
Richmond, H.W. (1941) *Amphibious Warfare in British History* (London: Historical Association).
Richmond, H.W. (1946) *Statesmen and Sea Power* (Oxford: Clarendon Press).

Richmond, H.W. (1953) (Ed. E.A. Hughes) *The Navy as an Instrument of Policy 1558–1727* (Cambridge: Cambridge University Press).

Roberts, Michael (1970) *Splendid Isolation, 1763–1780* (Reading: Reading University Press).

Rodger, N.A.M. (1976) 'The Dark Ages of the Admiralty: Pt II, Change and Decay, 1874–1880' in *Mariner's Mirror LXII*, pp. 33–46.

Rodger, N.A.M. (1979) *The Admiralty* (Lavenham: Terence Dalton).

Rodger, N.A.M. (1981) 'British Naval Thought and Naval Policy, 1820–1890' in *New Aspects of Naval History*, Ed. Craig L. Symonds (Annapolis, MD: USNIP) pp. 140–52.

Rodger, N.A.M. (1986) *The Wooden World: An Anatomy of the Georgian Navy* (London: Collins).

Rodger, N.A.M. (1992) 'The Continental Commitment in the Eighteenth Century' in *War, Strategy and International Politics: Essays in Honour of Sir Michael Howard*, Eds Lawrence Freedman, Paul Hayes and Robert O'Neill (Oxford: Oxford University Press) pp. 39–55.

Rodger, N.A.M. (1993) *The Insatiable Earl: A Life of John Montagu, Fourth Earl of Sandwich, 1718–1792* (London: Harper Collins).

Rodger, N.A.M. (1995) 'La mobilisation navale au XVIIIème siècle' in *Etat, marine et societé: hommage à Jean Meyer*, Eds Martine Acerra, Jean-Pierre Poussou, Michel Vergé-Franceschi and André Zysberg (Paris: Presse de l'Université de Paris-Sorbonne) pp. 365–74.

Rodger, N.A.M. (1996a) 'The West Indies in Eighteenth-Century British Naval Strategy' in *L'éspace Caraibe: théâtre et enjeu des luttes impériales, XVIe–XIXe siècles*, Ed. Paul Butel and Bernard Lavallé (Bordeaux: Maison de Pays Iberiques) pp. 38–60.

Rodger, N.A.M. (1996b) *Naval Power in the Twentieth Century* (London: Macmillan).

Rodger, N.A.M. (1997) *The Safeguard of the Sea: A Naval History of Britain 660–1649*, Vol. I (London: Harper Collins).

Rodger, N.A.M. (1998) 'Sea-power and Empire, 1688–1793' in *The Oxford History of the British Empire Vol. II, The Eighteenth Century*, Ed. P.J. Marshall (Oxford: Oxford University Press) pp. 169–83.

Rodger, N.A.M. (2000) 'George, Lord Anson (1697–1762)' in *The Precursors of Nelson: British Admirals of the Eighteenth Century*, Ed. Richard Harding and Peter Le Fevre (London: Chatham Publishing) pp. 177–99.

Rodger, N.A.M. (2001) 'Training or Education: A Naval Dilemma over Three Centuries' in Hore (2001) pp. 1–34.

Rodger, N.A.M. (2004) *The Command of the Ocean: A Naval History of Britain 1649–1815* (London: Allen Lane).

Roskill, S.W. (1954–1961) *The War at Sea 1939–1945* (4 vols) (London: HMSO, Vol. 1, 1954).

Roskill, S.W. (1962) *The Strategy of Sea Power* (London: Collins).

Roskill, S.W. (1963) 'Richmond in Retrospect' in *Naval Review*, Vol. 51.

Roskill, S.W. (1968) *Naval Policy Between the Wars* (2 vols) (London: Collins 1968, 1976).

Roskill, S.W. (1969) 'The Richmond Lecture' in *Naval Review*, Vol. 57.

Ryan, A.N. (1985) 'The Royal Navy and the Blockade of Brest 1689–1805: Theory and Practice' in *Les marines de guerre Européennes XVII–XVIIIe siècles*, Ed. Martine

Acerra, José Merino and Jean Meyer (Paris: Presse de l'Université de Paris-Sorbonne) pp. 175–94.
Schurman, D. (1965) *The Education of a Navy* (London: Cassell).
Schurman, D. (1981) *Julian S. Corbett 1854–1922* (London: Royal Historical Society).
Seager, R. (1977) *Mahan* (Annapolis, MD: Naval Institute Press).
Semmel, Bernard (1986) *Liberalism and Naval Strategy: Ideology, Interest and Sea Power during the Pax Britannica* (Boston, MA: Allen & Unwin).
Sims, William Sowden (1920) *The Victory at Sea* (London: John Murray).
Smollett, T. (1760) *Continuation of the Complete History of England*, Vol. 7 (London).
Soley, J.R. (1880) *Report on Foreign Systems of Naval Education* (Washington: US Government Printing Office).
Strachan, H. (1984) *Wellington's Legacy: The Reform of the British Army 1830–1854* (Manchester: Manchester University Press).
Sulivan, H.N. (1896) *Life and Letters of Admiral Sir B.J. Sulivan* (London: John Murray).
Sumida, Jon Tetsuro (1989) *In Defence of Naval Supremacy: Finance, Technology, and British Naval Policy* (Boston, MA: Unwin, Hyman).
Sumida, Jon Tetsuro (1997) *Inventing Grand Strategy and Teaching Command: The Classic Works of Alfred Thayer Mahan Reconsidered* (Baltimore, MD: Johns Hopkins University Press).
Sweetman, John (2000) *Tirpitz – Hunting the Beast: Air Attacks on the German Battleship 1940–44* (Stroud: Sutton).
Syrett, David (Ed.) (1970) *The Siege and Capture of Havana, 1762* (London: Navy Records Society, Vol. 114).
Syrett, David (1983) 'British Amphibious Operations During the Seven Years and American Wars' in *Assault from the Sea: Essays on the History of Amphibious Warfare*, Ed. M.L. Bartlett (Annapolis, MD: Naval Institute Press).
Syrett, David (1991) 'Home Waters or America – The Dilemma of British Naval Strategy in 1778' in *Mariner's Mirror LXXVII*, pp. 365–77.
Syrett, David (1998) *The Royal Navy in European Waters during the American Revolutionary War* (Columbia, SC: South Carolina University Press).
T124. (1940) *Sea Power* (London: Jonathan Cape).
Tegetthoff, Admiral (1878) 'Experiences of Steam and Armour' in *Fraser's Magazine*, June, pp. 671–92.
Thomson, Mark A. (1932) *The Secretaries of State, 1681–1782* (Oxford: Oxford University Press).
Till, G. (1979) *Airpower and the Royal Navy 1914–1915* (London: Jane's Publishing).
Till, G. (1982) *Maritime Strategy and the Nuclear Age* (London: Macmillan).
Till, G. (1984) *The Future of British Sea Power* (London: Macmillan).
Till, G. (Ed.) (1994) *Seapower: Theory and Practice* (London: Frank Cass).
Till, G. (1995) 'Retrenchment, Rethinking, Revival' in Hill (1995) pp. 319–47.
Till, G. (1996) 'Brothers in Arms: The British Army and Navy at the Dardanelles' in *Facing Armageddon: The First World War Experience*, Eds H. Cecil and P.H. Liddle (London: Pen & Sword) pp. 160–79.
Till, G. (1997) 'Passchendaele: The Maritime Dimension' in *Passchendaele in Perspective: The Third Battle of Ypres*, Ed. P.H. Liddle (London: Leo Cooper) pp. 73–87.
Till, G. (2001) (Ed.) *Sea Power at the Millennium* (Stroud: Sutton).

Till, G. (2003) 'The Gallipoli Campaign: Command Performances' in *The Challenges of High Command: The British Experience*, Eds G. Sheffield and G. Till (London: Macmillan).
Till, G. (2004) *Seapower: A Guide for the 21st Century* (London: Frank Cass).
Tracy, Nicholas (1974) 'The Gunboat Diplomacy of the Government of George Grenville, 1764–1765: in The Honduran, Turks Island and Gambian Incidents' in *Historical Journal, XVII*, pp. 711–31.
Tracy, Nicholas (1988) *Navies, Deterrence and American Independence: Britain and Seapower in the 1760s and 1770s* (Vancouver: Vancouver University Press).
Tracy, Nicholas (1991) *Attack on Maritime Trade* (Basingstoke: Macmillan).
Tracy, Nicholas (1996) *Manila Ransomed: The British Assault on Manila in the Seven Years War* (Exeter: Exeter University Press).
Tunstall, Brian (1936a) *The Anatomy of Nepture* (London: Routledge).
Tunstall, Brian (1936b) *The Realities of Naval History* (London: George Allen).
Tunstall, Brian (1936c) *Naval Warfare in the Age of Sail* (London: Conway, reprinted 1990).
Waddington, C.H. (1973) *OR in World War 2: Operational Research against the U-Boat* (London: Elek Science).
Waters, Lt Cdr D.W. (1957) *A Study of the Philosophy and Conduct of Maritime Warfare 1815–1945* (London: Naval Historical Branch).
Watt, D.C. (1980) *Greenwich Forum V: The North Sea: A New International Regime* (London: Westbury House).
Watt, D.C. (2001) 'The Sea in the 21st Century' in Till (2001).
Webb, Paul L.C. (1980) 'Sea Power in the Ochakov Affair of 1791' in *International History Review II*, pp. 13–33.
Welch, M.D. (1998) *Science and the British Officer: Its Early Days of the Royal United Services Institute for Defence Studies 1829–1869* (London: RUSI).
Welch, M.D. (1999) *Science in a Pickelhaube British Military Lesson Learning at the Royal United Services Institute for Defence Studies 1870–1900* (London: RUSI).
Wiest, A.A. (1995) *Passchendaele and the Royal Navy* (London: Greenwood).
Wilkinson, S. (1889) *The Brain of an Army* (London: Archibald Constable & Co.).
Williams, Mark (1979) *Captain Gilbert Roberts and the Anti-U-Boat School* (London: Cassell).
Wilson, Kathleen (1988) 'Empire, Trade and Popular Politics in Mid-Hanoverian Britain; The Case of Admiral Vernon' in *Past and Present, no. 121*, pp. 74–109.
Wilson, Kathleen (2002) *The Island Race: Englishness, Empire and Gender in the Eighteenth Century* (London: Routledge).
Woodfine, Philip (1988) 'Ideas of Naval Power and the Conflict with Spain, 1737–1742', in Black and Woodfine (1988).
Young, E. (1974) 'New Laws for Old Navies' in *Survival* November–December, 1974.

Index

Aboukir (battle 1798) *see* Nile (battle 1798)
Aboukir HMS 99
Acworth, Captain Bernard 116–17, 119, 123–4
Admiralty: in the 18th century 20; in the 19th century 30, 49, 81; in the 20th century 103, 109, 114, 115 *see also* Board of Admiralty
Airborne Early Warning (AEW) 177
aircraft carriers 124, 141
airpower 137, 148–9, 160, 164
American Civil War 41
American War of Independence 26–7, 72, 74, 85–6
amphibious operations 82–6, 110, 112; in Second World War 135, 138
Ampthill, Lord 106
Anatomy of Neptune (Tunstall) 127
anti-submarine warfare (ASW) 137, 170
Art of Naval Warfare (Bridge) 67
Armilla Patrol 172
Army: and conscriptionist homeland defence 51; higher level education in 52–4; in joint approach 82, 83, 84, 108; strategic role in 19th century 35, 40
Army Bureau of Current Affairs 14
Army Staff College 52, 53, 54, 55
Art of the Admiral (Grenfell) 107
Anson, Admiral George 21, 23
ASDIC (Anti-Submarine Detection Investigation Committee) 117
Asdic (sonar system) 100, 138
Ashigara (Japanese cruiser) 141
Aston, George 48, 52, 53, 53, 68, 82, 83, 84, 103, 107, 121, 128, 130–1
Atlantic, Battle of the 136, 138

atomic bomb 143
Audit of War (Barnett) 163

Ballard, George 49, 52
Ballard Committee 55
Barnett, Correlli 163
Battenberg, Prince Louis of 44–5, 49
battle cruisers 95, 96, 98
battleships 95, 96, 104; interwar capital ships controversy 122–4; in Second World War 138, 148
Beatty, Admiral Sir David 95, 97, 98, 99, 123
Bismark 135
Black, Jeremy 3, 7
blockades 62, 76, 105, 106, 119, 120–1, 147, 153
'bluewater' strategy 6, 65
Board of Admiralty 20, 39
Boer War 53
Booth, Ken 167–8
Bowles, Commander G.S. 6
Bowles, T. Gibson 119
BR1806 (1st edition) *see Fundamentals of British Maritime Doctrine* (1995) (BR1806)
BR1806 (2nd edition) *see British Maritime Doctrine* (1999) (BR1806)
BR1806 (3rd edition) *see British Maritime Doctrine* (2004) (BR1806)
Brain of an Army, The (Wilkinson) 53
Brest 24
Bridge, Admiral Sir Cyprian 48, 49, 66–7, 68, 69, 71–2, 76, 79, 83
Britannia Royal Naval College (Dartmouth) xiii, 8, 12, 14–15, 41, 50, 183
British Defence Doctrine (1996) 188

British Expeditionary Force: First World War 110, 112; Second World War 138
British Maritime Doctrine (1999) (BR1806) 188–9
British Maritime Doctrine (2004) (BR1806) 9, 189, 190
British Way of War (Liddell Hart) 105
Brown, David 182
Bullocke, John G. 14, 126
Burgoyne, Sir John Fox 35
Burrows, Montagu 36

Cable, Sir James 167, 187
Callender, Geoffrey A.R. 14, 15, 115, 125–6, 127
Callwell, Major General Sir Charles 66, 67, 72–3, 83, 84, 85, 103, 111, 130, 155
Campaign of Trafalgar, The (Corbett) 10
Camperdown, HMS 93
Cape St Vincent (battle 1797) 90
Capital Ship Enquiry (1921) 122
Carnarvon Commission on Colonial Defence 48
Chads, Captain Henry 39
Cherbourg, in British strategy of 1840s 39
Cherwell, Viscount *see* Lindemann, Frederick
Chesapeake (battle 1781) 27
Chiefs of Staff Committee 131
Childers, Erskine 75
Chile War (1891) 83
Churchill, Sir Winston xv, 8, 10, 11, 13, 55, 97, 104, 122, 146
Clarke, Sir George (later Lord Sydenham) 51, 52, 67, 103, 108
Clausewitz, Carl von 10, 52, 54, 70
Clerk of Eldin, John 1, 63
Clowes, Sir William Laird 7, 50, 66, 69
Cobden, Richard 61
Codner, Commander Mike 185
Cold War 165, 158
Collingwood, Admiral Lord Cuthbert 37
Colomb, Captain Sir John 42, 48, 63–4, 75, 82, 117
Colomb, Rear Admiral Philip 12, 49, 50, 63–5, 69, 75, 81–2, 107, 113
combined operations 142–3
command of the sea 79–82, 112, 113, 113–17, 150–3, 154, 169–70

Committee of Imperial Defence (CID) 51, 53, 131
Conjunct Operations (Molyneux) 63
'constabulary' maritime power 188
'continental' strategy 6, 71, 107, 109, 147
Convoy PQ17 143
convoy system 117–18, 151–2, 189
Corbett, Sir Julian xv, 1, 8, 12, 24, 31, 50–2, 53, 54, 55, 56, 65–6, 67, 69–70, 103, 104, 107, 126, 130, 151, 169, 187; amphibious operations 110, 112, 113; command of the sea 75, 80–2, 112, 114; influence of 126; joint approach 82–6, 111, 185–6; limited conflict 77–9; maritime strategy, 9–10, 70–3; trade protection 118
Cost of Sea Power, The (Pugh) 178
Cressy, HMS 99
Creswell, Commander John 106–7, 112, 115, 116, 117, 120–1, 123, 129
Crimean War 38–9, 72, 82
Crowe, Eyre 78
Culme-Seymour, Admiral Sir Michael 92, 94, 97
Custance, Admiral Sir Reginald 48, 49, 50, 54, 66–7, 68, 81, 116, 123, 124

Dardanelles, The (Callwell) 66
Dartmouth *see* Britannia Royal Naval College
de Grasse, Admiral Comte Francois 27
Defence of Great and Greater Britain, The (John Colomb) 64
Dispatches and Letters of Lord Nelson (Nicolas) 37
decisive battle 80–1, 89, 113–17, 152, 153, 157–8
Declaration of Paris (1856) 120
deterrence 170
doctrine 11, 90, 97, 131, 182–90
Douglas, General Sir Howard 52
Drake and the Tudor Navy (Corbett) 51
Drake, Sir Francis 70
Dreadnought, HMS 95, 96, 104
Dreyer, Admiral Sir Frederic xv, 145
Dundas, Henry 28
Dunkirk (battle 1940) 138

'east of Suez' debate 167, 175
Eberle, Admiral Sir James 168
Economy and Naval Security (Richmond) 104
Edmonds, James 54

Index

education *see* naval education
Effect of Maritime Command on Land Campaigns since Waterloo (Callwell) 66
England in the Mediterranean (Corbett) 51
England in the Seven Years War (Corbett) 52
Esher, Lord 7, 123
Esher Committee 53
Essay on Naval Tactics (Laughton) 45
Excellent, HMS 36, 39, 41, 43, 52
expeditionary operations 7, 82–6, 90, 112 *see also* maritime power projection

Falkland Islands: crisis of 1770 22; battle (1914) 98; War (1982) 163, 170, 172, 178
First World War 13, 74, 89, 97–101, 106, 115 *see also* Gallipoli campaign; Jutland
Fisher, Captain (later Admiral Sir) John 50, 53, 54, 55, 62, 64, 68, 75, 92, 94, 111; and flotilla craft for home defence 95–6
Flag Officer Sea Training 174
Foreign Intelligence Committee 48
'Forward Maritime Strategy' 187
France: in 18th century 22–6; in 19th century 28; invasion threat from 23, 61
Freedman. Lawrence xiv
French Navy: in 17th century 74; in 18th century 22, 26, 27; in 19th century 42, 61; in 20th century 95, 96, 99; Toulon Squadron 25, 26
Fundamentals of British Maritime Doctrine (BR1806) 182–8
Furse, Colonel George 68
Future Fleet Working Party 175
Future Navy Operational Concept 190
Future of Seapower, The (Grove) 168

Gallipoli campaign 110–11, 112, 113, 129
Gardner, Jock xiv, 17
Gat, Azar 64
Germain, Lord George 26
German Navy: Imperial German Navy 96, 97, 98–101; in Second World War 134, 135–6
Gordon, Andrew 17

Gorshkov, Admiral Sergei 156, 166, 170
Graf Spee 135
Grand Fleet 91, 95, 97, 98, 99, 101, 104, 122
Greenwich *see* Royal Naval College Greenwich
Greenwich Forum 165, 173
Grenfell, Russell 107, 108, 117–18, 123
Grenville, Lord William 28
Gretton, Admiral Sir Peter 144–5, 155, 156–7, 158
Grey, Sir Edward 6
Grove, Eric 17, 168–9
Gunboat Diplomacy (Cable) 167

Haines, Commander Steve 188
Hall, Rear Admiral Sydney Stewart 121
Hall, Captain William 48
Hankey, Sir Maurice 52
Hannay, David 67, 69, 71
Hardy, Thomas 8, 9
Harrier aircraft 175
Hartington Commission (1890) 53
Healey, Denis xiv, 167, 170
hedgehog (underwater weapon) 138
Henderson, Colonel G.F.R. 52, 53
Henderson, Admiral W.H. 103–4
Herrick, R.W. 166
Hill, Rear Admiral Richard xiv, 17, 168
Hogue, HMS 99
Hood, Lord Arthur 36, 45
Hornby, Captain (later Admiral Sir) Geoffrey Phipps 38, 45, 48, 92
Howard, Sir Michael xiv, 85
Howe, Lord Richard 37
Hurd, Archibald 6, 103, 107–8, 110, 114–15, 124
Hydrographer's Department 39–40, 41

Ikara (ASW system) 176
Imperial Defence and Capture at Sea in War (Richmond) 105
Imperial Defence College (IDC) 104, 129, 130, 144
Indian Ocean 140, 141, 142, 155
Inflexible, HMS 96, 98
Influence of Sea Power on History (Mahan) 30, 65
intelligence 135, 136–7, 142
International Law of the Sea 164, 167
invasion threat 23, 61
Invincible class cruisers 175, 176
Invincible, HMS 96, 98

James, William 37
James, Vice-Admiral William 129
Japanese Navy 139, 140
Jellicoe, Admiral Sir John 9, 95, 98, 99, 121, 182
Jervis, Admiral Sir John *see* St Vincent, Earl
joint approach 7, 71, 82–6, 129–31, 189
Joint Services Command and Staff College xiv, 12, 16
Joint Planning Committee 131
Joinville, Prince François de 61
Jungius, Vice-Admiral Sir James 166
Junior Naval Professional Association (JNPA) 43, 45
Jutland (battle 1916) 9, 91, 98, 99, 113, 114, 115

Kahn, Herman 171
Kennedy, Paul 155, 162, 163
Keppel, Admiral Augustus 26
Key, Sir Astley Cooper 12, 36, 44, 46, 64
Keyes, Admiral Sir Roger 123
King's College London 47, 50, 56, 185
Kitchener, Field Marshal Earl Horatio 111
Kolombangara (battle 1943) 145

Lambert, Andrew 12, 17, 66
Laughton, John Knox 7, 12, 42–3, 44–7, 48, 49–50, 51, 53, 54, 55, 69
Law, Andrew Bonar 122
Law, Force and Diplomacy (Booth) 167
Le Bailly, Vice Admiral Sir Louis 166
Leander, HMS 145
Letters and Despatches of Horatio, Viscount Nelson (Laughton) 45
Letters on Amphibious Wars (Aston) 68
Lewin, Admiral Sir Terence 173
Lewis, Michael 14, 119, 126, 157–8
Liddell Hart, Basil 10, 105–6, 107, 109, 113
limited operations 77–9, 167, 172
Lindemann, Frederick (Viscount Cherwell) xv, 145
Lissa (battle 1866) 41, 46, 82
Lloyd, Christopher C. 14, 126
Loss of Minorca, The (Richmond) 49
Luce, Admiral Stephen B. 47–8

MacDonald, Ramsay 3
Macey, Captain David 173
Mackinder, Sir Halford 2

Mahan, Alfred Thayer 1, 30, 42, 48, 49, 50, 54, 65, 70, 71, 127, 162
Malta 139–40, 141
Manadon *see* Royal Naval Engineering College Manadon
Manoeuvring Book (1874) 91, 93
Marder, Arthur J. xv, 127
'Maritime Contribution to Joint Operations' (MCJO) 189
maritime power projection 110–13
see also expeditionary warfare
Maritime Strategy: A Study of British Defence Problems (Gretton) 144
Maritime Strategy for Medium Powers (Hill) 168
Martin, Laurence 167
Martin, Sir Thomas Byam 38
Martin, Sir William 'Pincher' 92
May, Captain Henry 50–1, 52, 53
May, Admiral Sir William 97
McGwire, M.K. 166
Mediterranean: in First World War 92, 93; in Second World War 139, 140
Mends, Captain William 40
merchant marine 164
Midway (battle 1942) 82
Military Expeditions Beyond the Seas (Furse) 68
Military Operations and Maritime Preponderance (Callwell) 66
Molyneux, Thomas More 63, 83
Montgomery, John 70
Morris, Michael 169
Moulton, Major General J.L. 171
Mulgrave, Lord 20

Nailor, Peter 15–16
Napoleonic Wars 28
NATO 143, 161, 165–7, 170, 171–2, 175, 176
Naval Defence Act 1899 48
naval education 12–13; development from 1854–1914 34–56; in interwar years 124–9
Naval History (James) 37
Naval Intelligence Department (NID) 30, 48, 49, 50
Naval Policy: A Plea for the Study of War (Custance) 67
Naval Review xiv, 16, 50, 104, 123, 127, 161
Naval Side of British History (Callender) 125
Naval Staff 30, 41

Naval Tactics (Clerk) 63
Naval War Manual (1925) 157
Naval War Manual (1960s) 182–3
Naval Warfare (Philip Colomb) 64, 65
Naval Warfare: an Introductory Study (Creswell) 106
Naval Warfare in the Age of Sail (Tunstall) 127
Navies and Foreign Policy (Booth) 167
Navy and Seapower (Hannay) 67
Navy and the Nation (Clarke and Thursfield) 67
Navy as an Instrument of Policy 1558–1727 (Richmond) 105, 127
Navy in India, The (Richmond) 104, 108
Navy in the War of 1739–1748 (Richmond) 104
Navy Records Society 30, 49, 51
Nelson, Admiral Horatio 7, 27, 37, 45, 47; as a rule-breaker 9, 182
Newbolt, Sir Henry 54, 114
Nicolas, Sir Harris 37
Nile (battle 1798) 7
Nimrod 3 (AEW aircraft) 177
Nootka Sound Incident (1790) 22
North, Dudley 146
nuclear weapons 160, 163–4
Nugent, Robert (Earl Nugent) 2

Ochakov affair (1791) 22
O'Connell, Daniel 173
'offensive-defence' concept 168, 187
'offshore tapestry' 173
Official Naval History of the First World War (Corbett) 66, 113
On Escalation (Kahn) 171
Onslow, Admiral Sir Richard 166
'operational level of war' 10
operational research 136, 137, 142
Osgood, Robert 10
Ottley, Captain Charles 51, 52

Pacific campaign (1941–45) 140, 141–2, 155
Parkinson, C. Northcote 147
Pearl Harbor (battle 1941) 139, 140
Physical Geography in its Relation to the Prevailing Winds and Currents (Laughton) 42
Plymouth Dockyard 24
Polaris missile programme 16
pollution 164, 173

Prince of Wales, HMS 140, 143, 146, 155
Principles of Maritime Strategy (Corbett) 71
Protection of Our Commerce, The (John Colomb) 64
Pugh, Philip 178

radar 137–8
Ranft, Bryan xiii, xv, 17, 69, 77, 160, 161, 166, 169, 183, 187; career 14, 15, 16, 56, 192–3
Ranken, Commander Michael 173
Rawlinson, Colonel (later General) Henry 53, 54
Realities of Naval History (Tunstall) 126
Repulse, HMS 140, 143, 146, 155
Richmond, Sir Herbert xiv, xv, 31, 49, 50, 51, 52, 55, 103–31, 145; capital ships controversy 122–3; career 103–4; 'decisive victory' doctrine 115; maritime power projection 110–11; naval education 126, 127, 128, 129; service co-operation 108–9; trade protection, 118–20
Rise and Fall of British Naval Mastery (Kennedy) 155, 163
Robertson, George xiv
Rodger, Nicholas 7, 17, 61
Rodney, Admiral Lord George 27, 37
Roskill, Captain Stephen xiv–xv, 127, 145–58
Rossbach (battle 1757) 26
Royal Air Force 108, 130, 137, 164, 170
Royal College of Defence Studies xiv, 166
Royal Corps of Naval Constructors 177
Royal Marines 53, 170
Royal Military College Sandhurst 52
Royal Naval College Greenwich xiii, 8, 12, 13–16, 43–4, 45, 49, 54, 55, 64, 65, 69, 104, 129, 183, 184; Department of History and English 14; Department of History and International Affairs (DHIA) 15–16; Department of Nuclear Science and Technology 15; Junior Officers General Education and War Course (JOWC) 14; Lieutenants' Greenwich Course 15; Special Duties Officers' Course Greenwich (SDOGC) 15;

War Course 51–2, 54–5, 128; WRNS Officer Training course 15
Royal Naval College Portsmouth 35, 42, 54, 65, 69
Royal Naval Engineering College Manadon 8, 12, 15
Royal Naval Exhibition (1891) 49
Royal Naval Staff College 14, 15, 16, 125
Royal United Service Institution 30, 45–6, 49
Rules of Engagement 172
Russel, Admiral Edward 74
Russo-Japanese War 72

St Vincent, Earl (John Jervis) 89–90, 98
Saintes, the (battle 1782) 27
Sandhurst *see* Royal Military College 52
Sandwich, Lord 20, 26
Saumarez, Admiral Lord James 38
Scheer, Admiral Reinhard 99
Schwarzhoff, General Gross von 68
Scott, Admiral Sir Percy 121, 123
Sea in Modern Strategy, The (Martin) 167
Sea in Soviet Strategy, The (Ranft and Till) 166
Sea Kings of Britain (Callender) 125
Sea, Land and Air Strategy (Aston) 68
Sea Power and the Modern World (Richmond) 105
Sea Power of the State (Gorshkov) 166
Second World War 134–58
Selborne, Lord 12
Seven Years War 25, 26, 82
Sherman, General William T. 47
shipbuilding 165
Signal Book 91, 92, 93, 94, 97
Slade, Edmond 49, 51, 52
Slater, Admiral Sir Jock 182
Slave Catching in the Indian Ocean (Philip Colomb) 64
Small Wars: Their Principles and Practice (Callwell) 66
Social History of the Navy (Lewis) 126
Society for Nautical Research 125
Some Principles of Maritime Strategy (Corbett) 51, 66, 184, 185, 187
sonar 138
Southey, Robert 38
Soviet Navy 156, 166, 171
Spain, in 18th century 22, 25
Spanish Armada (1588) 49, 82

Spanish Navy: in the 17th century 74; in the 18th century 22, 26, 27; in the 19th century 28
Spee, Maximilian, Graf von 98
Spencer, Earl 90
Spratt, Captain Thomas 40
Stanford, Vice Admiral Peter 171
State Papers Relating to the Defeat of the Spanish Armada (Laughton) 49
Statesmen and Sea Power (Richmond) 105, 127
Stead, W.T. 61, 69
steam power 61, 91
Strategy of Sea Power, The (Roskill) 147, 154
submarines 98–100, 136, 140, 141, 176; nuclear powered 175; U-boats 99–101, 104, 118, 138, 139, 142, 143, 151–2; Upholder class submarines 177
Successors of Drake (Corbett) 51
Suez crisis (1956) 167, 170
Sulivan, Captain Bartholomew 40
Sumida, Jon 74
Switzer, Jeffrey xiv
Sydenham, Lord *see* Clarke, Sir George

T124 (naval commentator) 1, 8
Taranto (battle 1940) 139
technological advances: in Victorian era 91–2; in the interwar period 121–4, 127; in the Second World War 137–8, 148
Tegetthoff, Wilhelm von 46, 47
Thursfield, J.R. 67, 69, 103
Till, Geoffrey 165, 166
Tirpitz 135
trade, protection of 4; in 18th century 5, 6, 22, 23; in 19th century 22, 28–9, 76; in First World War 89, 117; in the interwar period 117–21; in the Cold War 165, 166
Trafalgar (battle 1805) 7
Trenchant, HMS 141
Trevelyan, G.M. 6
Tryon, Vice-Admiral Sir George 92–4
Tunstall, Brian 126–7
Turner, Stansfield 170, 186
Type 21 frigates 178
Type 42 frigates 178

U-1/*U-2* (German submarines) 99
U-boats *see* submarines
Ultra intelligence 135, 146

214 *Index*

underwater weapons 138, 164
United Nations Convention on the Law of the Sea 164, 168
United States Naval War College 47–8, 50
United States Navy 170, 171
University College London, Department of Naval Architecture 15
Upholder class submarines *see* submarines

Vernon, Admiral Edward 21, 23
Victoria, HMS 93
Victorious, HMS 141

Walker, Admiral Sir Baldwin 38
Walpole, Sir Robert 4, 5
War at Sea (Roskill) 146, 147
War of the Polish Succession 22
Washington, Captain John 38, 40
Waters, D.W. 170
Weddigen, Captain-Lieutenant Otto 99
Western Squadron 23–6, 74
Wilkinson, Spenser 53
Williams, Captain David 175
Wimbledon, Viscount 61

Young, Elizabeth 173

Zumwalt, Elmo 170